HOW THE GLOVES CAME OFF

COLUMBIA STUDIES IN TERRORISM
AND IRREGULAR WARFARE

COLUMBIA STUDIES IN TERRORISM
AND IRREGULAR WARFARE

Bruce Hoffman, Series Editor

This series seeks to fill a conspicuous gap in the burgeoning literature on terrorism, guerrilla warfare, and insurgency. The series adheres to the highest standards of scholarship and discourse and publishes books that elucidate the strategy, operations, means, motivations, and effects posed by terrorist, guerrilla, and insurgent organizations and movements. It thereby provides a solid and increasingly expanding foundation of knowledge on these subjects for students, established scholars, and informed reading audiences alike.

Ami Pedahzur, *The Israeli Secret Services and the Struggle Against Terrorism*

Ami Pedahzur and Arie Perliger, *Jewish Terrorism in Israel*

Lorenzo Vidino, *The New Muslim Brotherhood in the West*

Erica Chenoweth and Maria J. Stephan, *Why Civil Resistance Works: The Strategic Logic of Nonviolent Resistance*

William C. Banks, *New Battlefields/Old Laws: Critical Debates on Asymmetric Warfare*

Blake W. Mobley, *Terrorism and Counterintelligence: How Terrorist Groups Elude Detection*

Jennifer Morrison Taw, *Mission Revolution: The U.S. Military and Stability Operations*

Guido W. Steinberg, *German Jihad: On the Internationalization of Islamist Terrorism*

Michael W. S. Ryan, *Decoding Al-Qaeda's Strategy: The Deep Battle Against America*

David H. Ucko and Robert Egnell, *Counterinsurgency in Crisis: Britain and the Challenges of Modern Warfare*

Bruce Hoffman and Fernando Reinares, editors, *The Evolution of the Global Terrorist Threat: From 9/11 to Osama bin Laden's Death*

Boaz Ganor, *Global Alert: The Rationality of Modern Islamist Terrorism and the Challenge to the Liberal Democratic World*

M. L. R. Smith and David Martin Jones, *The Political Impossibility of Modern Counterinsurgency: Strategic Problems, Puzzles, and Paradoxes*

ELIZABETH GRIMM ARSENAULT

HOW THE GLOVES

CAME OFF

Lawyers, Policy Makers, and
Norms in the Debate on Torture

Columbia University Press / New York

Columbia University Press
Publishers Since 1893
New York   Chichester, West Sussex
cup.columbia.edu

Library of Congress Cataloging-in-Publication Data
Names: Arsenault, Elizabeth Grimm, author.
Title: How the gloves came off : lawyers, policy makers, and norms in
the debate on torture / Elizabeth Grimm Arsenault.
Description: New York : Columbia University Press, [2017] | Series:
Columbia studies in terrorism and irregular warfare | Includes
bibliographical references and index.
Identifiers: LCCN 2016021891 (print) | LCCN 2016034286 (ebook) |
ISBN 9780231180788 (cloth : alk. paper) | ISBN 9780231543255 (e-book)
Subjects: LCSH: Torture—Government policy—United States. |
Prisoners of war—United States—History.
Classification: LCC HV8599.U6 A77 2017 (print) | LCC HV8599.U6
(ebook) | DDC 364.6/7—dc23
LC record available at https://lccn.loc.gov/2016021891

Columbia University Press books are printed on permanent
and durable acid-free paper.
Printed in the United States of America

Cover design: Archie Ferguson

CONTENTS

ACKNOWLEDGMENTS

I AM DEEPLY grateful for the wisdom and encouragement from many friends and colleagues who helped me complete this project. During my graduate studies at Georgetown University, George Shambaugh, Colin Kahl, and, especially, Anthony Arend shaped my thinking about international relations and international law. In addition, special thanks are owed to the late Christopher Joyner, who helped motivate this project from the beginning, reading the first ten-page draft of this paper. He will be remembered by all who knew him as a man of unfailing enthusiasm and encouragement.

My dear friends Tricia Bacon, Dan Baltrusaitis, Sarah Cross, and John Sawyer provided countless hours of editing and unflagging support. Their wit, calmness, and counsel were necessary for writing this book.

I am grateful for the support of my colleagues in the Security Studies Program, in particular for the support of Bruce Hoffman, as well as former colleagues from the College of William and Mary, notably Dennis Smith and Sue Peterson.

I would also like to thank my teachers and mentors from the College of William and Mary, George Washington University, and Georgetown University.

For her early interest in the book and assistance in guiding it through the publication process, I am grateful to Anne Routon at Columbia University

Press. I am also indebted to Carole Sargent at Georgetown University for her guidance, encouragement, and feedback.

Thank you does not seem sufficient to express my gratitude to the incredible undergraduate and graduate students who have provided their research support to this project. To Colette Clark, Rosemary Pritchett-Montavon, Amanda Powers, Stephen Okin, Hijab Shah, and Trevor Nielsen: many thanks for their patience, time, and hard work. These brief sentences do not do justice to their sublime efforts in making this final product possible. Stephen Okin, in particular, questioned assumptions and provided essential feedback, strengthening the arguments presented in this book.

For everything—but especially his patience and love—I thank Jacques.

Lastly, for their love and unfailing support, I dedicate this book to my parents.

HOW THE GLOVES CAME OFF

PART ONE

BACKGROUND

1

INTRODUCTION

Now when we raise our heads and look in the mirror, we see an unfamiliar and hideous reflection . . . ourselves. Appalled, the French are discovering this terrible truth: that if nothing can protect a nation against itself, neither its traditions nor its loyalties nor its laws, and if fifteen years are enough to transform victims into executioners, then its behavior is no more than a matter of opportunity and occasion. Anybody, at any time, may equally find himself victim or executioner. Happy are those who died without ever having had to ask themselves:—If they tear out my fingernails, will I talk? But even happier are others, barely out of childhood, who have never had to ask themselves that other question:—If my friends, fellow soldiers, and leaders tear out an enemy's fingernails in my presence, what will I do?

—JEAN-PAUL SARTRE, *THE QUESTION*

THE IMMEDIATE ANSWER to the question of why the United States tortured in the aftermath of the 9/11 attacks is a surprisingly simple one: no one who could end the program, amend guidance, or overturn decisions said no. Throughout the duration of the program, many individuals—some known and scores who will remain unknown—pushed back. They challenged the notion that torture was an effective means to gain actionable intelligence. They argued that the use of these methods would imperil U.S. servicewomen and -men serving abroad. They insisted that torture defiled U.S. values and rendered vague the line between U.S. methods and the methods of the terrorists being fought. But still no one said no. In fact, many people—policy makers, lawyers, and interrogators—actively said yes.

The more interesting question to ask is not *why* the United States decided to torture but *how* we came to a place in U.S. history where techniques such as sleep deprivation, waterboarding, and rectal hydration would even be considered at the highest levels of government. How did we arrive at a decision point in which torture was even on the table? How did so many people say yes to these techniques? Answering these questions requires examining U.S. history and taking a deeper look at the actors and agencies involved in the decision-making process. Answering this question also requires investigating the importance of international humanitarian law and norms to U.S. values and identity. The United States did not casually or arbitrarily determine in the months after 9/11 that it was acceptable to slap detainees or to put them in cramped spaces with insects. Rather, the decision to torture individuals in U.S. custody was the result of deliberate decisions made by top policy makers and lawyers to challenge existing norms and laws. Despite the normative and legal constraints imposed by the Geneva Conventions and the United Nations Convention Against Torture (CAT), these actors again and again demonstrated the willingness and capacity to challenge the legal status quo.

Understanding the *how* of the torture question is more than an academic exercise. The decisions that led to cruelty against captured detainees significantly diminished U.S. values, legitimacy, operational effectiveness, and strategic interests. These actions imperiled members of the U.S. military as well as U.S. citizens abroad. Legal and moral legitimacy are not simply values that exist in a vacuum; while they are certainly ends worth pursuing in and of themselves, they also have important operational and strategic consequences. As a counterexample, as recently as 2004, the entire leadership of the Department of Justice (DOJ) threatened to resign in response to concerns about the legality of the Terrorism Surveillance Program, demonstrating that perceptions of legal and moral legitimacy affect government activities, personnel, and strategic goals.[1]

There is no question that the United States engaged in torture. Euphemisms such as "enhanced interrogation techniques" only serve to cloak hard facts with distracting and vague language. Following the 9/11 attacks, the administration of President George W. Bush authorized the Central Intelligence Agency and Department of Defense to use a range of extraordinary tactics—many adapted from Chinese methods used during the Korean

War against U.S. soldiers—to extract information from captured detainees. These techniques, some almost Orwellian in their creativity and cruelty, defied all legal and normative prohibitions in U.S. and international law.

An investigation of how this program came to be is timely because of recent developments in the torture debate. In December 2014, the U.S. Senate Select Committee on Intelligence (SSCI) released a 528-page declassified executive summary of its findings on U.S. interrogation practices after September 2001.[2] The executive summary provides detailed accounts of waterboarding, sleep deprivation lasting up to 180 hours, and ice-water baths, among other similarly brutal techniques. It states that multiple detainees who were subject to torture provided no actionable intelligence or simply lied to their interrogators. While the minority report issued by the SSCI and the official response from the CIA rebut many of the claims made, an opportunity was lost to engage the American public on the legality, efficacy, and morality of this program.

A nationwide poll conducted by the *Washington Post* after the report's release showed more than half of all Americans believe that torture of suspected terrorists can be often or sometimes justified.[3] The immediate response to the SSCI Report was a flurry of editorials and Sunday-morning roundtables, but it quickly faded from the headlines. The question of the U.S. public's quiescence to this deeply troubling report is outside the scope of this research; however, investigating how the United States came to embrace torture may begin to explain the public's view of the issue as well as shed some light on its conception of the broader debate on how to balance security and liberty in a democratic society.

Recent scholarship has succinctly and effectively answered the *why* of the torture question.[4] This robust literature from scholars such as Karen Greenberg, Jane Mayer, and David Cole has both effectively laid out the timeline of events and examined the motivations of the various actors involved in the decisions and actions. As a result, this book does not seek to replicate their findings. However, a large gap in the literature exists with regard to *how* the United States came to this place in history. How could the United States violate laws and norms that are so deeply internalized in its identity and practice? Under what conditions did these norms unravel?

A significant body of international relations scholarship examines the processes by which states comply with international norms and laws and the ways in which those tenets become part of the states' identity over time. However, fewer IR scholars examine the durability of norms after they have become embedded in a state's identity. How do norms change over time, and what causes these changes? The literature fails to account for how norms change domestically and the resulting gap between the tenets of the norm and the actions of the state.

In addition to these theoretical gaps, the book specifically explores the roles played by the three parties—policy makers, lawyers, and interrogators—that were involved in formulating and applying torture after 9/11. Previous reports, investigations, and books have examined in detail the roles played by these actors in implementing and executing the detainee-interrogation program. Looking at their actions through the lens of normative change, however, provides a unique understanding of how these groups' actions led to torture. Instead of examining the torture debate as simply a series of isolated policy decisions made over time, the theory of norm change reveals which actors played the crucial role of challenging the prevailing norm of humane treatment. Looking at the issue from the perspective of normative change reveals a number of critical insights, one of which is that the interrogators lacked the ability to challenge the preexisting norm. As such, despite being the group most punished for its actions, the interrogators actually deserve the least blame for the cruelty applied to detainees in the "Global War on Terror" (GWOT). Therefore, the book challenges the conventional wisdom offered by some commentators that torture was solely the work of a few "bad apples."

Previous accounts of the torture decisions either look at one set of actors involved or focus on the question of blame and accountability. This book seeks to examine the motivations, access, and influence of all three sets of actors involved—policy makers, lawyers, and interrogators—as well as to place their actions in historical context. Before turning to the future and asking whether this will happen again, it is essential to examine past instances of compliance and noncompliance with the laws governing detainee treatment.

In order to provide this alternative explanation for post-9/11 torture and fill these theoretical and empirical gaps, the book traces the evolution of U.S. norms on detainee treatment from Vietnam to today. Examining this history provides a detailed narrative context for how the ground-breaking decisions taken immediately after 9/11 occurred, and the book seeks to determine what impact this aberration may have on future U.S. detention policy.

As such, this book is an analysis of the dynamics of change in deeply held norms. Norms evolve through a process of "contestation"—the revision and transformation of beliefs and standards around detainee treatment over time—by actors with the access and influence to interpret and adapt their meaning. Examining how the United States abandoned its longstanding tradition of complying with human rights norms requires understanding how norms function and interact with power, especially during wartime. In addition to looking to the past for answers, equally important is examining whether and how the state will comply with international humanitarian norms in the future. Not only is the U.S. domestic and international identity at stake, but the very rule of law upon which the country was founded is also at risk. Is U.S. behavior in war simply a matter of opportunity or occasion? Or do the norms of international humanitarian law still guide U.S. decision making and actions?

THE ARGUMENT

This book examines how the norms governing humane POW treatment became embedded in U.S. practice and identity, how they unraveled, and what new normative frameworks emerged. The major theme is how, after centuries of commitment to humane prisoner treatment as a component of U.S. identity and decades of compliance with international humanitarian law, the United States came to a place in which policy makers, lawyers, and interrogators placed the gathering of intelligence over compliance with the law.

This theme is underpinned by a deceptively complex question: how do norms change? The first step in understanding this process of change is examining how the norm initially became embedded in domestic practice and identity. The second step is analyzing how ambiguities and actions trigger debate around the norm. The final step is consolidating around a new set of principles and beliefs to guide future decision making.

The process for norm change internationally is well documented in both IR and international legal scholarship. As laid out in Article 38 of the International Court of Justice Statute, new laws emerge from treaty conclusions, customary law (both state practice and *opinio juris*), and general principles of law. Taken together, these sources of law demonstrate that the international community has consolidated around a set of principles, standards of behavior, or interpretations of rules.

Less well known is the process for domestic norm change. After a state signs and ratifies a treaty, what happens? IR literature provides several explanations for how compliance with international law occurs. Compliance can range from mechanisms of coercion to "embeddedness."[5] On one end of the spectrum, rationalist literature argues that states comply with international law out of self-interest. In this view, primarily espoused by realist scholars, states comply with international law because of carrots and sticks wielded by other states. States rationally choose between the options of compliance and noncompliance, weighing the strategic costs and benefits. Based on this calculation, they "conform with international norms if it increases their political utility, and on the condition that the costs of adaptation are smaller than the benefits of external rewards."[6] Because state behavior is based on rational self-interest—which is reduced at its most basic level to national survival—norms, identity, and ideology play no deciding role in whether states comply with international law. State behavior may coincide with the law, but the tenets of the law do not affect the compliance decision or affect the identity of the state actor.

On the other end of the spectrum, constructivist scholars reject the notion that states comply with international obligations solely to maximize self-interest. Instead, they emphasize that compliance can occur as a result of the law becoming embedded in the states' domestic identity, norms, and processes.[7] As opposed to the instrumental argument detailed above, constructivists claim that compliance occurs because over time the law becomes a deeply held belief. Domestic practices, laws, and education consequently reflect these values. According to Cortell and Davis, a norm is considered embedded when: "The state has made concrete alterations in its policy choices, or has incorporated formal procedures into its domestic processes in an effort to be in accordance with the rule's prescriptions. In this case, the norm or rule comes to be embedded within the nation's own normative, juridical, or constitutional framework."[8] For other constructivist scholars such as Harold Koh, embeddedness requires more than implementation in domestic law—it also requires debate and discourse among the public, policy makers, and civil society, as well as engagement by nongovernmental organizations (NGOs) and transnational networks. Therefore, consistent with these constructivist theories, this book starts from the premise that norm internalization begins with a state's ratifying and implementing a treaty. The gradual process of embedding continues through deliberate political and social actions by various actors. Policy makers will refer to the law in speeches, memoirs, and decisions. Judges will eventually make reference to this law in their rulings and scholarly writings on the topic. Members of civil society will invoke this law in discourse and practice. Academic institutions—both military and civilian—will provide training and education in this law's contours and applicability. These actions, taken together, constitute the tipping point for the norm, as "a critical mass of relevant state actors adopts" it.[9] The process thus changes the identity of the state by including the law as one of its values.[10]

HOW DID THESE NORMS BECOME EMBEDDED?

Based on the last several decades of U.S. practice, scholars and practitioners could not have anticipated the gross misinterpretations of international humanitarian law that occurred after 9/11. The two prohibitions at stake—the Geneva Conventions and the CAT—were written, concluded, and

ratified with substantial support from the United States. They both constituted international laws to which the United States was not only a party but
also a leading supporter.

The United States ratified the 1949 Geneva Conventions only a few years
after their drafting. These laws do not seek to prevent war but rather to ameliorate its effects by protecting innocent bystanders, shielding soldiers from
unnecessary harm, and limiting the physical damage caused by conflict. The
four conventions are the cornerstone of the modern laws of war regime and
represent values so universal they are considered customary international
law binding on all states regardless of whether they are signatories to the
conventions. In fact, the Geneva Conventions represent the rare treaties
that have garnered—with the 2012 adherence of South Sudan—universal
acceptance.[11]

Similarly, the United States was instrumental in the promulgation of
the 1984 CAT.[12] The CAT defines torture and allows for no situation in
which its use is permitted.[13] Most significantly, the CAT requires signatories to criminalize torture in their domestic law. The U.S. Senate approved
the CAT in 1994, and that same year Congress fulfilled its obligations
under the treaty and criminalized the infliction of severe pain and suffering through the passage of 18 U.S.C. § 2340–2340A (hereafter "U.S. federal
antitorture statute").

Over the course of the last several decades, the norms and standards contained in these conventions became embedded in the United States through
deliberate political and social practice.[14] These norms have been included in
U.S. domestic law, from the U.S. federal antitorture statute and the Torture
Victim Protection Act of 1991—allowing victims, regardless of their citizen-
ship or the geographic location of the crime, to sue their torturers in U.S.
courts—to the federal War Crimes Act, which stipulates that abrogation of
Common Article 3 of the Geneva Conventions constitutes a federal felony.
As described in chapters 2 and 3, the tenets of the Geneva Conventions and
the CAT have also been included in U.S. military law, codes, doctrine, and
manuals. They have been added to the curricula of military academies and also
to training programs mandated before deployment. Importantly, the United
States translated its beliefs and values into practice, with detainee policies

improving from Vietnam to Grenada to Panama and finally reaching a peak of compliance in the 1991 Gulf War.

Taken together, these norms crossed the tipping point in U.S. policy and society: there was widespread agreement that individuals in U.S. custody during wartime were entitled—both legally and ethically—to humane treatment. These norms have constituted elements of U.S. identity and molded U.S. practice in war since the Revolutionary War, as chapter 2 will outline. The modern interpretation of the norm of humane treatment stems from the Geneva Conventions and the CAT as well as the impact of the Vietnam War. The United States thus entered the GWOT with significant institutional knowledge and lessons learned about the treatment of POWs, and the importance of following the laws of war in the conduct of military operations was widely accepted. Norms governing the humane treatment of detainees were embedded. The gloves were on.

HOW DID THE NORMS UNRAVEL?

The story begins in the aftermath of the U.S. war in Vietnam, in which the United States sought to improve its handling of POWs by taking steps to include the laws of war in military practice, education, and U.S. identity. As described in chapter 3, this set of norms and laws thus constituted the framework for U.S. decision making and action before 9/11. Consistent with constructivist theorizing, this framework guided actors' preferences and behavior in the intervening decades. However, all rules possess gaps that render existing interpretations vague or ineffective as new situations arise. The Geneva Conventions and the CAT are no exceptions. Questions about their applicability, who was specifically entitled to their protections, what type of conflict triggered their relevance, and the extent of the president's powers in deciding these issues emerged in the immediate aftermath of 9/11.

These were not new questions. Questions about who was entitled to Geneva Convention protections plagued U.S. deliberations regarding the ratification of the 1977 Additional Protocol I to the Geneva Conventions.

The United States signed the protocol, but President Reagan never submitted it to the Senate for approval because of fears that doing so would legitimize the claims of the Palestine Liberation Organization and other liberation movements.[15] Meanwhile, the extent of the president's powers in foreign affairs became a subject of debate in the 1980s, as criticism emerged of the post-Watergate reforms that had sharply limited the executive branch's prerogatives. Similarly, in the 1990s, the investigation of the International Criminal Tribunal for the Former Yugoslavia into NATO's compliance with the tenets of discrimination and proportionality—the cornerstones of the law-of-war regime—prompted questions about military objectives and target selection as well as about the legitimacy and fairness of international law.[16] This last point in particular became the focus around the turn of the twenty-first century of the so-called new sovereigntists, who drove debate about the appropriate constraints of international laws, such as the Rome Treaty, the Comprehensive Test Ban Treaty, and the Land Mines Convention (among others) on U.S. practice.[17] Nevertheless, despite these various debates, the general norm consensus before 9/11 was that humane treatment of civilians and combatants during wartime constituted a critical component of the U.S. identity. While there were certainly instances of noncompliance with the laws of war before 9/11, it is not as simplistic as assuming that compliance reinforces norms and noncompliance weakens them. Consistent with the judgment in the 1986 International Court of Justice case *Nicaragua v. United States of America*, if a state acts in a way that is incompatible with customary international law, "but defends its conduct by appealing to exceptions or justifications contained within the rule itself, then whether or not the state's conduct is in fact justifiable on that basis, the significance of that attribute is to confirm rather than to weaken the rule."[18] These instances of noncompliance with the laws of war, which will be addressed in chapters 2 and 3, never resulted in policy makers, lawyers, or interrogators debating the utility of the norm. As such, acts of noncompliance alone do not serve as evidence of norm contestation.

Full contestation would come with the election of George W. Bush in 2000. As president, Bush brought into the government political actors at various levels who questioned the applicability of international law to U.S.

practice and dismissed the legitimacy of restrictions on the executive's freedom to act during wartime. In the case of the Geneva Conventions, Bush administration lawyers almost immediately sought to clarify which authorities governed the conflict between the United States and members of al-Qaeda and the Taliban. Since the original four 1949 Geneva Conventions applied only to state parties, and al-Qaeda was not a state signatory, did the United States have to afford Geneva protections to al-Qaeda fighters? The Taliban controlled most of Afghanistan, which was a state signatory to the conventions, but was it entitled to Geneva's protections given its disregard for the laws of war? If the answer to these questions was no, what about the possibility of domestic criminal prosecution under the War Crimes Act? These were all new questions for the government to face as matters of policy; since 1949, the United States had never denied the applicability of the Geneva Conventions in an armed conflict.[19]

In the case of the CAT, the Bush administration raised different issues. What physical and mental acts qualified as torture? How long did the suffering have to last, and did the intent behind its application matter? These ambiguities—combined with the shock of an attack on the U.S. homeland—triggered contestation among the policy makers and lawyers inside the administration of the existing normative consensus on detainee treatment. The groups relied on different arguments to challenge the consensus, with the policy makers arguing "never again" and the lawyers arguing "anything goes." These arguments ultimately prompted a new norm framework around the utility and applicability of international humanitarian law.

POLICY MAKERS: "NEVER AGAIN"

In the aftermath of 9/11, the policy makers argued "never again." Never again should the United States be the victim of a terrorist attack on the U.S. homeland. Never again should terrorists strike at the nerve centers of U.S. economic, military, and cultural power. Never again should the United States know the shattering sense of vulnerability and powerlessness that so many other states have felt at the hands of extremists with no regard for noncombatant life. To operationalize this credo, the Bush administration consistently emphasized that confronting al-Qaeda required new ways of thinking. In a speech to Pentagon employees one week after 9/11, Bush stated:

> But I know that this is a different type of enemy than we're used to. It's an enemy that likes to hide and burrow in, and their network is extensive. There are no rules. It's barbaric behavior. They slit throats of women on airplanes in order to achieve an objective that is beyond comprehension. And they like to hit, and then they like to hide out. But we're going to smoke them out. And we're adjusting our thinking to the new type of enemy.[20]

Vice President Dick Cheney, in a speech on October 18, 2001, reiterated the novelty of the effort, declaring September 11 to be "a day like no other we have ever experienced, requiring a war like no other we have ever waged."[21] He continued:

> I spent four years at the Pentagon working with some of the finest men and women I have ever met. More people died there on September 11 than we lost in combat in the Gulf War. When you think of that attack and of the merciless horror inflicted at the World Trade Center, no punishment for the terrorist seems too harsh.[22]

These remarks were quickly translated into action. Three days after Cheney's speech, Bob Woodward reported for the *Washington Post* the remarks of an unnamed senior Bush administration official: "The gloves are off. The president has given the agency [CIA] the green light to do whatever is necessary. Lethal operations that were unthinkable pre–September 11 are now underway."[23]

President Bush also moved quickly to determine detention policy for the nascent conflict. In November 2001, he issued a Military Order regarding the "Detention, Treatment, and Trial of Certain Non-Citizens in the War

Against Terrorism," one of the first signals that this conflict represented a break with recent U.S. practice in wartime.[24] The text of the order invoked the president's new normative position:

> Given the danger to the safety of the United States and the nature of international terrorism, and to the extent provided by and under this order, I find consistent with section 836 of title 10, United States Code, that it is not practicable to apply in military commissions under this order the principles of law and the rules of evidence generally recognized in the trial of criminal cases in the United States district courts.[25]

When the White House announced the Military Order, the communications director Dan Bartlett couched it in terms of the developing narrative of extraordinary circumstances: "We have looked at this war very unconventionally," he said, "and the conventional way of bringing people to justice doesn't apply to these times."[26] The DOJ spokeswoman Mindy Tucker echoed the White House: "These are obviously extraordinary times and the president needs to have as many options as possible."[27]

The order established a set of procedural rules that differed both from the constitutional rights afforded U.S. citizens and from the process outlined in the Uniform Code of Military Justice (UCMJ).[28] The trials would be closed to the public, would prevent defendants from invoking the privilege against self-incrimination, would eschew the ordinary rules for presentation of evidence, would disallow any form of appeal, and would do nothing to prevent indefinite detention.[29] In addition, the original order included three even more drastic provisions that were ultimately amended by the DoD in 2002: the right to detain and try a defendant without informing him of the charges or evidence against him, the ability to convict without finding proof beyond a reasonable doubt, and the elimination of the defendant's right to choose his own counsel.[30] Previous terror convictions had occurred in civilian courts and with the benefits of proof beyond a reasonable doubt and trial-quality evidence, making this legal policy decidedly novel.[31] In fact, in 1996 the White House turned down a Sudanese offer to extradite Osama bin Laden for fear it would not be able to try him in a federal court.[32]

Alongside the release of this Military Order, the Bush administration also announced that it would be seeking the arrest of five thousand men suspected of being involved with or being supporters of a terrorist organization.[33] These men were by and large immigrants from Middle Eastern states.[34] The fact that many of these men had not committed any illegal act was deemed irrelevant given the possibility that they could simply be part of "sleeper cells" ordered to hide among the U.S. population.[35] The Military Order and the announcement of the arrests represented some of the initial steps in operationalizing the "never again" slogan. The policy makers saw 9/11 as an inflection point, a paradigm-changing event that required the United States to wage a new kind of war, one that required new rules and methods for victory. In the months that followed, as U.S. forces expanded their offensive and captured increasing numbers of Taliban and al-Qaeda fighters, this push for new methods and rules would be extended to countless aspects of the GWOT, including detainee-interrogation methods.

LAWYERS: "ANYTHING GOES"

The lawyers for the DOJ, along with lawyers in the Office of the Vice President, CIA, and DoD, adhered to a different narrative when faced with these normative gaps: "anything goes." Their views and legal conclusions were inextricably shaped by the conviction that in a time of war, there were few—if any—constraints on the power of the executive. In particular, they believed that the president's power as commander-in-chief and his position as head of the unitary executive gave him wide latitude to set detention policy as he saw fit. The position of "anything goes" was most powerfully and prominently laid out in a series of legal memos from the DOJ's Office of Legal Counsel. In a January 9, 2002, memo authored for DoD General Counsel Haynes, the OLC lawyers John Yoo and Robert J. Delahunty articulated the position that Taliban and al-Qaeda detainees were not legally entitled to the protections of the Third Geneva Convention, which addresses the rights and standards of POW treatment. Perhaps even more critically, the memo stated that any attempts to restrict the president's power and authority in wartime—including the treatment of prisoners—would be constitutionally dubious.[36]

The OLC then issued two opinions to the White House about the definition of torture under the CAT as embodied in the U.S. federal antitorture statute. These two memos were sent on August 1, 2002, and were written by Yoo, although they were signed by Jay Bybee, then–assistant attorney general for the OLC.[37] As such, they are popularly known as the "Bybee memos" despite Yoo being their principal author. The first Bybee memo provided an analysis of the conduct allowed under the U.S. federal antitorture statute. The memo concluded that "acts may be cruel, inhumane, or degrading, but still not produce the pain and suffering of the requisite intensity to fall within Section 2340A's proscription against torture."[38] In the case of mental suffering, acts qualify as torture if they result in "significant psychological harm of significant duration, e.g., lasting for months or even years."[39] In the case of physical suffering, acts constitute torture if they are "equivalent in intensity to the pain accompanying serious physical injury, such as organ failure, impairment of bodily function, or even death."[40]

In addition to this questionable threshold of physical and psychological pain applied as a legal justification, two other justifications in Bybee's first memo have come under legal scrutiny.[41] The first attempted to expand the provisions of self-defense to include efforts that were intended to prevent future attacks of unknown imminence to the United States.[42] While this argument is presented in the memo as unconventional, the memo fails to note that the plea of self-defense is specifically prohibited by the CAT's declaration that no exceptions or emergency situations legitimize the use of torture.[43] The second legal justification invoked the president's status as commander-in-chief, asserting that no limits can be placed on the president's authority to conduct war.

The second Bybee memo analyzed the legality of classified interrogation techniques requested by the CIA. This eighteen-page memo was addressed to John Rizzo, acting general counsel of the CIA, and examined the federal prohibitions against torture for a specific case: the interrogation of

Zain al-Abidin Muhammad Husayn Abu Zubaydah, a senior al-Qaeda leader captured in Pakistan in March 2002.[44]

The memo analyzed ten techniques—"attention grasp, walling, facial hold, facial slap (insult slap), cramped confinement, wall standing, stress positions, sleep deprivation, insects placed in a confinement box, and the waterboard"— and concluded that these methods, used either separately or as a course of increasing pressure, would not violate the U.S. federal antitorture statute.[45] The ten techniques outlined in this 2002 memo, specifically the use of insects in a confinement box, resemble techniques employed in Room 101 in Orwell's dystopian *1984*. The memo states: "You would like to place Zubaydah in a cramped confinement box with an insect. You have informed us that he appears to have a fear of insects. In particular, you would like to tell Zubaydah that you intend to place a stinging insect into the box with him. You would, however, place a harmless insect in the box."[46] It concluded with the assessment that CIA personnel, in interrogating Zubaydah using the above ten methods, would neither cause severe pain and suffering nor intended to do so.[47]

Taken together, the legal memos interpreted U.S. obligations under the Geneva Conventions and the CAT as being secondary to the president's national security obligations to the state. If the president believed the use of torture was necessary to protect the country against future attacks, he could authorize its use without congressional or judicial interference.

INTERROGATORS: A LACK OF ACCESS AND INFLUENCE

Lastly, many accounts of the torture debate have identified the interrogators as the source of the abuses committed after 9/11. In fact, top Bush administration officials consistently voiced the idea that torture was simply the product of "a few bad apples."[48] Despite the frequency of this claim, the life-cycle theory of normative change shows that the interrogators are the group *least* responsible for contesting the norm of humane treatment and for creating an environment in which torture could be used.

The reason for this is simple: unlike policy makers and lawyers, the interrogators lacked the access and influence to challenge the norm of humane treatment and contribute to its deterioration. As countless interviews, memoirs, and investigative reports have shown, DoD and CIA interrogators were motivated by a plethora of issues. Some wanted revenge; others lashed out in boredom. Some insisted they were operating under orders and saw themselves as the tip of the spear in the fight against terrorism; others pointed to a lack of official guidance and relied on their memories of interrogations from television shows or movies to fill in the gap. The interrogators, therefore, did not constitute a monolithic group united by a desire to overturn the normative consensus. They could not engage in normative contestation because they could not even agree on how to do so.

Cultural and organizational differences between the DoD and CIA further contributed to the interrogators' inability to act as agents of normative change. These differences meant that the DoD and CIA interrogators relied on a different set of historical precedents and cultural guidelines, leading their respective interrogation programs to widely different fates. As such, it is not possible to speak of a single, unified interrogation program composed of uniform interrogators. The programs were housed within and staffed by completely different organizations with different histories and cultures. Simply put, the interrogators were too diverse to act with unity of purpose. They lacked the access and influence to challenge the norm of humane treatment for detainees.

THE TAKEAWAY: SO WHAT?

These three groups of actors played different roles in implementing the use of torture after 9/11. While interrogators actually committed the cruel acts, it was the policy makers and lawyers who challenged the existing norm of humane treatment by disputing the prevailing interpretations of executive power and international humanitarian law. This opposition was aided along the way by shifting public attitudes, best represented by the popularity of casual displays of torture in culture, such as those depicted in Fox's television show *24*. As such, the challenges put forth by the policy makers and lawyers not only reflected the interests of each group but were also increasingly accepted as being in the interest of U.S. society in general.

According to the theory of norm change, after the arguments are developed, the final step in the process of normative development is consolidation around a new interpretation that will guide future actions. The disputes from the contestation period modify the norm by highlighting its ambiguities and problematizing its inadequacies. The new set of beliefs proposed to fill these gaps eventually influences political and social life by affecting legislation, doctrine, judicial precedent, and public debate. As this book will show, this is exactly what happened in the case of post-9/11 torture. The disputes around the preexisting norm had a wide-ranging effect on the policies, laws, and debates surrounding detainee treatment.

As such, this book starts from the assumption that norms play an important role in regulating the behavior of individuals, groups, and states, both domestically and internationally. By focusing on the evolution of detainee policy from Vietnam to today, it reveals that changes in norms can produce significant policy results. Given the moral values and strategic interests at play, understanding the life cycle of normative development is crucial to the future of U.S. identity and power. Norm change is a constant, not an aberration, and understanding the processes by which norms affect state behavior is necessary in order to assess the durability of norm frameworks. The cycle of norm change presented here posits one way that norms change and unravel in the domestic context. Using this analysis, the book's findings suggest:

- Norms around the use of torture have become more permissive
- Shocks and ambiguities catalyzed different normative arguments by policy makers and lawyers about the rules
- The interrogators, despite being the group most punished for its actions, bear the least responsibility for the abuses committed during the GWOT
- The proscriptions against torture and the prescriptions for humane treatment of detainees are not ironclad but rather are subject to the interpretations and normative arguments of the actors involved

Each empirical chapter will thus illuminate these findings through an illustrative theory-driven account of what led the United States to torture, guided by the answers to these core questions for each group:

- What were the existing norms in the minds of this group?
- What shocks and ambiguities drove the contestation of the norms within the group?
- What claims did each group invoke in their challenge of the normative framework?

The outline for this research proceeds according to Legro's "two-step" model: the process by which the POW norm came to be embedded in the U.S. domestic context will be examined in the first half of the book, and the process of decision making and action is considered in subsequent empirical chapters.[49] The book compares qualitative case studies in order to understand the norm framework for each group after the Vietnam War and the contestation (or, in the case of the interrogators, the lack of contestation) that occurred during the GWOT. It proceeds by developing structured, focused case studies in order to best capture variation across historical contexts and to isolate the causal arguments at work. The case studies are structured to the extent that they rely on a standard set of research questions to guide data collection for each case.[50] The case studies are focused to the extent that they are undertaken with a single research objective: to determine the conditions under which U.S. compliance decisions regarding the POW norm were debated, made, and ultimately executed.

LIMITATIONS OF PREVIOUS APPROACHES

The research questions engaged in this book draw upon both constructivist IR literature as well as international legal scholarship. Despite the widespread attention paid to detainee issues over the past decade in both academic and popular literature, we still lack a systemic understanding of the conditions under which the decisions to use torture were made and, importantly, whether similar decisions could be made again.

Constructivist scholars highlight the importance of legitimacy, discourse, and identity in international politics. Rather than positing that state interests are static, constructivists argue that shifting beliefs, new norms, and changing identities alter state preferences. In particular, scholars have examined the various processes by which compliance with international law influences not only state behavior but also state identity and preferences. In this view, the Geneva Conventions are not simply laws that restrict state behavior. Instead the conventions transform how the state constructs reality, thereby altering how the state determines its policy preferences. By participating in this regime, states come to view themselves as norm protectors dedicated to upholding their interests as represented in the new normative regime.

Despite the claim that "if constructivism is about anything, it is about change,"[51] many constructivist scholars overlook what happens to a norm *after* it has become embedded domestically. Some scholars, such as Vaughn Shannon, assume that "at some point norms become internalized so that conformity is not a matter of conscious choice but of second nature."[52] Similarly, in Finnemore and Sikkink's three-stage life cycle of norms, the third stage of the life cycle is "internalization." In other words, many constructivist scholars view embeddedness as the final word on norm development. In this view, after the norm has been embedded, it is "internalized by actors and achieves a 'taken for granted' quality that is almost automatic."[53] Thus, some scholars have overlooked the social change that occurs after norms are embedded and the ability of actors to interpret and reinterpret the norm. These theories generally overlook the possibility that international norms, once adopted and internalized domestically, are still subject to disputes about their meaning, application, and utility.

Other scholars, such as Sandholtz, have challenged this notion and put forward models of norm change.[54] This book seeks to build upon his claim that "normative change is continual" and to test and expand this model of norm evolution.[55] This research takes as a starting point his argument that actions will inevitably clash with norms, generating disputes and contestation, but applies his theory in the context of the laws of war. As U.S. treatment of detainees in the GWOT has demonstrated, there has been nothing "taken for granted" about the norms protecting the humanity of captives during war. The embedding of a norm is not the end of the story but rather just the beginning.

International legal scholarship, in contrast, has delved deeply into the legal arguments and personalities that shaped torture and detainee decisions. Scholars have provided ideological assessments of U.S. behavior,[56] educated the public about the use of enhanced interrogation techniques (EITs),[57] analyzed the legal debates put forward by the lawyers in the DOJ,[58] and some have even defended administration decisions based on constitutional precedent.[59] Notably, though, this scholarship as a whole does not present models for understanding the decision making, nor does it provide the reader with any predictive tools for assessing the conditions under which such contestation may occur in the future.

This book borrows critical insights from each field while simultaneously seeking to fill gaps within their existing research programs. Theoretically, this book moves the constructivist research program on compliance forward by examining the role of domestic actors and resurrecting the notion of agency. With few exceptions, constructivists have hindered their own research by overlooking the important role that domestic agents and contexts have upon state identity and interests.[60] Essentially, constructivism is—and should be—a theory about social life and change. Constructivism emerged from a gap in existing IR theories, which struggled to explain change in international politics. Whereas structural realists see the world as immutable, constructivists argue that individuals can transform the world through ideas that reconstruct reality. However, constructivism has failed in its promise of attributing agency to domestic actors. Constructivists are often unable to account for change because of their belief in the strict structure that embedded norms prescribe. Finnemore and Sikkink's three-stage life cycle of norms is the perfect example of this conventional understanding. In their words, through the process of embeddedness, "*States* are socialized to want certain things by international society in which they live and the people in them live."[61]

This book also argues that the compliance research program has counterintuitively generated "structure-specific" constructivist analysis. Whereas some research programs in constructivism do privilege the role of agency—namely the research that examines the role of norm entrepreneurs or transnational civil society activists—very few scholars examine the role of domestic agents. Unfortunately, constructivists have frequently "erected a black box around processes of social choice" and overlooked the reality that actors make choices all the time.[62] This book supports the conclusion that norms do not ossify in the domestic context. Embedded norms are in a state of constant evolution and progression; they provide a stable frame for guiding actors' behavior and simultaneously provide the frame for their own transformation.

Empirically, this work borrows from the rich process-tracing and investigative work done in the international legal field and seeks to formalize those findings into a workable model of decision making. It also seeks to contribute to the question about the utility of torture during wartime. Recent events, such as the death of Osama bin Laden, seemed to justify to some U.S. policy makers and citizens the value of extraordinary measures to obtain information. In 2011, Yoo wrote that the Navy SEAL operation in Abbottabad, Pakistan, "vindicates the Bush administration, whose intelligence architecture marked the path to bin Ladin's door."[63] Yet even former Bush administration officials acknowledge some of the harms caused by the torture decisions. At a minimum, Abu Ghraib—in the words of former secretary of defense Rumsfeld—was "unhelpful" to the efforts to stabilize Iraq.[64] As a result, it will take, according to Karl Rove, a "generation" for the United States' image to recover.[65] The ramifications of U.S. interrogation practices continue to haunt the United States. As recently as August 2014, the U.S. journalist and hostage James Foley was waterboarded several times by Islamic State of Iraq and the Levant (ISIL) jihadists, a decision almost certainly taken in response to the CIA's use of the same technique.[66] The orange jumpsuit he wore in the videos posted online by ISIL was also chosen purposefully: it served as a reminder to the United States of the harm done to the detainees at Guantánamo Bay, clad in similar orange jumpsuits. Given these consequences, understanding the full life cycle of the normative framework on detainee policy is needed now more than ever.

CASE SELECTION

This book examines the detainee decisions made in the GWOT against the backdrop of the norm framework cultivated after the Vietnam War. The justification for this case-selection framework begins from the premise that the conditions in the GWOT, in particular the two principal battlefields of Iraq and Afghanistan, bore many similarities to situations U.S. forces faced in Vietnam, notably the difficult task of confronting armed insurgencies and asymmetric conflict. With regards to prisoner treatment in each of these conflicts, for example, many U.S. opponents technically did not qualify for POW status because they did not wear uniforms, did not carry arms openly, and frequently violated the laws of war. As a result, the U.S military was under no international legal obligation to provide Geneva standards of treatment—as articulated in the Third Geneva Convention—to the captured fighters in these engagements. The lessons learned from Vietnam about the value of Geneva compliance, however, provide an important comparison to the recent conflicts within the GWOT.

In addition, these cases were chosen for comparison because the norms, rules, and guidelines promulgated after Vietnam provide the context for subsequent U.S. actions—and ultimately, disputes—regarding the laws of war. The lessons learned about humane treatment, the value of the Geneva Conventions, and the challenges incumbent in fighting an irregular guerilla force bear significant value for the contemporary issues facing the United States.

From the initial letter from the International Committee of the Red Cross (ICRC) in 1964 stating that the conflict in Vietnam had escalated to the level of "international armed conflict," the United States pledged its willingness not only to comply with the norm governing POW treatment but to develop broad definitions for POWs, definitions that were even more generous than those provided in the Geneva Conventions. President

Lyndon B. Johnson's administration argued that an expansive view of the Geneva Conventions should be taken for three primary reasons:

- the belief that extending Geneva protections was good for winning "hearts and minds";
- the belief that an expansive view of the conventions would "ameliorate domestic and international criticism of the war"; and
- the belief that if the U.S. military provided humane treatment for North Vietnamese and Viet Cong POWs, it would earn reciprocal treatment for captured U.S. soldiers and sailors.[67]

The goal of detainee policy in Vietnam was not merely to extract tactical intelligence from the belligerents. Rather, detainee treatment was envisioned as a critical component of the counterinsurgency campaign against the North Vietnamese and as an attempt to influence the postconflict outcome. The central importance afforded to detainee treatment was highlighted by initiatives such as the Chieu Hoi program, an operation to persuade captured North Vietnamese soldiers, Viet Cong, and North Vietnamese civilians to side with South Vietnam. Initiated in 1963 by President Ngo Dinh Diem and authorized by the United States in 1965, the Chieu Hoi program promoted the defection and neutralization of more than 194,000 North Vietnamese through vocational training, education, and political amnesty.[68] The Chieu Hoi program served two goals: depleting the manpower of North Vietnam and diminishing the effectiveness of communist ideology.

Compliance with the Geneva Conventions regarding prisoner treatment in Vietnam, however, was complicated by the fact that the United States did not directly maintain or administer detainee facilities. Reports of prisoner cruelty and abuse at the hands of South Vietnamese forces surfaced to the media, U.S. military leaders, and policy makers throughout the conflict. The United States bore some of the responsibility for these abuses because it supported the South Vietnamese counterinsurgency efforts.

Despite the importance of detainee treatment to the conduct of the counterinsurgency campaign in Vietnam, compliance with the Fourth

Geneva Convention—recognizing noncombatant immunity—was anything but exemplary. The most notable account of civilian victimization was the massacre at My Lai, in which U.S. infantry personnel, under the command of Lt. William Calley, killed approximately three hundred unarmed noncombatants including elderly civilians, women, and children. Civilian authorities and policy makers largely overlooked the events at My Lai until a year later, when the journalist Seymour M. Hersh published an account of the events based on his conversations with the Vietnam veteran Ron Ridenhour.[69]

The impact of Vietnam was felt widely throughout the government and broader U.S. society. For example, the DoD significantly altered its doctrine, training, and education programs to reflect the lessons learned in Vietnam, particularly about the value of compliance with the Third and Fourth Geneva Conventions. In order to determine the underlying causes of the My Lai massacre, General William Westmoreland commissioned a review led by General William Peers. The Peers Report concluded that systemic deficiencies existed in the military with regards to training and education of Geneva Conventions provisions, the handling and treatment of POWs, and the treatment and safeguarding of noncombatants.

The DoD consequently instituted the law-of-war program, driven by an organizational commitment within the Pentagon to protecting POWs and civilians during future international armed conflicts. In addition to the law-of-war program, U.S. military doctrine also adapted to reflect the legacy of Vietnam. Field Manual (FM) 19-40 ("Handling of Prisoners of War"), originally issued in 1952 and reissued in 1976, reinforced the idea that the objectives of the detainee program were to implement the Geneva Conventions with full accountability.[70]

The experience of Vietnam caused large changes for the three groups of actors examined here. A new consensus was reached on the importance of humane treatment of both prisoners and civilians—the gloves were on. The fracturing of this consensus constitutes the purpose of the book. It will reveal important insights not only about past actions but also about where norms on detainee treatment are today and where they could be tomorrow.

ROAD MAP

The book's organization mirrors the proposed model for norm change: the first section of the book examines how the norm came to be embedded, the middle section examines how it was challenged by various actors, and the conclusion examines what the effects of this norm change have been on U.S. reputation, foreign policy, and identity. To set the stage for the case studies examining the role played by the three sets of actors, the next two chapters survey the history of U.S. development of and engagement with the laws of war.

Chapter 2 begins with the importance given to treating prisoners humanely during the U.S. Revolutionary War. It then traces the influence of this conviction through the Civil War, during which the Union issued the Lieber Code, a set of instructions ordering field commanders to treat captured soldiers as POWs rather than as common criminals. It then reviews the broad pattern of U.S. compliance with the Hague Conventions and the Geneva Conventions up to the end of the Korean War, including the measures taken during these decades to incorporate the laws into domestic practice.

Chapter 3 starts by analyzing U.S. behavior during the Vietnam War in order to provide a comparison with contemporary decision making within the similar context of fighting an asymmetric opponent. This chapter assesses U.S. compliance with the Geneva Conventions during this conflict and explores the ways in which Vietnam compelled the DoD to develop new training, education, and doctrinal standards around the laws of war. The chapter will conclude with an assessment of how these rules came to constitute the norm standard that would endure until 2001.

Chapters 4 through 6 examine the process of normative change from the perspectives of the three groups of actors. Chapter 4 assesses the role of the lawyers; chapter 5, the role of the policy makers; and chapter 6, the role of the interrogators. For each chapter, the existing rule structure prior to 2001 will be presented before examining how each group either engaged in normative contestation or not following the shock of 9/11. The self-interests and arguments of the actors will be presented before looking at how these disputes drove a new understanding of the norm.

Chapter 7 concludes with the findings of the book: how does norm change occur, and why does it matter? As such, it investigates the harms imposed on various U.S. interests by the decision to use torture and covers the lessons learned from the life-cycle theory of normative change. This final chapter also examines the development of the new norm framework for detainee treatment by covering the various reviews—judicial, congressional, and executive—that occurred following the Bush administration's legal and policy decisions. It then concludes by assessing the potential durability of this framework and what it means for detainee treatment in the future.

This book engages one of the most important questions driving the studies of international security and international law: what limits exist on state behavior during wartime? How and under what conditions do the laws of war restrain states, especially powerful ones like the United States, in their use of force? The question of how to promote humanity at war is not simply a military concern: it is a matter of identity and leadership for the United States. Many of the decisions made in the GWOT not only called into question U.S. identity but also unintentionally undermined its counterterrorism goals. U.S. actions served as a recruiting tool for al-Qaeda and, more recently, ISIL, who pointed to images from Abu Ghraib and the continued existence of Guantánamo as evidence of U.S. inhumanity.

This research also seeks to understand how scholars, practitioners, and the public will remember and reflect upon the GWOT in the future. Will the United States—like France after the Algerian Civil War—hold up a mirror to its actions and recoil against the self-inflicted wounds it has cast in the name of national security? Will it choose to use this opportunity—as the U.S. military did after the Vietnam War—to amend its education, training, and doctrine to align U.S. values with practice more explicitly? Or will the United States do nothing?

How *did* the gloves come off after 9/11? Top policy makers and administration lawyers inside the Bush White House used their access and influence to probe ambiguities in the norms and laws governing detainee treatment, which had guided U.S. practice and decision making for hundreds of years. Guided by their arguments—"never again" and "anything goes"—U.S. policy was crafted that stripped detainees of their humanity.

The norms governing the humane treatment of those in U.S. custody during wartime are not static rules. They are living entities that engage, and occasionally collide, with power, national security, and state self-interest. How actors interpret those norms and the texts in which they are embedded provides the focus for this research examining U.S. compliance with the laws of war.

2

HISTORY OF POW TREATMENT IN THE UNITED STATES

From the Revolutionary War to the Korean War

Should any American soldier be so base and infamous as to injure any [prisoner] . . . I do most earnestly enjoin you to bring him to such severe and exemplary punishment as the enormity of the crime may require. Should it extend to death itself, it will not be disproportional to its guilt at such a time and in such a cause . . . for by such conduct they bring shame, disgrace and ruin to themselves and their country.

—ROBERT NOWLAN, "GEORGE WASHINGTON,
CHARGE TO NORTHERN EXPEDITIONARY FORCE, SEPTEMBER 14, 1775"

C USTOMS AND STANDARDS for handling POWs were conceptualized and accepted long before the United States became a sovereign state. Such customary law found its place in Continental Army military doctrine and in the thinking of leaders such as General George Washington about the relationship between prisoner treatment and state identity. The early authors of American wartime policy quickly adopted models steeped in these concepts, emphasizing just and humane treatment. The Revolutionary War proved a formative conflict for the first U.S. military leaders and policy makers to establish norms of compliance with this corpus of law. As such, despite lapses in compliance throughout the last 240 years and variations in the standards of prisoner treatment, it is not naïve to argue that humane POW treatment is a founding ideal of the United States.

Each U.S. conflict illustrates how these legal rules and norms were continually embedded in military tradition, education, law, and discourse. Examining the history of POW treatment by the United States in wartime outlines a narrative of a state that, faced with new and unexpected POW issues in conflict after conflict, sought to reinforce its founding principles and to match its practice with its values. In accordance with the life cycle of norm change, the United States entered each conflict up to 9/11 building on previous POW-treatment lessons learned. Because this book seeks to answer *how* the United States arrived at the post-9/11 decision to torture, an analysis of U.S. treatment of POWs throughout history is critical to establish the depth of internalization of these rules and norms. From the early adoption of the customary laws of war to the role played by the United States in developing the Geneva Conventions regime, compliance with these international laws has played an undeniably important role in U.S. decision making and military action.

It is instructive first to locate the norm governing POW treatment within the broader framework of the laws of war. The laws of war—or the laws of armed conflict—refer to the body of international law that governs the military's duties, responsibilities, and activities with regards to combatants and noncombatants in conflict. The modern law-of-war canon is divided into two constituent parts: *jus ad bellum*—the legal permissibility of the decision to go to war—and *jus in bello*—how the war may legitimately be fought. These criteria embody a calculus for determining if military action is morally justifiable and emphasize that the moral permissibility of the decision to go to war and the conduct of hostilities are inextricably linked.

The norms governing POW treatment are enshrined in *jus in bello*, justice in war, rules. In modern discourse, *jus in bello* includes the principles of discrimination and proportionality, which impose restraints on belligerents during the course of conflict.[1] "Discrimination" is the idea that combatants must make every effort to differentiate between legitimate and illegitimate targets in wartime and to direct their military force against legitimate targets. "Proportionality" is the concept that combatants must deploy commensurate force against legitimate targets and must weigh the accomplishment of a military outcome against the potential civilian lives lost. These guidelines are contained in both the Geneva Conventions and the Hague Conventions. The Hague Conventions of 1899 and 1907 stipulate the rules for what types of weapons can be employed; the Geneva Conventions outline how vulnerable parties in conflict need to be treated. The obligation to discriminate between combatant and noncombatant, as well as the obligation to weigh the military advantage against the potential civilian lives lost, is a moral calculus not just for military leaders but also for each individual soldier and sailor. *Jus in bello* rules underscore that once belligerents have laid down their arms, they no longer constitute a threat and rather become individuals who have a right to be protected and treated humanely.

This chapter provides a historical overview of U.S. POW treatment to set the stage for understanding how long-embedded *jus in bello* norms were so abruptly discarded in the face of a new and unknown enemy. By outlining the evolution of POW-treatment laws and norms from the U.S. Revolutionary War through the Korean War, this background offers a foundation to explore in depth the U.S. experience in Vietnam, put forward in chapter 3. This chapter also details the contours of the Geneva Conventions regime, a set of rules characterized by "conscious efforts to agree on their major provisions, explicit consent on the part of individual participants, and formal expressions of the results."[2] Following the examination of the 1949 Geneva Conventions, the chapter then explores the U.S. wartime experience in the Korean War, which will shape the context for a subsequent comparison of the decision making in Vietnam and the GWOT—two conflicts remarkably distinct in POW-treatment outcomes.

The common theme connecting the conflicts reviewed in this chapter is a clear U.S. effort to codify laws of war that emphasize the humanity of the enemy and the justice necessary in wartime to respect this ideal. Beginning with the Revolutionary War, U.S. policy makers established America's role in the world as a protector of human rights, a status not to be undermined by the brutish characteristics of war.

THE U.S. REVOLUTIONARY WAR

With the outbreak of the Revolutionary War, the Continental Army adopted the American Articles of War on June 30, 1775. For 176 years—until the adoption of the UCMJ—these articles, updated over time, governed the operations and conduct of war in the United States.[3] The articles stipulated the code of criminal law for the armed forces and were heavily based on the British Articles of War, themselves, according to John Adams, a "literal translation" of Roman law.[4] In addition, the ideals of the Enlightenment and, in particular, the writings of Emmerich de Vattel and Hugo Grotius on the laws of war impressed upon American military leaders the importance of fighting with civility and humanity. At Washington's request, Congress issued a set of general POW regulations on May 21, 1776. These regulations included providing prisoner rations equal to the rations issued to American troops, segregating officers from enlisted prisoners, offering employment possibilities to captured prisoners, and prohibiting prisoner enlistment in American armed forces.[5] Congress reinforced the importance of restraint in its commission to General Washington on June 17, 1775, which ordered him to "regulate your conduct in every respect by the rules and discipline of war."[6]

Following these regulations, Washington charged his troops to treat the captured Hessians who had surrendered following the Battle of Trenton in December 1776 "with humanity."[7] He ordered: "Let [the Hessians] have no reason to complain of our copying the brutal example of the British army."[8] Other examples exist of U.S. restraint in the treatment of British prisoners of war. In the Battle of Stony Point in July 1779, for example, Continental forces surprised the British Army and consequently spared the 543 prisoners who surrendered. According to one scholar, "Stony Point displayed American arms in a new light. Not only had the Americans proved their discipline and martial prowess, they had demonstrated a higher moral standard than their opponents."[9] This is not to imply that the Continental Army complied in every instance with customary international law. Atrocities did occur—on both sides—but the newly created United States sought to protect both its combatants and prisoners as well as abide by the customary rules of war. The legislative and executive decisions—and the subsequent actions of the Continental Army troops—first embedded the notion that humane treatment of captured combatants represented an American ideal.

Following the Revolutionary War, the United States concluded treaties with several states that included provisions for the protections of prisoners. In the 1785 Treaty of Amity and Commerce that the United States concluded with Prussia, Article 24 delineated rules and standards for the treatment of captured prisoners. It prohibited sending prisoners "into distant and inclement countries, or . . . crouding them into close and noxious places."[10] It further allowed each officer who was taken prisoner "as many rations, and of the same articles and quality as are allowed . . . [by the capturing power] to officers of equal rank in their own army."[11] This treaty was the first significant international attempt to protect war victims and would lay the groundwork for national military codes regulating the treatment of captured prisoners.[12] Successive treaties, such as the 1786 Treaty with Morocco, stipulated: "In case of a War between the Parties, the Prisoners are not to be made Slaves, but to be exchanged one for another, Captain for Captain, Officer for Officer, and one private Man for another."[13] While these treaties formalized concepts that had existed for centuries as customary international law, it is significant that the United States included provisions in these early treaties for prisoner treatment. The codification of these norms signaled U.S. recognition that limits existed on the use of force.

There is no doubt that the Revolutionary War served as a formative experience in developing U.S. interests and values. Notably, U.S. leaders began immediately codifying internationally accepted norms related to human rights in wartime, as demonstrated by the ample attention paid to POWs in the American Articles of War and the several bilateral treaties adopted in the post-Revolution period. Together, Washington and his fellow civilian and military leaders founded the United States on the ideals of restraint and respect for human dignity, developing an implicit U.S. moral code that would translate explicitly to forthcoming legislation as well as conflict behavior.

WAR OF 1812

The War of 1812 was caused in large part by the capture and treatment of U.S. civilians by the British Navy. During this time, Britain needed additional bodies for its ongoing conflicts with Napoleon's France. The British Navy's practice of removing U.S. sailors from merchant vessels and impressing them into British service antagonized the United States. For their part, the British invoked British Common Law, which claimed that individuals born as British subjects would always remain British subjects; "naturalized" U.S. citizens were not recognized.[14] While the causes of the war are complex, the issue of impressment directly contributed to the outbreak of war between the United States and Britain.[15]

Throughout the conflict, treatment of U.S. prisoners varied significantly. Many prisoners—such as Winfield Scott—were paroled and returned home; others languished in prisons such as Dartmoor, in England, where 270 Americans died from disease and pneumonia.[16] POWs captured by U.S. forces were immediately evacuated from the war zones and either sent "deep into U.S. territory"[17] or given quarter in private homes.[18] Canadian government archives hold original letters and documentation of British POWs held by the United States. One chronicles the capture of Captain Henry Nelles and outlines his lenient terms of parole in Massachusetts.[19] Another shows correspondence between Captain William Hamilton Merritt and his girlfriend. She writes: "It is very gratifying to me to know that you enjoy so much tranquility in your new situation."[20]

U.S. treatment of POWs during the War of 1812 included a famous instance of retaliation. In October 1812, British soldiers captured a number of longtime U.S. residents and naturalized citizens of Irish descent. Considered to be British subjects, these twenty-three American Irishmen were set to be tried in Britain for treason.[21] In response, the United States confined twenty-three British prisoners and threatened retaliatory execution. The British responded by confining forty-six more Americans, and the process spiraled to such an extent that by 1814 all officers held by the United States were kept in close confinement. This retaliatory policy cooled, however, before any prisoners were harmed.

In comparison to the Revolutionary War, the treaties concluded in the aftermath of the War of 1812 failed to codify explicitly additional POW-treatment laws. The Treaty of Ghent, which ended the conflict, mentioned prisoners only insofar as it stipulated that prisoners taken on either side should be returned as soon as possible.[22] The treaty neither resolved the impressment concerns that gave rise to the conflict nor included any tenets regarding humane treatment for surrendering combatants. Perhaps with the Revolutionary War still serving as a recent example and the continued applicability of the American Articles of War, U.S. leaders found little need to elaborate on POW treatment in this repeat bilateral clash, as the retaliatory escalation ended without widespread harm to prisoners on either side.

MEXICAN–AMERICAN WAR

Following the War of 1812, the U.S. Army was reduced in size, and scant training was offered to officers at the nascent U.S. Military Academy on the laws of war.[23] Soldiers received no practical training in prisoner handling and treatment; what education did exist consisted of scholarship from de Vattel and Grotius.[24] Thus, by the time the United States annexed Texas and subsequently clashed with Mexican troops on the Rio Grande, the U.S. military had internalized few lessons learned from previous conflicts.

During the war, concerns about reciprocity and the potential treatment of captured U.S. combatants in Mexican hands abounded. Prior to the declaration of war, Mexican treatment of Texan combatants had been infamous; as is well known, the Mexican general Antonio López de Santa Anna did not take any prisoners at the Battle of the Alamo in March 1836.[25] Later that month, he similarly ordered the execution of all prisoners taken at Goliad.[26] When Santa Anna threatened to execute Texans—some of whom were U.S. citizens—who had been captured during their raids into Mexico, the U.S. minister to Mexico highlighted current U.S. thinking when he argued: "They are human beings and prisoners of war, and it is the right and duty of all nations to see that Mexico does not violate the principles and usages of civilized war—more particularly it is the duty of the United States to maintain those laws and usages on this Continent."[27]

After sweeping U.S. victories led to the capture of thousands of Mexican soldiers, many enlisted prisoners were released on a parole of honor in order to decrease the burden the United States faced in retaining all of its captives.[28] This act of clemency was revoked only for those Mexicans who reentered the war in violation of parole. When captured, these combatants were executed.[29] General Winfield Scott also oversaw the execution of a number of American deserters who were captured after joining the war on the side of Mexico.[30]

Despite these instances of extreme punishment, prisoner treatment during the Mexican–American war is generally regarded as "civilized."[31] Newspapers from the time include stories of prisoner capture, noting that prisoners received the best treatment "known amongst civilized nations to prisoners of war," that "people on both sides are capable of behaving with great kindness and courtesy,"[32] and that "officers while prisoners were well treated."[33] Stephanie Carvin attributes this behavior to Washington's desire to portray itself as benevolent to the Mexican citizens in its conquered territory, in order to ease the U.S. military victories, and to the parties' shared cultural understanding of war derived from their mutual European inheritance.[34] As the war came to an end, General Zachary Taylor concluded an agreement with Mexico to exchange hostages immediately, and he even went so far as to parole the Mexican captives early, allowing them to return to their homes before the prisoner exchange was formalized.[35] As a result of Taylor's early parole and the similar actions of other U.S. commanders, the U.S. military accrued little practical experience handling prisoners during the war with Mexico. While U.S. treatment of Mexican POWs was largely positive, U.S. POW policy remained largely ad hoc and rooted in ancient and European philosophy and theology. The American Articles of War again served as the basis for prisoner treatment during the Mexican–American War and functioned effectively in this conventional fight between two sovereign states. However, as the nation descended into civil war just a few years later, a gaping hole existed in U.S. military doctrine regarding how Union troops should handle captured Confederate soldiers. To fill this gap, the Union would issue the Lieber Code in 1863.

THE LIEBER CODE AND THE U.S. CIVIL WAR

The Lieber Code, developed during the Civil War by Dr. Francis Lieber, a German immigrant, drew on norms of humane treatment on the battle-field that already existed in the nineteenth century. According to the scholar Richard Hartigan, "Restraint [in war prior to the Lieber Code] did not stem from a conscious articulation of principles of international law so much as a kind of soldier's honor not unlike the medieval chivalric code of fair fight."[36] Despite the customary practice of respecting the laws of war, the Lieber Code, also known as General Orders No. 100, was the first formal codifica-tion of these practices. The code was the first modern military field man-ual.[37] While earlier historical examples had prescribed and codified the rules of warfare—such as the Book of Deuteronomy, the Third Lateran Council, the Hindu Code of Manu, the law of Szu-ma in China's Chou dynasty, and the proclamation of Caliph Abu Bakr in 634 AD—the Lieber Code was the first attempt by a modern, Westphalian sovereign state to place formal limitations on the activities of soldiers in battle.[38] The code was a series of instructions issued by President Abraham Lincoln to the Union forces that ordered field commanders to treat captured soldiers as POWs rather than as common criminals. It drew upon historical international law,[39] existing state practice,[40] contemporary precedents,[41] and Lieber's own experience as a soldier in Europe fighting both against Napoleon at Water-loo and in the Greek Civil War of 1824–1825.

The catalyst for Lieber's authorship of the code was the Battle of Bull Run, in which the following question was raised: could prisoners be exchanged without recognizing Confederate sovereignty? The Union did not recognize the Confederate fighters as professional soldiers but rather as armed insurgents. Yet, as increasing numbers of Union forces were captured, it became evident that military doctrine was needed to protect the rights of both sides' forces. Recognizing a lacuna in the current military code, Secretary of War Edwin Stanton commissioned a panel of army officers and international legal experts in 1862 to develop a manual on the rules of war. As a personal friend of Secretary Stanton and Major General Henry W. Halleck, the general-in-chief of U.S. land forces, Lieber, who was a noted legal scholar at Columbia College of Law, was asked to participate on the panel. Lieber, the only civilian member, drafted the code of military conduct. He believed that further formal regulation of war was needed: "Ever since the beginning of our present War, it has appeared clearer and clearer to me, that the President ought to issue a set of rules and definitions providing for the most urgent cases, occurring under the Laws and Usages of War, and on which our Articles of War are silent."[42]

The Lieber Code lays out the rights of POWs as well as the obligations of the capturing troops in an attempt to codify *jus in bello* standards. In particular, Article 56 of the code states: "A prisoner of war is subject to no punishment for being a public enemy, nor is any revenge wreaked upon him by the intentional infliction of any suffering, or disgrace, by cruel imprisonment, want of food, by mutilation, death, or any other barbarity."[43] Lieber clearly articulates that POWs are not criminals or thugs but rather are individuals who suffer in war and are thus deserving of protection. The code further articulates the prisoner-exchange system, the punishment for deserters and spies, the meaning of flags of truce and flags of protection, and the rights of black POWs that were captured by Southern troops and often forced into hard labor or slavery.

Fundamentally, the crux of the Lieber Code can be found in Article 15, which states: "Men who take up arms against one another in public war do not cease on this account to be moral beings, responsible to one another and to God."[44] Equally significant, one of the innovations of the code was the recognition that the purpose of laws governing POWs "was the prevention of things being done in war which might hinder the return to peace."[45]

Despite its codification during the Civil War, the code did not have an immediate impact on battlefield behavior and did not enjoy universal socialization. Confederate troops, in fact, dismissed the Lieber Code as

Northern propaganda and refused to accept its tenets as binding on their military conduct.[46] Though the code laid the groundwork for future international humanitarian agreements, it unfortunately had little practical effect for the prisoners captured during the course of the war.

Though they were not universally applied during the Civil War, the tenets of the Lieber Code became integrated in U.S. practice through judicial decisions immediately following the war. Upon the cessation of hostilities between the North and the South, the judicial branch began to hear cases that challenged former president Lincoln's suspension of civil liberties during the war. One of the cases was *Ex Parte Vallandigham*, a Supreme Court case in which Clement Vallandigham, a candidate for the governor's race in Ohio, was convicted by a military commission of expressing sympathy for the Confederacy. He sought to have this conviction overturned by the Supreme Court and though the court denied his writ of certiorari, the justice assessing his case referred to the Lieber Code in his decision. Justice Wayne stated that Vallandigham's trial by military commission was valid because the commander acted "in conformity with the instructions for the government of the armies of the United States, approved by the President . . . which were prepared by Francis Lieber."[47] According to one scholar, "For the military, Lieber's Code may have been informational rather than directory, but for the [Supreme] Court, it was law, binding and prescriptive."[48] In addition, Supreme Court Justice Salmon Chase wrote to Lieber and called the code a "great work."[49]

The development of the Lieber Code represented a watershed event in the history of prisoner treatment, signaling that states do not have unlimited means at their disposal to handle captured combatants and that prisoner treatment has a causal effect on the peace-building process after the conflict has concluded. The Lieber Code successfully formalized U.S. ideals of humane and just prisoner treatment and received praise from the country's highest court—a signal of internalization for U.S. wartime norms articulated originally by George Washington. As America's role in the world expanded, the Lieber Code and other U.S. military doctrines would influence international legal norms throughout the twentieth century, beginning with the Hague Conventions.

THE HAGUE CONVENTIONS AND WORLD WAR I

In the words of the scholar Geoffrey Best, the Lieber Code was "so good and comprehensive that it became the prototype and model for Europe's emulation in the succeeding decades."[50] In 1899, Czar Nicholas II of Russia convened a conference at The Hague in order to address arms limitations and legal standards for warfare. The result of this effort was the Hague Convention of 1899, which sought to balance respect for the laws of war against emerging warfare technologies and the "ever increasing requirements of civilization."[51] During the conclusion of the 1899 Hague Convention, a new conference was also called to revise the Geneva Convention of 1864, which emerged from the efforts of Henri Dunant to form the ICRC to protect victims of warfare and to establish rules to prevent the widespread neglect of sick and injured soldiers.[52] This second Geneva conference took place in 1906 and established one of the few sources of international law in place throughout World War I.[53] The following year, the 1899 Hague standards were revised with the 1907 Hague Conventions, again dedicated to establishing limitations on the methods and means of warfare. Hague Convention IV contained a section dedicated to the rights of POWs, stating: "Prisoners of war are in the power of the hostile Government, but not of the individuals or corps who capture them. They must be humanely treated."[54] These standards of humane treatment for POWs governed military conduct during World War I.

In addition, the United States issued its first Rules of Land Warfare manual in April 1914.[55] This document, issued because U.S. officials assessed that the Hague and Geneva Conventions were not exhaustive, was based largely on the still highly regarded Lieber Code.[56] Despite signing and ratifying both of those conventions and providing an even more comprehensive rulebook of its own, the United States entered World War I proclaiming that neither the Geneva nor Hague Conventions were applicable to the conflict.[57] This exception was drawn from Article 24 of the Geneva Convention and Article 2 of the Hague Convention, both of which stated that the agreed-upon laws applied only in situations in which all belligerents were convention signatories.[58] While the major players in the war were signatories, some minor participants such as Costa Rica and Liberia were not. This fact allowed U.S. officials to claim exception.[59] Alvey Adee, second assistant secretary of state, mentioned to the American Red Cross as early as August 1917 that the Hague Convention was nonbinding.[60] However, he appeared to see no real import to this nuance, stating that customary international law would cover most relevant topics: "In so far as the rules set forth in the convention are declaratory of international law, they are of course obligatory as being a part of the law of nations, but not by virtue of the convention in which they are laid down."[61]

By November 1917, the U.S. legal interpretation was creating friction between the belligerents and between Washington and the ICRC. The German government, attempting to negotiate an exchange of medical personnel, wrote that Germany "will bring stipulations of these international agreements [the Hague Conventions of 1907 and Geneva Convention of 1906] into execution according to their letter, as well as according to their spirit . . . and look[s] forward to a statement of this kind by the Government of the United States."[62] In response, U.S. Secretary of State Robert Lansing replied in early 1918 that the U.S. government "does not consider the provisions of the Geneva Convention of 1906, or of the Hague Convention No. X of 1907, as binding on the United States in the present war."[63] However, Secretary Lansing went on to say that the vast majority— all but two—of the two conventions' articles would be accepted as a modus vivendi. Still, this assertion elicited a sharp rebuke from the ICRC, whose officials wrote later that year, "We cannot help thinking that America's action is a dangerous precedent. As for us it would prevent us from doing anything in favor of her prisoners."[64] Nevertheless, similar arguments were made with regards to the nonapplicability of the Hague Convention by Germany and Great Britain when the respective states found such legal arguments expedient.[65]

Regardless of the political opposition to applying the conventions, accounts indicate that the U.S. military generally operated as if the conventions were binding.[66] Indeed, U.S. General John J. Pershing ordered his forces to treat captured enemy combatants as if the relevant treaties were legally in force.[67] Still, there are some reports of U.S. soldiers killing wounded or surrendering enemy combatants,[68] and U.S. officials sometimes attempted to ensure good treatment for U.S. POWs by threatening reciprocal treatment on German captives.[69] Josephus Daniels, secretary of the navy, wrote to the secretary of state, saying, "While, in the interests of humanity, reprisal is an act which the Navy Department would only advocate as a last resort, yet it must be borne in mind that this government has at its disposal a weapon which is quite as efficacious as any which Germany might be able to bring to bear on any of our prisoners."[70]

On the whole, however, failures to provide proper treatment often stemmed not from bad intentions but simply from economic and logistical realities.[71] When the United States entered the war, the War Department was ill prepared to provide for the rapid influx of enemy prisoners, and the resulting POW program was largely improvised.[72] Ultimately, the United States was able to negotiate POW issues with Germany based on treaties concluded between the United States and Prussia in 1799 and 1828.[73] The war's end also saw the United States and Germany establish bilateral treaties to clarify POW treatment and exchange, most notably in the German-American POW treaty of 1918.[74]

In terms of prisoner-treatment norms, World War I functioned as a vehicle for the U.S. military to test its capacity to handle POWs on an international scale. It is significant to note the precedent set by U.S. military orders to abide by the Hague and Geneva Conventions, despite their declared nonapplicability by civilian leaders to the conflict. This difference in approaches to POW treatment between military and civilian leaders would mirror debates in the United States almost a hundred years later, with military leaders initially assuming full compliance with the Geneva Conventions in the field in Afghanistan in 2001 even while civilian leaders were debating their applicability. In an attempt to prepare for future conflicts, after World War I the United States acknowledged the pitfalls in its botched handling of POWs through both negotiations with Germany and a subsequent revision of the Geneva Conventions.

THE GENEVA CONVENTIONS AND WORLD WAR II

The abuses of World War I, the incredible scale and devastation of that war, and the numbers of prisoners captured on both sides made evident that further refinement of the laws of war was needed. The 1929 Geneva Convention Relative to the Treatment of Prisoners of War expanded the baseline standard of humane treatment for POWs established in the Hague Conventions of 1899 and 1907, stipulating—among other issues—the hygienic standards in POW camps, the intellectual and moral needs of the prisoners, the organization of work and pay for prisoners, and the penal and judicial sanctions for misbehavior. In one famous passage, it stated:

> Prisoners of war are in the power of the hostile Government, but not of the individuals or formation which captured them. They shall at all times be humanely treated and protected, particularly against acts of violence, from insults and from public curiosity. Measures of reprisal against them are forbidden. Prisoners of war are entitled to respect for their persons and honour. Women shall be treated with all consideration due to their sex. Prisoners retain their full civil capacity.[75]

In addition, the 1929 Convention improved on its predecessors by including the provision in Article 82 that the humane standards articulated in the treaty applied to all signatories whether or not their opponent had signed it.[76]

Despite these improvements, the 1929 Convention fared little better in World War II than the earlier conventions had in World War I. The Japanese government, under pressure from the international community, signed the 1929 Convention but never ratified it. To the Japanese, concern for the humane treatment of captured prisoners was a foreign concept; in their view, surrendering soldiers represented a disgrace to the military profession.[77] Early in the war, the U.S. government sought to convince the Soviet government that it was in its best interest to sign and ratify the convention; the Soviet Union, however, informed the U.S. ambassador in Moscow that it would comply with the 1907 Hague Conventions, the 1925 Gas Protocol, and the 1929 Geneva Conventions only with assurances of reciprocity from the German government.[78] As the Soviet government refused to sign the 1929 Conventions, German forces refused to apply humane standards of treatment to captured Soviet troops.[79]

Most accounts cite U.S. treatment of POWs in World War II as being generally positive and in adherence to the Geneva Convention of 1929.[80] Indeed, the U.S. public at the time even complained that prisoners being held in the United States were being treated so well as to be "coddled."[81] A *New York Times* article from 1944 quotes Brigadier General Charles "Chuck" Eager denying the "talk of 'molly-coddling,'" saying prisoners received only cast-off goods, rather than being clothed and housed in newly produced lodging and clothes. "The idea certainly is not to coddle them," Eager said.[82]

Upon further inspection, a number of issues arose regarding U.S. treatment of enemy prisoners, and to exclude them from the discussion would be a dangerous oversimplification. The primary issues at hand were U.S. political indoctrination of German captives, accounts of U.S. servicemen killing captives in the Pacific theater, secretive military trials for accused spies, the conversion of POW status after Italy and Germany surrendered in order to facilitate using prisoners as a source of labor, and extremely poor conditions for German soldiers captured at the war's close.

Many of the enemy soldiers captured by U.S. forces were brought to the United States, where U.S. authorities had to adapt quickly to the influx of prisoners. In addition to establishing legal work programs, U.S. officials began a program of political indoctrination that attempted to de-Nazify the German captives in the U.S. system. A unit of the U.S. Army's Special Projects Division, self-dubbed "The Factory," developed a "crash course in democracy" for German POWs.[83] The program was so widespread that at the end of the war, roughly 74 percent of prisoners returned to Germany "with an appreciation of the value of democracy and a friendly attitude toward America."[84] While this program might not have violated the letter of the 1929 Geneva Conventions, since they do not contain stipulations regarding reeducation or prisoner indoctrination,[85] Paul Springer notes that the program "certainly violated the spirit" of these international legal frameworks.[86] In fact, U.S. officials kept the program's existence secret until June 1945, after it had already been running for one year.[87] This secrecy was likely maintained because of the controversial nature of reeducation.[88] The secretary of war publicly rejected the notion of education programs in November 1944, despite the program being underway at that time.[89] The effects of this program would come to haunt U.S. personnel during the wars in Korea and Vietnam, when U.S. POWs were routinely subjected to political indoctrination by enemy captors that cited U.S. practice during World War II as justification for the effort.[90] Interestingly, one German escapee cited the program as the motivation for his getaway: "We'd been lectured to death about the virtues of democracy; it was time to see them for myself."[91]

Serious challenges to U.S. credibility arose in the Pacific theater after allegations that U.S. servicemen were shooting and killing enemy combatants rather than accepting their surrender and taking them captive.[92] At the time of Japan's surrender, Allied governments held a total of 38,666 Japanese combatants.[93] The most common explanation given for these low numbers is that surrender was unacceptable in Japanese culture at the time.[94] The Imperial Japanese Army Military Field Code of 1941 directed soldiers to "never live to experience shame as a prisoner."[95] Those who did live to experience POW shame were treated as nonpersons and erased from Japanese records.[96] In an internal letter, the Japanese foreign minister stated, "As you know, our Army maintains the position that Japanese prisoners of war do not exist."[97] As such, it has been speculated that the low number of Japanese POWs may have stemmed in part from Japanese suicides in the face of surrender.[98] However, allegations still surfaced that U.S. forces killed Japanese servicemen signaling surrender. Robert Doyle attributes this brutality in part to an ethos of self-defense, spurred by U.S. experiences of being ambushed or trapped by Japanese soldiers pretending to surrender.[99] While this justification may have existed, the stain on the U.S. record caused by the illegal killings remained.

Back in the United States, another act of questionable legality occurred in 1942, when eight German spies were captured on U.S. soil during an attempt to disrupt communication lines and attack businesses owned by Jewish Americans.[100] President Roosevelt tried the eight men in a secret military tribunal instead of in a civilian court, a decision supported by the Supreme Court. As a result, six of the eight men were sentenced to death. Years later, the precedent set by *Ex parte Quirin* would be used by the Bush administration to justify the sentencing of individuals captured during the GWOT by military commission.

As World War II drew to an end, legal nuances and logistical challenges contributed to a worsening of conditions for Italian and German captives in U.S. hands. After Italy renounced its ties to Germany and joined the Allies in late 1943, Italian prisoners held in the United States were put in a strange position, as were U.S. officials. Despite protests from the new Italian government, the United States decided to form noncombat service units out of the captured Italians.[101] These units performed duties such as munitions handling and military port work, which, because the United States maintained their POW status, were incompatible with Geneva Convention Article 31,[102] which stated: "Work done by prisoners of war shall have no direct connection with the operations of the war. In particular, it is forbidden to employ prisoners in the manufacture or transport of arms or munitions of any kind, or on the transport of material destined for combatant units."[103]

German soldiers captured after the German surrender also underwent a change in status. The Allied powers, including the United States, argued that the Geneva Conventions were rendered inapplicable by the surrender, as the German Third Reich had ceased to exist.[104] Captured Germans became "Disarmed Enemy Forces" under U.S. jurisdiction rather than "Prisoners of War."[105] This semantic change came with grave material consequences, as 426,000 German prisoners were "loaned" to France for years after the war's end and forced to work in poor conditions that led to malnutrition and disease, killing tens of thousands of German soldiers.[106]

While POWs in U.S. hands are generally considered to have been well cared for, the five cases detailed above illustrate the nuances contained within that broad generalization. The conversion of POW status after the Italian and German surrenders, and especially the precedents set by *Ex parte Quirin*, point to ambiguities in the law that were exploited for national security considerations. Ultimately, gross prisoner abuses occurred at the hands of both the Axis and Allied forces, actions that prompted the expansion and codification of the laws of war in the four Geneva Conventions of 1949.[107]

1949 GENEVA CONVENTIONS

In February 1945, the ICRC convened talks in Geneva for the purpose of modifying the existing Geneva Conventions. The results of this diplomatic conference were the four Geneva Conventions of 1949.

Dunant and his associates initially drafted the First Convention in 1864, which addressed wounded and sick combatants in the field. The Second Convention, governing those wounded at sea, was initially developed in 1906 and underwent revision in 1949. The Third Convention, covering POW treatment, emerged first in 1929 and was revised in 1949. The 143 articles and five annexes of the Third Convention specifically protect those individuals who can no longer fight, such as POWs and wounded troops. This convention regulates, among other things, the medical care, working conditions, discipline, internment standards, and trial of captured fighters. It safeguards prisoners' rights by allowing the pursuit of religious, intellectual, and physical activities; by prohibiting "outrages upon personal dignity"; and by punishing "grave breaches" of the convention.[108] The Fourth Geneva Convention, which safeguards the rights of noncombatants, was developed as a direct response to the barbarity suffered by civilians in World War II at the hands of the Nazi regime.

In addition to the introduction of the Fourth Geneva Convention, the inclusion of Common Article 3—so called because it is included in all four conventions—represented the international community's condemnation of practices not previously prohibited in the conventions. One of the goals of the Geneva Conventions was to ensure that no one was outside the law's protection: combatants are accorded rights based on the Third Geneva Convention; noncombatants are guaranteed rights based on the Fourth Geneva Convention. Article 4 of the Third Geneva Convention defines combatants who are entitled to POW status as those who fulfill the following conditions:

- individuals who are commanded by a person responsible for his subordinates;
- individuals who wear fixed distinctive signs recognizable at a distance;
- individuals who carry arms openly; and
- individuals who conduct their operations in accordance with the laws and customs of war.[109]

Common Article 3 prohibits practices such as degrading treatment and torture and also establishes basic humane standards from which no derogation is permitted:

> In the case of armed conflict not of an international character occurring in the territory of one of the High Contracting Parties, each party to the conflict shall be bound to apply, as a minimum, the following provisions:
>
> Persons taking no active part in the hostilities, including members of armed forces who have laid down their arms and those placed hors de combat by sickness, wounds, detention, or any other cause, shall in all circumstances be treated humanely, without any adverse distinction founded on race, colour, religion or faith, sex, birth or wealth, or any other similar criteria.
>
> To this end the following acts are and shall remain prohibited at any time and in any place whatsoever with respect to the above-mentioned persons:
>
> - Violence to life and person, in particular murder of all kinds, mutilation, cruel treatment and torture;
> - Taking of hostages;
> - Outrages upon personal dignity, in particular, humiliating and degrading treatment;
> - The passing of sentences and the carrying out of executions without previous judgment pronounced by a regularly constituted court affording all the judicial guarantees which are recognized as indispensable by civilized peoples.

The wounded and sick shall be collected and cared for. An impartial body, such as the International Committee of the Red Cross, may offer its services to the Parties to the conflict. The Parties to the conflict should further endeavor to bring into force, by means of special agreements, all or part of the other provisions of the present Convention. The application of the preceding provisions shall not affect the legal status of the Parties to the conflict.[110]

The innovations of both Common Article 3 and the Fourth Geneva Convention represent an interest on behalf of the international community to take human rights seriously and to ensure that no matter what their status, all persons in war are afforded humane standards of treatment.

Despite these changes, much of the text of the 1949 Geneva Conventions does not differ dramatically from its predecessors, although a number of provisions were clarified and expanded. The definition of "humane treatment," for example, was bolstered from the original standard of "they must at all times be humanely treated"[111] to a much deeper description of what *inhumane* treatment looked like. The revision stated:

Any unlawful act or omission by the Detaining Power causing death or seriously endangering the health of a prisoner of war in its custody is prohibited, and will be regarded as a serious breach of the present Convention. In particular, no prisoner of war may be subjected to physical mutilation or to medical or scientific experiments of any kind which are not justified by the medical, dental or hospital treatment of the prisoner concerned and carried out in his interest.[112]

Prisoner labor was also further defined, with specific acceptable industries spelled out.[113] Food rations, rather than being provided on a basis determined by the detaining state, were standardized to ensure the continued health of all detainees.[114] Prisoners accused of crimes committed before their capture were granted Geneva Convention protections during their trials and up to their convictions.[115] Importantly for the following conflicts in East Asia, the delegations agreed that repatriation of all prisoners must be undertaken "without delay" upon the conflict's conclusion.[116] In addition, signatories agreed to bolster the efficacy and enforcement mechanisms of the new treaties by complementing the international agreements with accompanying domestic legal structures.

Following the destructiveness of two world wars in three decades, the international community mobilized to expand and deepen the protections enshrined in law for the most vulnerable populations in wartime. The Geneva protections were incorporated into many aspects of U.S. legislation as well as into military and executive orders.[117] However, conflicts in the Cold War and post–Cold War eras would test the ambiguities in these protections.

KOREAN WAR

Similar to the wars that preceded it, the Korean War was characterized by discussions of inequality of treatment, with U.S. treatment of captured communists lauded as exemplary in comparison to the treatment U.S. servicemen received at communist hands.[118] Again, concerns arose domestically that captured combatants were given *too many* liberties under American control. In a hearing with General Matthew Ridgway, supreme U.S. and UN commander in Korea, Senator Wayne Morse of Oregon asked for confirmation that captors were "limiting their liberties and their prerogatives to the Geneva Convention," noting that "one would judge from the newspaper comments that apparently we have been soft on these prisoners."[119]

At the war's immediate outset, U.S. soldiers were sometimes reluctant to take prisoners, establishing an "unofficial policy of no quarter."[120] U.S. military historians attributed this reluctance to reciprocity: U.S. servicemen were aware of the poor treatment their comrades endured in enemy captivity.[121] One month later, in July 1950, General Douglas MacArthur ordered all U.S. forces to treat captives "in accordance with the humanitarian principles applied by and recognized by civilized nations."[122] Later that same year, this order was clarified to specify compliance with the Geneva Conventions of 1949, despite the fact that the U.S. Senate would not give its consent to these new treaties until two years after the conclusion of the war. MacArthur stated:

My present instructions are to abide by the humanitarian principles of the 1949 Geneva Conventions, particularly the Common Article three. In addition, I have directed the forces under my command to abide by the detailed provisions of the prisoner-of-war convention by all concerned and have fully accredited the ICRC delegates accordingly.[123]

As the conflict continued, concerns about prisoner riots, issues of repatriation, and prisoner education dominated decision making. Prisoner actions prompted further issues with POW treatment. Initially, all prisoners were grouped together in large camps, following a Third Geneva Convention directive that "all prisoners of war shall be treated alike."[124] Communist prisoners, however, were trained to consider themselves combatants even under capture and to continue to fight via subversive activities within the POW compounds.[125] Indeed, some officers deliberately surrendered in order to assume positions of command within these POW organizations.[126] As the polarization and danger became clear to U.S. captors, they sought to implement a program of screening whereby prisoners could be separated by ideological leanings for the purposes of their immediate safety and for future ease of repatriation.[127] This decision provoked a violent backlash from hardline communist prisoners that devolved into deadly riots. One of the most memorable incidents occurred in May 1952, at Compound #62 on Koje-do Island. During this prisoner uprising, a U.S. Army general was captured and held captive as prisoners made numerous demands, including the cessation of the screening program that separated POWs and a forced confession of U.S. violations of Geneva protections.[128] Faced with extreme violence of this kind, U.S. guards used force to quell the uprisings, and dozens of prisoners were killed over the course of the war.[129] During ongoing negotiations seeking the war's conclusion, communist negotiators presented these killings as atrocities deserving of negotiation concessions.[130]

Despite the indoctrination efforts of hardline prisoners at the POW camps, U.S. officials discovered that some prisoners were strongly anti-communist, to the point where some were eager to assist in the UN effort. As a result, some of these prisoners were recruited as spies, and others assisted in translating pamphlets to be used in psychological operations.[131]

As William White writes in *The Captives of Korea*, "Geneva strictly forbade us to give them the guns they asked. Yet there are other ways of fighting the communist idea, and Geneva did not bar education, provided there was no compulsion."[132] Consequently, President Harry Truman's administration quickly moved to approve an extensive education program, justified under Geneva Convention Article 38, which stated that "the Detaining Power shall encourage the practice of intellectual, educational, and recreational pursuits."[133] The most important legitimization for these programs came from the ICRC verification of their voluntary nature.[134]

Still, the knowledge that U.S. captives were undergoing intense communist indoctrination produced some uncertainty about the morality—if not the legality—of the U.S. program. Some scholars argue that the voluntary nature made the "Indoctrination, USA style" acceptable. "Yes, we also offered our viewpoint to the prisoners we held on Koje-do," argues White, "but starvation was never one of our education tools."[135] Others saw the courses in democracy and the aims of the United Nations as a continuation of a dangerous international precedent. In the words of Major George S. Prugh, a U.S. Army lawyer during the conflict,

> Naturally both sides will justify their use of techniques, will claim that the captives being indoctrinated do so voluntarily, and will vehemently deny any attempt at wrong-doing in the program. Whether one, both or neither of the combatants is telling the truth about this is immaterial. The important thing is that the program is under way at all.[136]

By attempting to create democratic-norm entrepreneurs out of former communists, Prugh argued that the United States was failing in its duty fully to remove the prisoners from further participation in the war.[137] Indeed, some U.S. officials agreed and refused to implement the program.[138] These critiques highlight a potentially questionable U.S. practice in an otherwise well-conducted war effort.

As the conflict drew to a close, the discrepancy between strongly communist and anticommunist prisoners continued to prove problematic. The Truman administration, recalling that the USSR's POWs were sent to the gulags upon returning from World War II,[139] was determined not to repatriate any Korean or Chinese captives who did not wish to return to communist lands.[140] This determination, however, contradicted the 1949 Geneva Conventions, which mandated repatriation "without delay." Against the protests of the Chinese and North Korean negotiators, U.S. officials argued that the Geneva Conventions were intended to protect individual liberties and safety and were not meant to serve the greater interests of the prisoner's native state.[141] While this proclamation was fought bitterly by the North Koreans and Chinese during negotiations, a ban on forced repatriation ultimately prevailed and was endorsed by the ICRC and the UN General Assembly.[142] Prisoners were then transferred to the custody of neutral India and given the opportunity to meet with representatives of their home states. Ultimately, about half of the POWs in UN hands elected to remain in noncommunist lands.[143]

All in all, POW issues during the Korean War dominated—and indeed, prolonged—the armistice talks that began in 1951.[144] General Ridgway stated in a U.S. Senate hearing that "prisoner-of-war repatriation is the crux of the whole thing."[145] The paramount importance of prisoners in this conflict propelled POW issues to the frontlines of conflict diplomacy and demonstrated the United States' commitment to humanitarian treatment for all POWs, U.S. or otherwise. It is on this footing that the United States would enter the conflict in Vietnam and navigate a complex enemy in an offensive fueled by the fear of communism. The Korean War set an important precedent for the U.S. conflict in Vietnam—both in the handling of prisoners broadly but also in the difficulties of navigating the ideological tendencies of the captured prisoners more specifically.

CONCLUSION

Taken together, U.S. military history spanning from the Revolutionary War through the Korean War weaves a complicated story of POW treatment and the development of U.S. military doctrine in accordance with relevant international treaties and conventions. The origin of these norms of humane and just treatment for POWs is undeniably tied to the experiences of the American Revolution and the adoption of the American Articles of War. However, it was not until the introduction of the Lieber Code during the U.S. Civil War that these founding ideals, born out of international customary law, were formally integrated into U.S. military doctrine. In the subsequent decades, the U.S. perspective on the importance of humane prisoner treatment, as embodied in the Lieber Code, heavily influenced the drafting and revising of the Hague and Geneva Conventions and the development of international humanitarian law in general.

However, as the life cycle of norm change predicts, some of the standards for humane POW treatment were questioned, ignored, and reimagined throughout this history as the United States faced new conflicts that highlighted ambiguities and gaps in the prevailing normative consensus. Questions about how to treat Confederate soldiers, try captured unlawful combatants, and separate ideologically diverse prisoners all prompted changes in POW policies and eventually the norms governing POW treatment. What remained consistent throughout this history, however, was the U.S. commitment to achieving as just and fair treatment as possible. In other words, while the United States struggled at times to adapt to new and unforeseen scenarios, it always worked to address these ambiguities from the perspective of reinforcing rather than challenging the norm of humane treatment. As such, with ample lessons learned from its many conflicts, the United States entered the Vietnam War ready to abide by the prevailing norms of humane treatment. Unfortunately, these good intentions quickly broke down, as U.S. forces faced difficulties in confronting the irregular forces of North Vietnam and the challenges of partnering with a state such as the Republic of South Vietnam. The next chapter covers this experience and shows how the lessons learned in Vietnam laid the groundwork for U.S. military doctrine, legislation, and norms regarding prisoner treatment in the late twentieth and early twenty-first centuries.

3

MODERN POW TREATMENT IN THE UNITED STATES

The Vietnam War, the Geneva Conventions,

and the Pre-9/11 Era

*The authority of international law rests on a reasonable congruence
between formally articulated norms and State behavior; when the two
diverge too sharply, the former must adapt or lose their relevance.*

—DAVID WIPPMAN, "KOSOVO AND THE LIMITS OF INTERNATIONAL LAW"

T HE HISTORICAL FOUNDATION of U.S. POW treatment covered in the previous chapter proved its staying power in the latter half of the twentieth century. The application of the 1949 Geneva Conventions in the Korean War was just the beginning. U.S. ideals codified by the conventions continued to guide legal and policy debates as the U.S. government navigated a new style of conflict in Vietnam. Events in Vietnam, however, would reveal flaws, ambiguities, and gaps in existing U.S. POW policies. As was the case in previous conflicts, the U.S. government responded to these challenges by refining its military doctrine, standard operating procedures, and education programs—all toward the goal of further embedding the norm of humane treatment into U.S. practice and identity. As Vietnam was a generation-defining conflict, the POW-treatment norms embedded by the war then defined the U.S. approach to subsequent conflicts until they were contested by the Bush administration following the attacks of 9/11.

Analyzing U.S. treatment of POWs in Vietnam requires understanding two key issues. First, many U.S. opponents in the war technically did not qualify for POW status because they did not meet Geneva's strict requirements for lawful combatants. As a result, the U.S. military was under no international legal obligation to provide POW standards of treatment—as articulated in the Third Geneva Convention—to many of the fighters it captured. Nevertheless, policy makers inside the Johnson administration successfully argued in favor of applying POW status to all combatants for three reasons. First, U.S. officials believed that extending Geneva protections was good for winning "hearts and minds." Chester Cooper, a member of the administration's National Security Council (NSC) staff, explained the hearts-and-minds ideal when he said, "At issue here is how the war should be fought. . . . Our object is not so much to destroy an enemy as to win a people."[1] Second, policy makers believed that an expansive view of the conventions would, in the words of Staff Judge Advocate Colonel Prugh, "ameliorate domestic and international criticism of the war."[2] Third, the United States hoped that humane treatment of North Vietnamese and Viet Cong POWs would earn reciprocal treatment for captured U.S. soldiers and sailors. A telegram from the U.S. embassy in Vietnam to the Department of State on October 20, 1965, explicitly states: "His [South Vietnamese Prime Minister Nguyen Cao Ky's] treatment of prisoners concerned us very intimately because of the fate of our own prisoners."[3]

Compliance with the Geneva Conventions regarding prisoner treatment in Vietnam, however, was complicated by a second key issue: the fact that the United States did not directly maintain or administer detainee facilities. Instead, the United States handed over captured fighters to the government of South Vietnam, which consistently flouted Geneva's requirements. The United States, therefore, bore some of the responsibility for these abuses because it supported the South Vietnamese counterinsurgency efforts. However, over the course of the war the United States would make several efforts to improve Saigon's treatment of enemy prisoners, mostly to no avail.

Together, these two characteristics provide the framework for understanding POW treatment in Vietnam. This is significant because, as a case study, Vietnam is particularly applicable to the contemporary context of the GWOT. Vietnam represented the first challenge to the traditional state-versus-state paradigm of conflict within the context of the modern laws-of-war regime and consequently had a significant effect on U.S. military thinking about combat, training, and the laws of war. Furthermore, like Vietnam, the GWOT occurred in an untraditional battle space where the frontline was undetermined and the definition of a combatant was even more ambiguous. In addition, the relationship between the U.S. and South Vietnamese governments posed legal and logistical challenges that would mirror tensions between the United States and many of its allies after 9/11. Lastly, international perception of Washington's actions in Vietnam brought increased attention to the laws of war and U.S. behavior in wartime—a situation that would foreshadow international scrutiny of U.S. actions in the GWOT several decades later.

To explain the importance of Vietnam and the postwar reforms that it spawned, this chapter starts by analyzing U.S. behavior during the war in order to provide a comparison with contemporary decision making within the similar context of fighting an unconventional opponent. This chapter not only assesses U.S. compliance with the Geneva Conventions during Vietnam but also explores the ways in which the war compelled the DoD to develop new training, education, and doctrinal standards around the laws of war. It then examines U.S. compliance with the laws of war throughout the conflicts of the 1980s and 1990s, before concluding with an assessment of how these rules came to constitute the norm standard that would endure until 2001.

LEGAL CHALLENGES IN THE VIETNAM WAR

Absent the traditional characteristics of conventional warfare exhibited in conflicts such as the Korean War or World War II, the Vietnam War raised several questions about the scope of the Geneva Conventions with regard to prisoner treatment. U.S. military planners and legal scholars had never previously engaged many of the international legal issues that arose during

the conflict. The issues faced by U.S. policy makers and military commanders would mirror many of the same challenges and concerns faced by the
United States in the GWOT. Staff Judge Advocate Prugh summarized the
challenges faced in Vietnam:

> The battlefield was nowhere and everywhere, with no identifiable front
> lines, and no safe rear areas. Fighting occurred over the length and
> breadth of South Vietnam, on the seas, into Laos and Cambodia, and in
> the air over North Vietnam. It involved combatants and civilians from
> a dozen different nations. Politically, militarily, and in terms of inter-
> national law, the Vietnam conflict posed problems of deep complexity.
> The inherent difficulty of attempting to apply traditional principles of
> international law to such a legally confusing conflict is well illustrated by
> the issue of prisoners of war.[4]

The challenges were manifold. First, ambiguities existed regarding the
legitimacy of the partitioned governments. The United States—along
with eighty-seven other states—recognized the legitimacy of South
Vietnam yet refused to recognize the legitimacy of the North Vietnamese government. In addition, neither Vietnamese government recognized
the legitimacy of the other.[5] Similar to the concerns faced by the Union
forces during the Civil War, the South Vietnamese government feared
that classifying any captured North Vietnamese fighters as POWs would
legitimize the Northern government. Instead, Saigon treated captured
fighters as illegitimate insurgents acting against a legitimate government.[6] They subsequently refused to accord prisoners from North Vietnam POW status, trial in a military court, or even imprisonment in a
military prison.[7]

In addition, the fighting forces in the conflict involved a range of combatants, many of which did not constitute sovereign-state militaries. Most
of the participants in the conflict represented signatories of the Geneva
Conventions: the Free World Military Assistance Force (FWMAF),
composed of the United States, South Vietnam,[8] the Republic of Korea,
the Philippines, Thailand, and Australia; and North Vietnam.[9] The Viet

Cong, however, did not represent a sovereign state and, as such, did not constitute a signatory to the conventions. The combat forces involved in the conflict thus included the regular forces of the FWMAF, the regular forces of North Vietnam, as well as the main and local forces of the Viet Cong, the secret self-defense corps of the Viet Cong, the civilian irregular defense group of South Vietnam, and the regional and popular forces of South Vietnam.[10] Since the conventions define a lawful combatant as someone who is "commanded by a person responsible for his subordinates," possesses "a fixed distinctive sign recognizable at a distance," carries "arms openly," and conducts his "operations in accordance with the laws and customs of war," they do not account for the Vietnam War's range of participants.[11]

Despite these ambiguities—and the repeated claim by the North Vietnamese government that the conflict was a domestic struggle—the U.S. government assessed that the war in Vietnam represented an international armed conflict and made the policy decision to apply the Geneva Conventions to the full range of participants, including those that did not meet Geneva's standards as lawful combatants. Furthermore, Washington did not hesitate to pressure Saigon to comply similarly.

POW TREATMENT

As U.S. policy makers debated the extent of their military commitment to South Vietnam during the summer of 1965, the ICRC determined on June 11 that "the hostilities raging at the present time in Vietnam both North and South of the seventeenth parallel have assumed such proportions recently that there can be no doubt they constitute an armed conflict to which the regulations of humanitarian law as a whole should be applied."[12] Secretary of State Dean Rusk responded to this statement by affirming that the United States was already applying "the provisions of the Geneva Conventions [in Vietnam] and we expect the other parties to the conflict to do likewise."[13] The government of South Vietnam responded on August 11, 1965, that it was "fully prepared to respect the provisions of the Geneva Conventions and to contribute actively to the efforts of the ICRC to ensure their application."[14]

North Vietnam responded that it would treat captured U.S. pilots humanely but that it would not grant them POW status. According to Hanoi, U.S. pilots were "pirates" engaging in unprovoked attacks against North Vietnam.[15] The government in Hanoi also tried to justify its refusal to apply the Geneva Conventions on the basis that their protections did not apply in the absence of a formal declaration of war,[16] despite the clear language in Article 2 stating that the conventions apply "even if the state of war is not recognized"[17] by a party. Following the North's refusal to apply the conventions, the Viet Cong also unequivocally rejected their applicability.[18]

The execution of U.S. POWs in 1965 solidified the U.S. commitment to providing Geneva Convention protections to captured Vietnamese belligerents. On September 26, 1965, the Viet Cong executed Captain Humbert R. Versace and Sergeant Kenneth M. Roraback as a reprisal for the killings of Viet Cong prisoners by the government in Saigon. The Department of State took immediate action and protested the executions as violations of the Geneva Conventions at the ICRC's Twentieth Conference in Vienna on October 7, 1965.[19] At the conference, the ICRC condemned the executions and called upon "all authorities in an armed conflict to ensure that every prisoner is given the treatment and full measure of protection prescribed by the Geneva Convention of 1949 on the Protection of Prisoners of War."[20] Following this condemnation by the ICRC, Secretary Rusk sent a cable to the U.S. embassy in Saigon on October 13, 1965, stating: "[We] can neither submit tacitly to these actions or threatened actions, nor can we ignore them. However, [the] problem is to find ways and means of bringing effective pressure against DRV [Democratic Republic of Vietnam] and VC [Viet Cong] to move them to treat prisoners in accordance with 1949 Geneva Convention."[21]

Seeking to demonstrate full compliance with the Geneva Conventions in order to place pressure on the North Vietnamese and the Viet Cong to reciprocate, a joint U.S.–South Vietnamese military committee was appointed in late 1965 to develop guidelines for the application of the Geneva Conventions by U.S., South Vietnamese, and other FWMAF forces.[22] Ultimately, the joint committee agreed to interpret the provisions of the conventions broadly and to apply all of their provisions to Viet Cong and North Vietnamese personnel.[23] As a result, in October 1965, guidelines consistent with the Geneva Conventions were distributed on the appropriate handling of North Vietnamese and Viet Cong prisoners.[24]

U.S. MILITARY AND MACV POW POLICY

In drafting these guidelines and other detainee policies, the U.S. military initially relied on its substantial existing doctrine on POW treatment and later updated its policies to account for the new challenges presented by the war. FM 19-5 (1945) addressed the responsibilities of military police in POW handling and emphasized the importance of the conventions based on the reciprocal treatment that U.S. forces should expect to receive. It further highlighted that any violations of the Geneva Conventions would "subject this nation to unfavorable criticism in the public opinion of people throughout the world."[25] FM 27-10 (1956) contained an extensive discussion of the rights of POWs, including working hours, religious freedom, rights of POWs who are officers, and rights to medical care.[26] Lastly, FM 19-40 (1964), which served as the operational guide for military police throughout the war, consistently reinforced the notion that POWs must at all times be treated with humanity.[27]

Other field manuals addressed the wartime obligations incumbent on military intelligence personnel in their interactions with POWs. FM 30-15, entitled "Military Intelligence: Examination of Enemy Personnel, Repatriates, Documents, and Matériel," was issued during World War II and established basic U.S. Army doctrine for POW interrogation by military intelligence officials from 1943 to 1987.[28] While the military made several revisions to FM 30-15 throughout the Vietnam War, it is critical to note that the 1967 revision was the first to introduce a paragraph that justified the prohibition of force during interrogations because it was deemed "unnecessary to gain a subject's cooperation and may induce subjects to fabricate information to end the force being applied."[29]

To complement existing U.S. military policy, the U.S. Military Assistance Command, Vietnam (MACV), developed its own directives for POW treatment and handling. Most notably, MACV Directive 381-11 established the baseline of treatment for captured fighters, Directive 381-46 created the criteria to be applied when screening captured fighters, and Directive 20-5 outlined the composition of Article 5 Geneva Convention tribunals.[30]

Directive 381-11, issued in March 1966, stipulated that detainees were to receive humane treatment consistent with Common Article 3 of the Geneva Conventions. In August 1966, General William Westmoreland, the commander of MACV from 1964 to 1968, personally wrote to all of his major commanders to declare it "vital" that "prisoners of war and combat captives are properly processed and handled in accordance with International Law."[31]

MACV Directive 381-46, issued in December 1967, stated that all detainees must be classified either as POWs or non–prisoners of war, including civil defendants, returnees, and innocent civilians.[32] In accordance with official U.S. policy, which had afforded Geneva protections to all participants in the conflict, the MACV determined the following groups to be POWs: Viet Cong main forces, Viet Cong local forces, North Vietnamese Army units, and irregulars, a category that included guerrillas, the self-defense force, and the secret self-defense force.[33]

To address cases in which a detainee's POW status was in doubt, the MACV issued Directive 20-5 in March 1968 in order to establish detailed procedures for standing up Article 5 tribunals. Directive 20-5 also provided captured fighters with other safeguards, such as fair and consistent recording procedures, rights to an interpreter, and rights to testify or not during the POW screening process.[34] Under this directive, the MACV ensured that all fighters captured by U.S. and Vietnamese forces were treated initially as POWs and that the capturing units retained responsibility for the prisoners until they were turned over to Vietnamese authorities.[35]

The final broad MACV directive guiding U.S. military behavior toward POWs during Vietnam was Directive 190-6, which was issued in 1969 and stipulated that the ICRC and any Protecting Power representatives would have full access to the POW camps maintained by the Detaining Power, in this case South Vietnam.

TRAINING AND EDUCATION ON POW TREATMENT

In order to deal with the new challenges inherent in the Vietnam War, training and education in POW treatment reflected the importance of complying with the Geneva Conventions, both in the letter and the spirit of the treaties. In August 1965, Westmoreland directed that all forward-deployed soldiers receive an orientation in the Geneva Conventions and that they be issued four 3×5-inch informational cards.[36] One card, titled "The Enemy in Your Hands," reminded servicemen that "as a member of the U.S. military forces, you will comply with the Geneva Prisoner of War Conventions of 1949 to which this country adheres," and it went on to state that soldiers could not and must not do any of the following: "Mistreat your prisoner, humiliate or degrade him, take any of his personal effects which do not have significant military value, refuse him medical treatment if required and available." In sum: "Always treat your prisoner humanely."

Later that year, a list of "Do and Don'ts" was published by the MACV, a sixty-minute class on acceptable POW treatment was developed,[37] and the "Nine Rules"[38] were issued to U.S. and Vietnamese personnel.[39] The rules commanded forces to:

1. Remember that we are guests here: We make no demands and seek no special treatment.

2. Join with the people! Understand their life, use phrases from their language and honor their customs and laws.

3. Treat women with politeness and respect.

4. Make personal friends among the soldiers and common people.

5. Always give the Vietnamese the right of way.

6. Be alert to security and ready to react with your military skill.

7. Don't attract attention by loud, rude, or unusual behavior.

8. Avoid separating yourself from the people by a display of wealth or privilege.

9. Above all else, you are members of the U.S. Military Forces on a difficult mission, responsible for all your official and personal actions. Reflect honor upon yourself and the United States of America.[40]

In addition, under Army Regulation 350-216 (1967), all U.S. Army commanders needed to ensure that those in their command had received instruction on the Geneva Conventions in the previous year.[41] Each incoming serviceman also received training on the laws of war within seven days of assignment to Vietnam, and supplemental training was required quarterly.[42] Taken together, these training and education standards ensured that all deployed personnel had received significant training on POW treatment and the importance of treating all captured individuals humanely.

SOUTH VIETNAMESE PRISONER ABUSE

Despite the efforts of the U.S. government—and the clear guidelines issued by the MACV—South Vietnamese forces consistently committed prisoner abuses. In a letter dated August 14, 1965, to the commander of the Third Marine Division, Westmoreland stated:

> We have no command authority over the Vietnamese troops that accompany U.S. troops on operations but we must try to moderate the conduct of the Vietnamese in their treatment of prisoners so that it conforms to the spirit of the Geneva Conventions. . . . In any case we should attempt to avoid photographs being taken of these incidents of torture and most certainly in any case try to keep Americans out of the picture.[43]

In addition, Staff Judge Advocate at MACV Headquarters Colonel Prugh learned from U.S. soldiers departing Vietnam that both the Viet Cong and South Vietnamese forces often killed wounded and captured enemy fighters.[44] U.S. elected officials as well began to notice this startling pattern of abuse by the South Vietnamese. Senator Stephen Young (D-Ohio) argued for an end to the policy of turning Viet Cong prisoners over to the South Vietnamese, saying:

> It is well known that not only are these prisoners of war taken in combat by Americans mistreated following the time they are turned over to the South Vietnamese authorities, but also . . . many of these prisoners of war are executed. Probably more of these prisoners of war are executed than are permitted to survive. How can we Americans evade responsibility for the mistreatment of these war prisoners?[45]

As a result of these reports, on October 22, 1965, the ICRC informed Secretary of State Rusk that South Vietnam was not in compliance with the Geneva Conventions.[46]

Members of the executive branch also paid close attention to South Vietnamese noncompliance with the conventions. An October 25, 1965, memorandum from Abba Schwartz, the administrator of the Department of State's Bureau of Security and Consular Affairs, to Chester Cooper of the NSC staff stated that South Vietnam's failure to comply with the conventions was alarming because public opinion of the war might fall after an ICRC condemnation, because the United States might lose its ability to transfer prisoners, and because noncompliance inhibited efforts to obtain better treatment for U.S. POWs. The memo recommended that the United States place itself "squarely on the side of the Conventions" and convince South Vietnam to comply.[47]

On November 27, 1965, the joint U.S.–South Vietnam military committee developed a solution to bring all FWMAF combat forces into compliance with the Geneva Conventions. This plan included constructing five POW camps staffed by South Vietnamese police with Americans as POW advisors; identifying and removing all captured North Vietnamese and

Viet Cong prisoners from civil prisons; increasing training on the provisions of the Geneva Conventions for all forces; establishing a program of repatriation for the POWs; developing effective POW accountability procedures and record keeping; and adhering to the Conventions as accurately as possible, with regards to health and labor standards, visiting privileges, and required ICRC visits.[48] To that end, by mid-1966, the South Vietnamese government constructed five suitable prisoners-of-war camps.[49]

Despite these efforts and frequent pleas by U.S. advisors, compliance by the South Vietnamese was variable. In one example, ICRC visits to the island prison of Phu Quoc revealed many signs of prisoner abuse,[50] including nutritional deficiencies,[51] scars, burns, and shortages of food and water.[52] Because of this and similar reports, the United States continually exerted pressure on South Vietnam, both bilaterally and internationally, to treat captured prisoners according to the standards stipulated in the Geneva Conventions. These efforts, unfortunately, were mostly futile. Part of the problem stemmed from the fact that during Vietnam, judge advocate generals (JAGs) were largely relegated to their traditional role as providers of in-country legal services, such as dispensing military justice and adjudicating claims. Despite the pressing problems with POW treatment, the JAG Corps as an institution "failed to view its years in Vietnam as a basis for engaging in any substantial modification of the way in which it had traditionally practiced military law."[53] As a result, the corps did not direct JAGs to provide legal advice on military operations or POW treatment. This would slowly change after Vietnam, as the JAGs were increasingly relied upon to implement the Pentagon's renewed interest in international humanitarian law.

POST-VIETNAM EDUCATION AND LEGAL REFORMS

The United States' struggles with POW issues in Vietnam prompted major changes across the government. The Pentagon sought to improve its performance by instituting new educational programs that grounded instruction in international humanitarian law in real-life examples rather than simple legal instruction. Meanwhile, the government as a whole embarked on a mission to help strengthen the international human rights regime by negotiating the UN CAT in 1984 and ratifying it into U.S. domestic law a decade later.

THE LAW-OF-WAR PROGRAM

While South Vietnamese compliance with the Geneva Conventions was poor, the United States' performance was far more encouraging. For example, a 1970 study conducted by the Army Concept Team in Vietnam determined that, from the period of initial capture to the delivery of the enemy prisoner to South Vietnamese forces, U.S. forces complied with the Geneva Conventions.[54] Even as North Vietnamese and Viet Cong forces captured greater numbers of U.S. troops between 1964 and 1968, there is no evidence that any U.S. group advocated denying Geneva protections to North Vietnamese and Viet Cong personnel as a form of reprisal. Nevertheless, despite the importance accorded to detainee treatment as an integral component of the counterinsurgency campaign in Vietnam, U.S. compliance with the Fourth Geneva Convention recognizing noncombatant immunity was anything but exemplary and led to major reform efforts inside the U.S. government.

In addition to atrocities such as the My Lai massacre, routine U.S. military operations contributed to countless civilian casualties in Vietnam. In particular, U.S. bombing operations—including the use of Agent Orange, napalm, and carpet bombing—had severe and often lasting consequences on Vietnamese society. Additionally, in the late 1960s, the United States expanded its bombing campaign to Cambodia and Laos, where carpet bombing of densely populated civilian areas became routine for the U.S. Air Force.[55]

As a result of these experiences, in the aftermath of Vietnam the DoD recognized the need to provide law-of-war training for soldiers and sailors. While the U.S. military had long recognized the importance of abiding by the laws of war, it was not until DoD Directive 5100.77, originally issued in

November 1974, that the DoD established a universally required training and education program to prevent violations of the laws of war. The law-of-war program sought to clarify and institutionalize the Geneva norms in U.S. military behavior and identity. DoD Directive 5100.77 states:

It is DoD policy to ensure that the law of war obligations of the United States are observed and enforced by the DoD Components; an effective program to prevent violations of the law of war is implemented by the DoD Components; and all reportable incidents committed by or against U.S. or enemy persons are promptly reported, thoroughly investigated, and, where appropriate, remedied by corrective action.[56]

The law-of-war program emphasized real-life scenarios and case studies and placed the onus for training and implementing the program on the individual service components.[57] According to the directive, each component was required to "institute and implement" a law-of-war training program.[58] It also dramatically increased the role of the JAGs in advising and promoting compliance with the Geneva Conventions. Overall, the law-of-war program sent an important message that the military recognized the mistakes it made in Vietnam and was trying to rectify them. The Pentagon, however, was not the only part of the government dedicated to ensuring the future humane treatment of prisoners. In the 1980s and 1990s, the executive branch and Congress would take action to augment both the international and domestic legal frameworks providing for the humane treatment of POWs and noncombatants.

THE UNITED NATIONS CONVENTION AGAINST TORTURE AND THE WAR CRIMES ACT

A decade after the conclusion of the Vietnam War, the international community turned its attention to universal efforts to uphold human rights and prevent torture. Previous international agreements, such as the Universal Declaration of Human Rights (UDHR), which the United States helped draft, and the International Covenant on Civil and Political Rights

(ICCPR) had forbidden torture. By the 1980s, the ban on torture as expressed in the UDHR and ICCPR was broadly accepted as reflecting customary international law. All that remained was to flesh out the details and provide enforcement mechanisms.[59] The CAT was designed to complete this process by requiring the criminalization of torture in signatories' domestic legislation. The United States played a critical role in drafting the convention, as detailed in J. Hermann Burgers's handbook on the CAT.[60]

The first preliminary draft of what would become the CAT was received well by the United States with regard to expanded international jurisdiction to combat torture. This draft was also reflective of multilateral discussions that supported a convention against both torture and other acts of cruel, inhuman, or degrading treatment or punishment. However, on this point, the United States preferred the convention be focused solely on torture, presenting an alternative article that eliminated the Swedish proposal to ban torture as well as any cruel, inhuman, or degrading treatment or punishment.[61] The U.S. commentary argued that "cruel, inhuman, or degrading treatment or punishment" were relative terms, making the creation of international standards and evaluations difficult, especially in comparing practices in times of peace and hostility.[62] This effort to delete the clause was eventually successful; however, the CAT does contain a "saving clause" in Article 16 that alludes to other treaties prohibiting ill treatment, such as the Geneva Conventions of 1949.[63]

The U.S. delegate also advocated strongly for the inclusion of universal jurisdiction; he explained that leaving the punishment of officials who conduct torture to their respective states "would be a formula for doing nothing."[64] U.S. advocacy for universal jurisdiction, along with support from other delegates, instigated a revision of Article 7, which influenced the interpretation of aspects of Articles 5 and 6.[65] Together, these articles provided a robust system of universal jurisdiction that built upon the following requirements of Article 129 in the Third Geneva Convention:

> The High Contracting Parties undertake to enact any legislation necessary to provide effective penal sanctions for persons committing, or ordering to be committed, any of the grave breaches of the present

Convention defined in the following Article. Each High Contracting Party shall be under the obligation to search for persons alleged to have committed, or to have ordered to be committed, such grave breaches, and shall bring such persons, regardless of their nationality, before its own courts. It may also, if it prefers, and in accordance with the provisions of its own legislation, hand such persons over for trial to another High Contracting Party concerned, provided such High Contracting Party has made out a *prima facie* case.

In addition, the United States played a critical role in adding language to the CAT that ensured that denunciation of the treaty would not terminate any liability for violations committed before the date of exit.[66] As a result of these efforts, U.S. Representative to the UN Commission on Human Rights Richard Shifter called the vote to adopt the CAT by consensus on December 10, 1984, a "significant achievement."[67]

After the United States ratified the CAT in 1994, Congress passed the enacting legislation—the U.S. federal antitorture statute—to fulfill its obligations under the treaty. In addition to the federal antitorture statute, the War Crimes Act of 1996 (18 U.S.C. §2441) criminalized grave violations of the Geneva Conventions, specifically when those violations are either committed by or against a U.S. national or member of the U.S. armed forces. The act was intended to address the "grave breaches" mentioned in Article 129 of the Third Geneva Convention, defined in Article 130 as:

Willful killing, torture or inhuman treatment, including biological experiments, willfully causing great suffering or serious injury to body or health, compelling a prisoner of war to serve in the forces of the hostile Power, or willfully depriving a prisoner of war of the rights of fair and regular trial prescribed in this Convention.[68]

Taken together, U.S. action in the aftermath of Vietnam to improve its military training programs, enhance the international humanitarian legal regime, and strengthen its domestic enforcement legislation indicated a firm commitment to the norm of humane treatment. These changes were also translated into action on the ground. In the conflicts occurring between 1975 and September 11, 2001, the U.S. military made concerted efforts to apply and further refine the lessons it learned in Vietnam. While compliance in these conflicts was not without fault, the overall narrative is of a military slowly improving its performance with regard to detainee treatment.

KEY U.S. MILITARY ENGAGEMENTS, 1975–2001

In the conflicts following Vietnam, the United States endeavored to put its renewed commitment to humane POW treatment into practice. Early struggles in Grenada gave way to improved performances in Panama and the war in the Persian Gulf. However, as the century was coming to a close, the conflict in Kosovo reignited domestic debates over the role of international humanitarian law. As such, by the time President Bush entered the White House in 2001, a foundation existed for some of the contestation that his administration would engage in after 9/11.

GRENADA (1983 URGENT FURY)

The U.S. intervention in Grenada was the first major U.S. military operation following the end of the Vietnam War. The conflict helped define the role of the JAG Corps in military conduct, especially regarding detainees. Colonel Quentin Richardson, the Eighty-Second Airborne Division's staff judge advocate, anticipated from the beginning "that there were going to be a number of JAG-related problems" and expected fighting to "generate a large number of refugees and prisoners, or rather detainees since the United States was not at war with either Cuba or Grenada."[69] Colonel Richardson was correct. However, despite the lessons learned from Vietnam, detainee handling posed operational issues because of poor planning, lack of training, and operational mistakes.

To begin with, U.S. commanders repeated many of the mistakes they had made in Vietnam with regard to detainee policy. First, despite the increased attention given to law-of-war issues, the JAGs were excluded from advanced operational planning. The first JAG on the ground in Grenada had little more than twelve hours' notice for his deployment.[70] Edgar Raines Jr. notes in a review of the logistics operations of the invasion: "The exclusion of the civil affairs officer and the staff judge advocate from pre-alert planning meant that their concerns had not surfaced earlier and that these officers had not had any opportunity to interact with the division logisticians."[71] Similar shortcomings would be repeated in planning for other aspects of the military operation.

Second, the exclusion of the JAGs was indicative of the low priority they received from high-level commanders. On October 24, two hours after the notification to troops to begin the loading sequence to invade (N-hour $+2$, shortened to "N$+2$"), Major General Edward Trobaugh, commander of the Eighty-Second Airborne Division, briefed his men on operational orders and the conditions on the ground. Despite the days of planning in advance, it was not until this N$+2$ briefing that General Trobaugh "addressed the problem of detainees and refugees for the first time in a substantive fashion."[72]

Lastly, the Pentagon initially tasked the Caribbean peacekeeping forces that accompanied the U.S. military invasion with the job of holding and processing detainees. Much like in Vietnam, these local forces proved inadequate for the task—no surprise given that the Caribbean peacekeepers comprised mostly "policemen-turned-soldiers" who lacked training in handling detainees despite being skilled in handling civilian refugees.[73] While the Caribbean forces did not engage in widespread POW violations, there was some concern expressed in the media and by human rights NGOs such as Amnesty International regarding camp conditions.[74] These concerns were echoed by senior U.S. officers who visited the camp. Raines notes, "Almost every senior officer who landed on the island inspected the detainee camp and found conditions wanting."[75] As a result, three days after the invasion, responsibility for POW handling was transferred from the Caribbean forces to the 118th Military Police Company, which immediately set out to improve conditions and release innocent prisoners.[76] As part of this process, that same day, U.S. officials determined that all detainees would receive POW status, regardless of the categorization provided by the Geneva Conventions.[77]

Nevertheless, U.S. treatment of detainees was far from perfect. For example, the ICRC came close to denouncing U.S. treatment because its representatives were initially not given access to the detainee camp, U.S. staff being "too busy" to accommodate them.[78] Additionally, there was concern that a U.S. psychological-operations force had made posters of the ex-leaders of Grenada bound and blindfolded and spread them around the island to humiliate them.[79] There were also reports of U.S. military police conducting warrantless searches and detaining suspects on flimsy grounds.[80] Finally, according to the *New York Times*, at the end of U.S. operations in December 1983, forty-eight detainees were still being held with no charges or chance of trial.[81]

In sum, Grenada served as an important warning to the military that its law-of-war problems remained fully unresolved. To begin with, it again proved that outsourcing detainee operations was not a wise decision, as the United States would be in the worst of all positions: not in control but still receiving all the criticism for the actions of its partners. More importantly, however, the invasion of Grenada revealed the need for a larger role for the JAGs. Stephanie Carvin notes:

> Although Operation Urgent Fury was short (major operations lasted just over a week), it indicated that there was still room for improvement regarding the role of military lawyers and operational law. Military commanders reached the decision that judge advocates must be included in the planning of contingency operations from the beginning. The lack of notice given to military lawyers hindered preparation for potential legal problems, especially as giving correct and complete legal advice depends on having a full understanding of the nature and purpose of the deployment.[82]

Several years later, Congress would aid this process by dramatically increasing the authority and responsibility of legal advisors via the 1986

Goldwater-Nichols Act.[83] As a result of this reform and the lessons learned from Grenada, U.S. detainee operations in Panama would go much more smoothly.

PANAMA (1989 JUST CAUSE)

As a result of Grenada, legal planning for the U.S. invasion of Panama started almost a year and a half in advance of the actual operation.[84] Moreover, once the invasion was underway, U.S. forces remained in control of detainee operations rather than outsourcing them to a third party.[85] Senior U.S. military officials were also actively involved in POW issues, with the commanding officer, Lt. General Carl Stiner, consulting with the staff judge advocate and the Sixteenth Military Police brigade commander before choosing the location for the detainee camp.[86] Additionally, the media and ICRC officials were given access to the camp facilities without problem.[87]

Colonel James Smith, the Eighty-Second's staff judge advocate, was the first U.S. Army lawyer deployed with U.S. troops to Panama. With FM 27-10, *The Law of Land Warfare*, at the top of his pack, Colonel Smith immediately began navigating legal and humanitarian issues surrounding the interrogations of civilians by U.S. military police. As in Operation Urgent Fury, each detainee was initially granted POW status until the person's status could be determined.[88] This approach contributed to the accurate classification of all detainees and a positive review from the ICRC when a delegation visited on December 29, "noting U.S. compliance with both the spirit and the letter of the law."[89]

The expansion of authority and responsibility of U.S. Army lawyers in Panama reflected the institutional recognition of the need for legal advice at every stage of military conduct. After the issues in Grenada, the Pentagon's performance in Panama represented a serious improvement with regard to the humane treatment of detainees. Carvin notes, "To military lawyers, Operation Just Cause demonstrated that the Department of Defense was taking the laws of war seriously."[90] This renewed sense of direction on POW issues would reach its apogee just a few years later in the 1991 war against Iraq.

PERSIAN GULF WAR

The Persian Gulf War of 1990–1991 represents for many the last time the U.S. military fought a traditional state-on-state war. According to the DoD's Final Report to Congress on the Conduct of the Persian Gulf, "Coalition care for enemy prisoners of war was in strict compliance with the 1949 Geneva Conventions relative to the treatment of Prisoners of War."[91] In fact, relative to the length of the military campaign, the Persian Gulf War was the most extensive U.S. POW operation since World War II.[92] U.S. forces captured enemy combatants from one month before the commencement of ground operations until the March 3, 1991, surrender of Iraqi forces.[93] In total, U.S., French, and British forces captured and held 69,882 Iraqi prisoners during the conflict.[94]

The 800th Military Police Brigade, which would a decade later be investigated for the abuses at Abu Ghraib prison, conducted tribunals to determine the status of captured individuals who claimed to be displaced civilians. During the conflict, 1,196 Article 5 tribunal hearings were conducted, resulting in 310 persons being granted POW status and the rest treated as refugees and released to U.S.- and Saudi-operated refugee camps.[95] In fact, following the conclusion of U.S. custody of Iraqi prisoners, ICRC officials reported that the treatment of Iraqi prisoners by U.S. forces complied more fully with the Geneva Conventions than the treatment provided by any other state in any previous conflict.[96] A monograph assessing the role of U.S. Army reservists in the Persian Gulf War stated that "the United States had to demonstrate to the World—and to Iraq—that it played by the rules and treated its prisoners with respect and humanity. This was essential to influence global public opinion positively to U.S. policy and U.S.-led actions against Iraq."[97] The monograph concluded with an overall assessment of POW policy in the Persian Gulf War and argued:

- Approval by the ICRC is an important asset for U.S. foreign policy.
- There was a distinct linkage between our treatment of the Iraqis and the release by Iraq of the Coalition prisoners.

- Even more important is that humane treatment of enemy prisoners of war is consistent with our beliefs and our principles.

- Good treatment of the Iraqi prisoners will also have beneficial long-term effects. The United States Army took good care of almost 70,000 Iraqis and put to rest the propaganda of their own Government. Surely this good—even kind—treatment has some positive effect and left some positive feelings toward the United States, which just might be helpful in the future.[98]

Given these concerns and the amount of attention shown to them, one legal advisor to General Norman Schwarzkopf described the Persian Gulf War as "the most legalist war [the United States] ever fought."[99]

In fact, the U.S. Army affirmed the centrality of the Geneva Conventions in the conduct of military operations in a training circular issued six months after the conclusion of major fighting operations in Iraq. The Army Training Circular "Prisoners of War" TC 27-10-2 (1991) stated that U.S. Army servicemen and women should abide by the laws of war "because you have a duty to defend the Constitution and uphold the laws of the United States."[100] Furthermore, it linked military activity with the identity of the United States. The circular unequivocally lays out the individual duty incumbent on all members of the U.S. Army to follow the laws of war: "In your hands is the reputation of the United States as a law-abiding member of the community of nations."[101] Following the Persian Gulf War, the military also took steps to embed further the notion that the use of force during POW interrogations was not only unnecessary but also counterproductive. FM 34-52, which was drafted in 1992 to account for the lessons learned from the Gulf War, superseded FM 30-15, which had guided interrogation procedures during the Vietnam War. The new manual contained an expansive section on the prohibition of the use of force during an interrogation. FM 34-52 states bluntly:

Experience indicates that the use of prohibited techniques is not necessary to gain the cooperation of interrogation sources. Use of torture and other illegal methods is a poor technique that yields unreliable results, may damage subsequent collection efforts, and can induce the source to say what he thinks the collector wants to hear. Revelation of the use of torture by U.S. personnel will bring discredit upon the U.S. and its armed forces while undermining domestic and international support for the war effort. It may also place U.S. and allied personnel in enemy hands at a greater risk of abuse by their captors.[102]

The manual then provides an extensive list of the activities that constitute physical and mental torture.

While legal questions did surface during the conflict regarding POW issues, no legal issues arose regarding the application of the Geneva Conventions and subsequent humane treatment of the Iraqi prisoners. The captured fighters were members of the Iraqi uniformed military, and Iraq was a signatory to the Geneva Conventions. This legal clarity would cease to exist in the subsequent conflicts that made up the GWOT, and the Vietnam-era precedents for dealing with such ambiguity would be disregarded.

CONFLICTS IN THE BALKANS

The exception to this narrative of gradual improvement in international legal compliance was Kosovo. The issue was not with POW treatment, which NATO had limited involvement with, or noncombatant casualties, which NATO worked hard to minimize, but rather the overall perception of international law within the United States. As will be explored in greater detail in the following chapter, Kosovo aroused serious concerns within the United States regarding the role of international law in U.S. policy making. In particular, the expanded role of lawyers in operational decisions was seen as having inhibited military effectiveness, and the decision by international prosecutors after the conflict had ended to investigate NATO war crimes in its bombing campaign was seen as an abuse of power and a manipulation of international law. The result was the denigration of independent operational lawyers and international law in the eyes of many influential Americans, thereby laying the groundwork for much of the post-9/11 contestation.

The breakup of the former Yugoslavia was marked by two conflicts that involved NATO intervention with U.S. participation: the Bosnian War and the Kosovo War. In August 1995, Operation Deliberate Force proved critical in bringing the belligerents to peace talks hosted in Dayton, Ohio. The bombings of Serbian military targets ended the Bosnian War quickly, despite Western reluctance to intervene. Four years later, the United States led a NATO air campaign, Operation Allied Force, in Kosovo, under the auspices of humanitarian imperatives. The belief among NATO leaders that reluctance in Bosnia had cost many innocent lives, such as the Srebrenica massacre, coupled with the assumption that Slobodan Milošević would concede quickly to the threat of NATO force, instigated this intervention with minimal longitudinal planning. Ultimately, despite the relative success of the intervention, U.S. involvement in the Kosovo War sparked questions about the role and applicability of international law in dictating U.S. war-time behavior.

In the words of President Clinton, the United States had long-term strategic, economic, and humanitarian motives for its involvement in Kosovo, including the restoration of a "stable, free Europe."[103] Nonetheless, Operation Allied Force was a clear departure from the previously expressed U.S. interest in serving as a beacon for international-law authorship and compliance. NATO proceeded with the bombing campaign despite the failure to secure approval from the UN Security Council. These details "created an irresolvable tension between the formal law of the UN Charter and the actual practice of States whose conduct is central to international lawmaking."[104]

Because the United States participated only by air, the Pentagon had no responsibility for enemy combatants detained on the ground. However, three U.S. Army soldiers were captured in Macedonia by Serbian forces.[105] Despite initial reports of violent handling, U.S. prisoners received humane treatment, as evidenced by a note left by Staff Sergeant Christopher Stone, one of the U.S. captives, for his Serbian jailers after he found out he was to be released. Stone wrote: "To all the Serbian guards of this prison. Thank you for your kindness and respect. I have much liking for Serbian people after this."[106] The holding of U.S. servicemen was intended by Yugoslavia "as the moral equivalent of those killed in the bombings," according to Reverend Jesse L. Jackson, who traveled to Belgrade to negotiate for the prisoners' release.[107] It is apparent, however, that POW issues were of lesser significance than the questions raised about the legality of force as a result of Operation Allied Force.

CONCLUSION

The norm of humane POW treatment was solidified by U.S. experience in Vietnam as well as U.S. POW activities during the 1980s and 1990s. Military practice and doctrine from Grenada, Panama, and the Persian Gulf War indicate a strong commitment to upholding the Geneva Conventions and the CAT. By integrating U.S. Army lawyers into operational planning and crafting a policy of widely extending POW status, the improvement in detainee treatment that occurred during these conflicts strongly reflects the redress for U.S. lapses in Vietnam. As with the broader narrative of U.S. history, starting with the Revolutionary War, U.S. practice following Vietnam illustrates an undeniable tradition of iterative improvement in international-law authorship and compliance.

While in general the U.S. experience following Vietnam reveals a deep embedding of the norm of humane treatment, the period before 9/11 was not without its challenges. The NATO intervention in Kosovo is just one example of an event that highlights the shift in the normative regime. The attacks of 9/11 would serve as the external shock that catapulted these concerns into a full-scale challenge of the post-Vietnam normative regime. September 11 seemed to erase U.S. institutional memory—learned from and embedded after the Vietnam War—of POW treatment, explicitly defined in the Geneva Conventions, the CAT, and domestic military doctrine. How did this shock cause so much damage to U.S. ideals embedded over two hundred years? Why was the outcome in the face of another ambiguous enemy so different from U.S. behavior in Vietnam?

In the next three chapters, the decision-making processes and players that led to the U.S. decision to torture will be analyzed in detail. Examined from the lenses of the lawyers, the policy makers, and the interrogators, the life cycle of norm change explains the *how* of U.S. torture polices in the GWOT. Each lens offers an alternative narrative to explain the divergence in normative consensus reached during the GWOT. This section begins with the lawyers because the normative arguments they made were incredibly powerful, persuasive, and influential. Any discussion of *how* the United States came to torture detainees after 9/11 must begin with them.

PART TWO

EVOLUTION OF NORMS AROUND POW TREATMENT

4

POW TREATMENT AND LAWYERS

As you have said, the war against terrorism is a new kind of war. . . .
In my judgment, this new paradigm renders obsolete Geneva's strict lim-
itations on questioning of enemy prisoners and renders quaint some of
its provisions.

—ALBERTO GONZALEZ, IN *THE TORTURE PAPERS: THE ROAD TO ABU GHRAIB*

T HE 1970S PROVED challenging—and defining—for the second branch
of government. In the eyes of the U.S. public, Vietnam, Watergate, and
the Pike Committee and Church Committee investigations painted
a picture of a cynical and at times almost rogue executive branch. Together,
these crises revealed a pressing need for reform, particularly in the area of
legal authorities and the role of law in political decision making. Because
these crises portrayed a White House and executive branch acting above and
beyond the law, the logical remedy was to augment the role of the law in
government functions. This effort was particularly pronounced in the realm
of foreign policy; in addition to eroding public trust, these scandals revealed
glaring deficiencies in the country's foreign policy decision-making process
and implementation. In subsequent decades, significant resources would be
poured into improving these competencies. As such, the 1970s saw the beginning of a determined, three-pronged effort to rein in executive power. First,
Congress would exercise greater oversight and restraint of executive authority
by instituting wide-ranging reforms to the foreign policy decision-making
process. Second, a number of academics would publish influential works
supporting the idea that the Constitution mandates a separation of powers in foreign affairs just as it does in domestic affairs. Finally, a widespread
effort emerged throughout the government to increase the number of lawyers serving in executive departments and to augment their authority in the
policy process. Within the military, these lawyers would increasingly view

compliance with international law as an integral part of a department-wide effort to improve the Pentagon's reputation. In sum, these efforts represented the growing importance of law in the decision-making process.

Together, these efforts constituted a new normative regime for how the U.S. foreign policy process should function. However, by the mid-1980s, a backlash against these initiatives began to materialize and gain strength. It is within the context of this backlash that the legal decisions on detainee treatment were made following the attacks of 9/11. The normative challenges put forth by the lawyers inside the Bush administration consisted of two main arguments: that international law should play less of a role in dictating U.S. policy, and that the executive branch has primary control over setting U.S. foreign policy. For the lawyers involved in deciding whether the EITs requested by the administration constituted torture or not, these were the fundamental issues at play. The decision of whether to treat captured members of the Taliban and al-Qaeda humanely became just another battleground in a series of legal debates between competing scholarly camps.

Equally significant, the decisions on detainee treatment would not have occurred without the justification provided by the lawyers in the executive branch. These men wielded formidable intellects, access to key decision makers, and positions of influence within key offices such as the OLC in the Justice Department to shape U.S. detainee policy in the GWOT. As such, this chapter begins by detailing the development of the post-Vietnam consensus on the role of law in foreign policy decision making. It then describes in detail how this consensus began to break down in the years before 9/11. Lastly, it examines the significant role that Bush administration lawyers played in successfully challenging the existing norm framework on humane treatment following the 9/11 attacks.

EMBEDDED NORM: NORM CONTEXT BEFORE 9/11

The existing norm framework for the lawyers arose from the efforts to rein in the executive branch following the scandals of the 1970s. Vietnam,

Watergate, and the various investigations of the intelligence community (IC) created a portrait of an executive branch that was out of sync with the domestic public. From illegal bombing campaigns in Southeast Asia to allegations of CIA assassination attempts, a question emerged of who was guarding the guards. As a result of these crises, three initiatives developed that constituted the existing norm framework for the lawyers prior to the 9/11 attacks: greater congressional oversight of intelligence functions and activities, the revival of academic arguments in favor of a separation of foreign affairs authorities, and an increase in the number and prominence of lawyers inside the executive branch.

GREATER CONGRESSIONAL OVERSIGHT

The current system of oversight for executive activities was developed largely in response to the executive branch's abuses of power in the 1970s. Why was such a system of oversight developed? Because, in the words of the Church Committee report, "the fear of war, and its attendant uncertainties and doubts, has fostered a series of secret practices that have eroded the processes of open democratic government."[1] IC activities came under peak scrutiny in the wake of the Watergate Scandal, and this scrutiny helped push for greater oversight by the Church Committee.[2] The committee was able to "draw the Congress more deeply into the making of intelligence policy through the detailed review of budgets, the offering of policy suggestions (usually in executive hearings), and even votes on sensitive operations."[3] While the Church Committee constituted a vital element of the oversight regime, it was only one of many efforts to put checks on the seemingly unfettered expansion of executive power and privilege.[4]

One of the first measures put in place to achieve greater oversight of the executive branch was the 1973 War Powers Resolution (WPR). Drafted in response to concerns about the Nixon administration's secret war in Laos and the persistence of an illegal bombing campaign in Cambodia, Congress sought to reassert its perceived primacy over war powers. The authors of the WPR claimed that the founding fathers had deliberately rejected the British model of foreign policy, in which a sole executive could take the country to war.[5] Arguing that Congress, and only Congress, was the branch of government authorized to decide whether to initiate war, the WPR attempted to reassert congressional prerogatives over foreign policy. It demanded that the president—"in every possible instance"—consult the legislative branch before the initiation of hostilities.[6] In this and several other key provisions, its authors sought to fight the "nature of war to increase the executive at the expense of the legislative authority" and put Congress back in charge of the decision to go to war.[7] This measure sought to align the United States with the concerns expressed by James Madison in a letter to Thomas Jefferson in 1798: "The constitution supposes, what the History of all Governments demonstrates, that the Executive is the branch of power most interested in war, and most prone to it. It has accordingly with studied care vested the question of war to the Legislature."[8]

The second category of measures, prompted by the negative effects of executive secrecy in an era of profound mistrust of the presidency, included legislation to reform the intelligence community. These efforts included the Hughes-Ryan Act of 1974, requiring the reporting of all CIA covert activity to Congress, as well as the work of the Church Committee and Pike Committee, which investigated the CIA and other intelligence agencies in response to the Watergate scandal and revelations of illegal domestic-surveillance programs. Both committees found evidence of the CIA spying on U.S. citizens, illegal wiretapping, and cover-ups. As a result, Senate Resolution 400 in 1976 and House Resolution 658 in 1977 established the select intelligence committees to prevent future abuses of power and maintain ongoing and regular oversight of the IC. These efforts together sought to ensure that intelligence policies and activities fell within the bounds of the law.

One of the last major pieces of legislation to establish greater oversight of the IC was the Foreign Intelligence Surveillance Act of 1978 (FISA). FISA was passed in order to reaffirm constitutional safeguards for the civil liberties of U.S. citizens against the charges of illegal wiretapping by agencies in the IC. It permitted electronic surveillance for up to one year for the purposes of collecting foreign-intelligence information if there is "no substantial likelihood that the surveillance will acquire the contents of any communication to which a United States person is a party."[9] On top of the changes mandated by Congress, the IC itself also took measures to improve its compliance with the law as well as its public perception. For example, the CIA changed how it interacted with many sectors of the U.S. public, including the media, the clergy, academia, and corporate America, in response to the scandals of the 1970s.[10]

These three major efforts, along with other important pieces of legislation that improved public access to executive information—such as the Freedom of Information Act, the Inspector General Act, and the Presidential Records Act—created a comprehensive oversight system for the executive branch. Unlike in other states where key national security activities such as intelligence collection and war making are handled as purely executive functions, these measures gave extensive oversight responsibilities to the legislative branch. For a brief period from the mid-1970s to the mid-1980s, these laws and this system of oversight seemed so consequential that many worried, in the words of Gerald Ford, that the presidency had become "imperiled, not imperial."[11]

ACADEMIC SUPPORT

The need for greater oversight of the executive branch was accompanied and supported by scholarly arguments that the presidency had grown too powerful and had exceeded its constitutional limits. Despite having ordained a system of government composed of three different branches, the framers of the Constitution included very few details about how national security should be coordinated among them. While the actual text of the Constitution seems to tilt national security powers to Congress—ascribing to it the appropriations powers, the power to declare war, to raise and support armies, to provide and maintain a navy, and to regulate commerce—it often fails to detail where one branch's foreign affairs powers begin and the other's ends. As a consequence, academic debate since the late eighteenth century has examined the assignment of powers in the realm of foreign affairs between these two branches.

Two books in particular, *The Imperial Presidency* (1973) and *Foreign Affairs and the U.S. Constitution* (1972), would challenge the notion of a powerful president in the realm of foreign affairs. Arthur Schlesinger Jr.'s *The Imperial Presidency* explicitly takes a side in the centuries-old debate about war powers between the branches. Schlesinger argues that the president was given the day-to-day management functions of foreign policy—such as negotiating treaties and recognizing governments—and the power to defend the country against attack as well as to guide the military in any war declared by Congress. Congress in turn had the power to initiate war, with the exception of self-defense (where the president was equally powerful), appropriate funds for the armed forces, and approve treaties.[12] His view solidly supported the academic camp that the founding fathers were "men who had the war-making propensities of monarchs in mind, so they took care to assign vital foreign policy powers to Congress."[13] Similarly, Louis Henkin's *Foreign Affairs and the U.S. Constitution* describes how the failures of the Articles of Confederation spurred the founding fathers to create the position of president, but he cautions against reading into this history any support for a powerful presidency. "The Framers were hardly ready to replace the representative inefficiency of many with an efficient monarchy," he writes. "Unhappy memories of royal prerogative, fear of tyranny, and reluctance to repose trust in any one person kept the Framers from giving the President too much head."[14]

The argument put forward by these two influential works was further advanced by another important book written almost two decades later by the lawyer (and future legal advisor to the secretary of state) Harold Koh. In his 1990 book *The National Security Constitution*, Koh argues that the Iran-Contra affair revealed a persistent flaw in U.S. politics: the aggregation of foreign affairs powers by the executive branch. He blames the various commissions investigating the scandal for focusing too much on the facts of the story and assigning blame, rather than unpacking what he views as the underlying constitutional causes for the scandal. The solution to this problem, Koh argues, is to return to the vision of foreign affairs powers the framers originally intended. This vision is contained in what he calls the National Security Constitution, which is composed of explicit and implicit powers provided by the Constitution as well as significant Supreme Court cases, statutes, and important constitutional norms that have developed over the centuries.

By consulting these various sources, Koh claims that a singular and unifying principle regarding the Constitution's foreign affairs powers becomes clear: that it provides for a separation of powers between the branches much like the Constitution does in domestic affairs. The National Security Constitution, he argues,

> rests upon a simple notion: that the power to conduct American foreign policy is not exclusively presidential, but rather, *a power shared* by the president, the Congress, and the courts. The constitutional system of checks and balances is not suspended simply because foreign affairs are at issue. To the contrary, in foreign affairs as well as domestic affairs, our Constitution requires that we be governed by separated institutions sharing policy powers.[15]

Koh often saw eye to eye with these scholarly predecessors. He considered himself and Henkin among the scholars that shared concerns about "executive overreaching in foreign affairs."[16] In *The National Security Constitution* and again in 1996, Koh demonstrated this belief when he called for, in the words of Schlesinger, "a strong Presidency within the Constitution."[17]

Despite their strong arguments for a separation of powers between the branches, both Schlesinger and Koh altered their positions regarding presidential power during wartime. In 1950, while teaching at Harvard, Schlesinger defended President Truman's decision to send troops to Korea without declaring war.[18] Decades later, Schlesinger later adjusted his opinion on Truman's actions in *War and the American Presidency* and claimed these actions represented "growing executive imperialism."[19] Schlesinger grouped Truman's decision together with Nixon's 1970 campaign in Cambodia when discussing presidents that did not believe their dispatch of troops required the explicit approval of Congress.[20]

Koh too altered his views on presidential power. As dean of Yale Law School, Koh challenged the Bush administration's claims that the president's foreign affairs and commander-in-chief powers gave him the ability to implement secret domestic wiretapping programs, detain captives indefinitely, and order the use of EITs to compel confessions, among other controversial counterterror policies.[21] However, while serving as legal adviser to the State Department under the Obama administration, Koh supported the president's right to use military force against Libya without congressional approval.[22] In his June 2011 testimony before the Senate Foreign Relations Committee, Koh advocated for the primacy of executive power in national security decision making when defending the president's right to continue operations in Libya without congressional approval.[23] Noting the limited mission, exposure of U.S. troops, risk of escalation, and military means employed, Koh supported the president's conclusion that operations in Libya did not fall under the WPR's sixty-day pullout rule absent congressional authorization.[24]

Despite his change of view once in the executive branch, Koh's previous academic work, combined with Henkin's and Schlesinger's, defined the academic state of the art on the Constitution's foreign affairs powers in the post-Vietnam era. Their writings would constitute a key component of the normative framework on how the U.S. foreign policy process should function. This approach would become a central target for pushback from the supporters of alternative theories that contested this new norm.

INCREASED ROLE OF LAWYERS

In addition to the statutory accountability measures enacted by Congress, executive branch agencies also underwent internal reforms to enhance the role of lawyers in the decision-making process. In the decades following Vietnam, both the CIA and the DoD made great efforts to increase the number of lawyers in their ranks.

In the CIA, the effect of the increased number of lawyers was reinforced by their expanded role as gatekeepers. One of the recommendations of the Church Committee, in the words of former acting CIA general counsel Rizzo, was that an "influx of lawyers without any CIA 'baggage' would bring more objectivity and rigor, with an ability and willingness to spot and deter any future abuses."[25] According to Rizzo, the hiring of new lawyers almost always followed the same pattern: after a crisis, "the cry would ring out, from Congress and/or the CIA leadership: By God, the Agency needs more lawyers! Inside the CIA, it would become a truism: A scandal would be awful for the Agency institutionally, but it would be great for the Office of General Counsel's growth potential."[26]

In fact, even the cutbacks across the IC during the 1990s could not reverse the growth in the CIA's legal corps.[27] As the restrictions on CIA activities grew, additional lawyers were needed to parse the growing web of regulations and assess the legality of CIA operations. In the CIA, as the number of lawyers in the Office of the General Counsel grew, so did the influence they wielded over decision making. For example, in his memoirs, Rizzo tells a story about how as a lawyer in the Directorate of Operations (DO) he was forced to interpret one of President Carter's Findings on covert action in Afghanistan. The Finding limited CIA aid to the Afghans to "cash" and "logistical support." However, the resistance fighters were in desperate need of donkeys to help them carry arms and attack Soviet bases. Rizzo had to make an on-the-spot decision as to whether donkeys constituted logistical support, which would be permitted, or lethal aid, which would not.[28] After a while, Rizzo's superiors in the DO "passed the word down through their staffs that virtually every proposed operation of any significance had to be run by me first."[29]

For the DoD, not only did the number of lawyers increase, but their role in dictating operations grew as well—creating what came to be known as operational law or "oplaw." As discussed in chapter 3, the years after the Vietnam War saw a significant expansion in the role of lawyers in the training and education of all DoD personnel on the laws of war. According to Carvin, the effect of this process "was to create a 'legal revolution': training in the laws of war was made more practical and lawyers, over the next fifteen years, fought their way into the 'war room.'"[30] Lawyers became included in battlefield decision making, including targeting, maneuvering decisions, and the decision to use force in the first place. In particular, during the range of U.S. force actions in the 1990s, lawyers were integral in determining the appropriate legal contours of U.S. behavior in combating drug trafficking, upholding human rights norms, addressing genocidal regimes, and separating warring parties during peacemaking negotiations.[31] Additionally, JAGs were involved in complex legal, social, and political decisions in Somalia, Haiti, Bosnia, and Rwanda.[32]

A significant reason for the increased prominence of the JAGs was that they were seen as a crucial tool for restoring honor to the military. Vietnam was widely seen as having tarnished the reputation of the armed forces, and "noncompliance with the law was seen as part of the problem."[33] As a result, the JAGs became the guardians of the military's integrity, and in the decades following Vietnam they accrued an unprecedented level of independence inside the Pentagon. This autonomy was on full display in the JAGs' pushback against the Bush administration's legal policies. In the words of Jack Goldsmith:

> In a testament to the JAG's reputation and independence, and to the mistrust of the Bush administration by this point [2004], the stories about the law fights inside the Pentagon were not generally treated as military subordination or affronts to civilian control. They were, rather, treated as JAGs standing up to the law-defying Bush administration in the name of the rule of law.[34]

A key component of the JAGs' effort to restore military honor and execute operational effectiveness was an increased dedication to upholding international law. In 1996, General Anthony Zinni recognized this trend when he predicted that "operational law and international law are the future."[35] As the body of international humanitarian law expanded in the post-Vietnam era, it spawned a growing recognition of a large and complex body of customary international law relating to the use of military force. This body of customary law was promoted by a growing network of parties interested in the promulgation of international law. The rise of activist NGOs dedicated to promoting human rights, the creation of international tribunals such as the International Criminal Court (ICC), and the increasing reliance on international legal precedent in some U.S. courts all contributed to the heightened significance of customary international law within the United States, even if U.S. policy makers had explicitly rejected many of this body of law's provisions.[36] Seeking to promote its reputation as a responsible actor, "the U.S. military—with the guidance and encouragement of military lawyers— followed many aspects of this customary law, and wrote it down in ever-expanding legal and policy manuals that military lawyers interpret and apply."[37] The result was a growing role for international law in all levels of military decision making.

The JAGs' increased status and authority complemented the growing number of both military and civilian lawyers inside the military. The CIA was not the only agency to face increased reporting and oversight requirements to Congress: the DoD also was required to subject its activities to a growing web of congressional restrictions and oversight mechanisms. This maze of new laws and rules required an increasing number of lawyers to understand. According to Goldsmith:

> When Donald Rumsfeld entered the Pentagon as Secretary of Defense in January 2001, a quarter-century after his first tour in that job in the Ford administration, one of the first things he noticed was many more lawyers. When he asked why, he was told that they were needed to interpret the mountain of new laws that had been imposed on the military since the 1970s.[38]

The increased number and prominence of JAGs and civilian lawyers inside the military eventually affected DoD policy, leading to new doctrine designed to apply strictly humane standards of treatment to detainees. This policy was primarily recorded in FM 34-52, which was originally published in 1987 and was updated in 1992 to reflect the lessons learned from the Persian Gulf War. FM 34-52 reflected the DoD's commitment to complying with the laws of war governing detainee treatment and strictly prohibited the use of force and threats in detainee interrogations. In the words of the legal scholar Philippe Sands, "Until September 11 no one thought FM 34-52 was quaint or obsolete. It reflected the finest traditions of valor."[39]

Following Vietnam, a new normative consensus on numerous key legal issues was developed and embedded in U.S. society. Executive power was reined in by new congressional legislation, academic arguments supported the idea of shared competencies in foreign affairs, and the number and influence of lawyers increased within the executive branch. The role of lawyers took on an increasingly significant role, not only as protectors of institutional honor within the military and intelligence communities but also as key facilitators of operational goals. Lawyers became an integral part of the executive branch's functions and had an independence that allowed them to act as honest brokers and arbiters. These lawyers, especially the JAGs within the military, became increasingly convinced that compliance with international law constituted an important criterion for U.S. reputation. As the 1990s progressed, however, it became clear that a group of scholars was putting forth an equal and opposite argument to this embedded norm.

AMBIGUITY/SHOCK: WHAT WAS THE ACTION OR INACTION THAT CAUSED ARGUMENTS?

Reaction to the normative consensus was grounded in two main arguments. First, a small but growing number of politicians and scholars believed that the post-Watergate reforms instituted by Congress to improve oversight of the executive branch were unconstitutional. Congress, they argued, had overstepped its bounds by reducing the executive's ability to manage powers that were solely the domain of the president. These concerns would begin to be voiced prominently in the wake of the Iran-Contra scandal.

Second, a number of conservative legal scholars questioned the role of international law in U.S. policy making. As referred to in chapter 3, the war in Kosovo greatly accelerated this reaction. At the same time, debates were occurring within the U.S. government about the proper legal tools to use against terrorism. The emerging threat from al-Qaeda prompted a gradual shift from prosecuting terrorists as criminals within the civilian legal system to treating them as combatants under the laws of armed conflict. As a result, by September 10, 2001, the post-Vietnam normative consensus was already under strain in many areas. Critics increasingly viewed the post-Vietnam norms on executive power and international law as outdated, providing a firm foundation for the contestation that would come following the attacks of 9/11.

MINORITY REPORT ON THE IRAN-CONTRA AFFAIR

During the proceedings investigating the Iran-Contra affair, testimony from key witnesses revealed a creative and operational NSC, funding the Contra militants in Nicaragua despite the Boland Amendment prohibiting such activity, and selling arms to Iran in exchange for the potential release of six Americans held by Lebanese Hizballah. The hearings before the special joint Senate and House investigating committee crystallized for many a view of an executive branch run amok. However, not everyone shared this perspective. The minority report on the Iran-Contra affair would forcefully articulate an opposing view premised on a contrasting argument about the constitutional separation of powers. The authors stated:

> The bottom line, however, is that the mistakes of the Iran-Contra Affair were just that—mistakes in judgment, and nothing more. There was no constitutional crisis, no systematic disrespect for "the rule of law," no grand conspiracy, and no Administration-wide dishonesty or coverup. In fact, the evidence will not support any of the more hysterical conclusions the Committees' Report tries to reach.[40]

Rather than blaming the White House, the authors of the minority report blamed the "aggrandizing theory of Congress' foreign policy powers" for the view that the executive branch had overstepped its authorities.[41] Whereas the majority concluded that "policies formed through consultation and the democratic process are better and wiser than those formed without it,"[42] the minority report is a testament to presidential prerogative in the area of foreign policy. What caused Iran-Contra? In the view of the authors and supporters of the minority report, it was caused by the "ongoing state of political guerrilla warfare over foreign policy between the legislative and executive branches."[43] In the view of the report's authors, Congress was the party at fault for this state of conflict between the branches because "much of what President Reagan did in his actions toward Nicaragua and Iran were constitutionally protected exercises of inherent Presidential powers."[44]

The ranking House Republican on the committee was Dick Cheney, then-representative from Wyoming, and David Addington (future counsel and chief of staff for Vice President Cheney) was a member of the minority's legal staff as well. Together, they constituted two of the chief architects of the report's argument. This report was not a meaningless government document; for the authors and supporters of the minority report, it represented a critical opportunity to articulate their views on presidential power and the dangers of allowing congressional checks on presidential decision making in foreign affairs. It based these claims on a specific reading of U.S. history that directly clashed with the view put forth by Koh, Henkin, and Schlesinger:

> This history speaks volumes about the Constitution's allocation of powers between the branches. It leaves little, if any, doubt that the President was expected to have the primary role of conducting the foreign policy of the United States. Congressional actions to limit the President in this area therefore should be reviewed with a considerable degree of skepticism. If they interfere with core presidential foreign policy functions, they should be struck down. Moreover, the lesson of our constitutional history is that doubtful cases should be decided in favor of the President.[45]

While the views in the minority report failed to convince Congress, they revealed an area of strong disagreement about the separation of powers within the Constitution. More significantly, the report foreshadowed how this group of individuals would behave once it was in the majority.

ROLE OF INTERNATIONAL LAW

The second significant ambiguity existed around the importance and meaning of international law. Despite—or because of—the zeitgeist in the 1990s around the growing relevance of international law, a counterreaction arose to it. Fueled by the belief that international law was deeply flawed, a school of academics arose to critique its importance in crafting state actions. Notably, this school would include scholars who would later populate the Bush administration's legal ranks, including John Yoo, Jack Goldsmith, and John Bolton.

Various claims were made about international law during this decade, including the charge that it was too vague, that it lacked accountability metrics, that it infringed on issues that were purely domestic concerns, and that it flouted the primacy of the U.S. Constitution.[46] None of these were new charges against international law. They had been leveled from the time of Thucydides to Machiavelli to Hans Morgenthau. Many of the charges against international law stem from foundational issues with this body of law itself: as international law is grounded in state consent, unless a state voluntarily restrains itself by consenting to the rule, it is free to act in violation of the rule. There is no enforcement mechanism and no higher sovereign to obligate compliance. Thus, it inherently lacks the power and enforcement of domestic rules.

Similar to previous claims about international law, these scholars warned that compliance with international law was not only foolish but dangerous. Similar to E. H. Carr, who once warned, "Blind trust in institutionalism is at best dangerous and at worst catastrophic,"[47] these scholars warned of cooperation with international institutions. John Bolton, then of the American Enterprise Institute, cautioned: "For every area of public policy there is a globalist proposal, consistent with the overall objective of reducing individual nation-state autonomy, particularly that of the United States."[48] John Yoo, then a professor at the University of California at Berkeley, warned against the antidemocratic tendencies of international law, declaring that "novel forms of international cooperation increasingly call for the transfer of rulemaking authority to international organizations that lack American openness and accountability."[49]

These concerns over the place of international law in U.S. policy making would accelerate as a result of the war in Kosovo and its aftermath. In his review of General Wesley Clark's memoirs, Professor Richard Betts famously turned a critical eye to the groundbreaking role that lawyers played in the NATO conflict. "One of the most striking features of the Kosovo campaign," he writes, "was the remarkably direct role lawyers played in managing combat operations—to a degree unprecedented in previous wars." During the conflict, "NATO lawyers constrained even the preparation of options for decisive combat. . . . Carried to this extreme, NATO lawyers thus became, in effect, its tactical commanders." This was, in his words, a development that should "shock any student of wartime command."[50]

This criticism was frequently repeated. In an issue of *The National Interest* published immediately after the conclusion of the NATO bombing campaign, David Rivkin Jr. and Lee Casey warned that international law "threatens" U.S. sovereignty. Echoing Carr, these authors ominously state, "If the trends of international law are allowed to mature into binding rules, international law may become one of the most potent weapons ever deployed against the United States."[51] This warning took on increased significance following the decision by the International Criminal Tribunal for the former Yugoslavia to investigate possible war crimes committed by NATO's bombing campaign. The investigation infuriated the United States and other Western powers. It was seen by many as an action representative of a broader "system in which independent prosecutors and judges, answering to no state or institution, wield unfettered power to sit in judgment of the foreign policy decisions of Western democracies."[52] The intransigence of such a system would have consequences, warned Judith Miller, DoD general counsel during the Kosovo operations. "I fear," she wrote, "that the reservations of the United States with respect to the International Criminal Court are well-founded, based on the aftermath of the Kosovo Conflict."[53]

At the same time as this pushback against international law was gaining strength, there was also growing pressure to begin treating international terrorism as acts of war rather than as criminal actions deserving due process via the civilian judicial system. While the norm of treating terrorists as criminals was not a product of the post-Vietnam reform effort, it is nonetheless worth mentioning as it played such a pivotal role in the arguments put forward by Bush administration lawyers following 9/11. In the mid-to-late 1990s, the Clinton administration intensified its efforts to locate Osama bin Laden, particularly after al-Qaeda's attacks on the U.S. embassies in Kenya and Tanzania in 1998. Initially, the Clinton OLC ruled that bin Laden had to be captured and that lethal force could only be used against him if the forces on the ground felt it was necessary for self-defense. Over time this position was seen as insufficient, leading the

OLC to issue a new opinion that gave U.S. forces the right to hunt down and kill bin Laden without attempting to capture him first.[54] The central argument of the memo, according to Benjamin Wittes, was that "under the law of armed conflict, killing a person who posed an imminent threat to the United States would be an act of self-defense, not an assassination."[55] This view—that terrorists constituted legitimate military targets—represented a paradigm shift in how the U.S. government could legally combat terrorist groups and operatives.[56]

This was the context in which 9/11 occurred. By September 10, 2001, many of the post-Vietnam measures and norms put in place regarding executive power, international law, and the role of lawyers in government operations were being challenged on multiple fronts. Likewise, the longstanding precedent of defaulting to the criminal justice system for targeting terrorists was being eroded in the face of operational necessities. That said, the contestation had not yet reached the level of overcoming the previous normative regime. Wittes notes:

> In the years before September 11, nobody was arguing—as the Justice Department claimed in the infamous "Torture Memo" of August 2002— that the legal definition of torture was limited to pain "equivalent in intensity to the pain accompanying serious physical injury, such as organ failure, impairment of bodily function, or even death" or that enforcing the statute in the context of fighting terrorists could "represent an unconstitutional infringement of the president's authority to conduct war."[57]

September 11 would constitute the final shock that allowed the critics of international law to triumph. It was thus the ideal environment for the critics' vision of an executive branch not beholden to Congress or international law. In a speech at Harvard just two months after the attacks, General Charles Dunlap, an Air Force lawyer and scholar, declared:

> I believe the air campaign against Kosovo and Serbia may represent something of a high-water mark of the influence of international law in military interventions, at least in the near term. The aftermath of that

conflict, along with the repercussions of the terrible events of September 11th, seem to have set in motion forces that will diminish the role of law (if not lawyers themselves) much beyond the hyper-legalisms to which Betts objects.[58]

Dunlap goes on to state that

> Americans are much more concerned about finding and stopping the perpetrators of violence than they are about the niceties of international law. Despite the President's statements to the contrary, many pundits called for the outright killing of those responsible, and derided the notion of trying to bring the perpetrators to justice in a criminal court. Unlike international law devotees, many Americans are exasperated with the law, especially when traditional applications of it proved to be an inadequate guarantor of basic security on September 11th.[59]

Dunlap realized that the shock from 9/11 meant international humanitarian law would not only be less salient for the public but that the normative regime must adapt to a new era if it were to stay relevant.

Dunlap's comments proved prescient. At the same time as he was giving his speech, lawyers inside the Bush administration were contesting the application of the Geneva Conventions to captured members of al-Qaeda and the Taliban. Empowered by access and influence to shape administration policy and presented with a prime opportunity to put their beliefs into action, the lawyers would not hesitate to push their arguments as far as they could.

CONTESTATION: WHAT ARGUMENTS WERE MADE?

Post-9/11 challenges from lawyers inside the Bush administration were grounded primarily in an extensive vision of executive power in general and in foreign affairs and war powers in particular. To begin, lawyers such as

John Yoo, William Haynes, and David Addington fervently believed that 9/11 constituted an act of war triggering the president's war powers as commander-in-chief. As such, the criminal justice system, with its protections for civil liberties and human rights, was no longer the appropriate venue for combating al-Qaeda and its sponsors. Moreover, the lawyers argued that the president is the head of a unitary executive, meaning that his writ is law inside the executive branch. As such, challenges to presidential initiatives were not only unwanted nuisances on a policy level but were also an acute threat to their vision for how the executive branch should function. For these men, this argument was based as much on practicality as ideals. Their reading of the Constitution, as well as the events of 9/11, convinced them that the founding fathers wanted an executive branch capable of acting quickly and secretly in order to protect the nation in a dangerous world. Thus, the normative regime put in place following Vietnam undermined the president's ability to act decisively and constituted a dire threat to U.S. national security.

This contestation would take many forms in the years following 9/11, with administration lawyers using their vision of executive power to argue for specific policies on domestic surveillance, military commissions, the use of force, and countless other aspects of the White House's counterterrorist agenda. However, the most prominent example and by far the most significant with regard to challenging the post-Vietnam normative consensus was the administration's detainee-treatment policy. Using their access and considerable intellectual firepower, by 2003 the lawyers had largely succeeded in implementing an interrogation policy that ignored international law, defanged the notoriously independent JAGs inside the Pentagon, and relied on a broad reading of executive power in wartime.

ACCESS AND INFLUENCE

The key in contesting any existing norm framework is having the access and influence to do so. A small handful of lawyers—Yoo, Addington, Haynes—were able to challenge the norm framework because they wielded an incredible amount of power in the executive branch. The OLC, in which both

Yoo and Goldsmith worked, "is, and views itself as, the frontline institution responsible for ensuring that the executive branch charged with executing the law is itself bound by law."[60] In this capacity, it is therefore the equivalent of the Supreme Court for the executive branch. The OLC decides what the law says, thereby defining the policy boundaries for the president. This is a powerful tool under any circumstance, but even more so in the hands of intelligent and ambitious personnel.

Yoo certainly fit this description. While he never served as the head of the OLC, he was "clearly the Bush administration's designated go-to guy in the OLC for the most important and sensitive post-9/11 legal issues."[61] Part of this authority derived from the fact that when the planes hit on 9/11, Yoo was one of the only people in the OLC who possessed expertise on matters of national security and presidential powers.[62] As deputy assistant attorney general of the OLC from 2001 to 2003, Yoo was involved in the drafting of the so-called Bybee memos providing legal cover for torture and authorizing which techniques could legally be used against Abu Zubaydah.[63] In addition to these memos, he is believed to have authored the memo entitled "The President's Constitutional Authority to Conduct Military Operations Against Terrorists and Nations Supporting Them," regarding the justification for preventive war, on September 25, 2001;[64] the legal justification for the 2001 NSA "Terrorist Surveillance Program";[65] the memo entitled the "Authority for Use of Military Force to Combat Terrorist Activities Within the United States" in October 2001, which determined that the president could order the use of military force domestically and "generally" not be subject to the Fourth Amendment;[66] and the January 2002 Geneva applicability memo.[67] In addition, he wrote a six-page letter addressed to Alberto Gonzales that states that U.S. treaty obligations, for example under the CAT, do not go beyond the U.S. federal antitorture statute.[68] Together, Yoo's position inside the OLC, his knowledge of national security law, and the clarity of purpose with which he wrote his opinions made him one of the most influential architects of the administration's counterterror policy.

The only lawyer who possessed greater influence than Yoo was David Addington. Addington was one of the first two employees hired by Cheney and, at the young age of forty-three, had already served "as staff attorney to three House committees, assistant general counsel of the CIA, a deputy assistant to the president under Ronald Reagan, and general counsel of Cheney's Pentagon."[69] Given his vast experience in national security law—and, perhaps most importantly, the unwavering trust Cheney placed in him—Addington as the vice president's counsel wielded more power than any of his predecessors and commanded more authority within the White House than the president's own counsel, Alberto Gonzales.[70] According to Barton Gellman,

> There was not a lawyer in government, of more than three dozen interviewed, who doubted Addington's status as first among equals. He had a size on him, everything writ large—the physical presence, the booming anger, the cutting intellect, the certainty of belief, the presumption of purview over whatever caught his eye. Addington attended pretty much every meeting of significance in Gonzales' wood-paneled office, the two of them facing the visitor's sofa in matching chairs. Often he did most of the talking.[71]

Addington used this influence to shape the administration's legal policy on detainee treatment. While he was not directly involved in the drafting of the OLC opinions, Addington worked through proxies to request "OLC opinions on subjects calculated to elicit broad replies. Addington insisted on strict secrecy, preventing the circulation of drafts to agencies that might challenge Yoo's analysis. With the rulings in hand, the vice president's counsel wrote the regulations, directives, and executive orders that changed events."[72]

Together, Yoo and Addington were the key players in shaping the Bush administration's legal policy after 9/11. However, they had help from important lawyers in other departments, chief among them William Haynes, general counsel in Rumsfeld's DoD. Haynes and Addington were incredibly close, with Addington having served as best man at Haynes's wedding.[73] This bond was more than personal. They shared a similar view of the unitary executive and, as the top lawyer in the DoD, Haynes was in a prime position to implement this vision, as he would show in his manipulation of the review process for the EITs. Other significant lawyers, such as John Rizzo at the CIA, would go along with the legal rationales put forth by Addington and Yoo, seeking to ensure that agency personnel would be protected from prosecution and never truly challenging the legal arguments supporting the interrogation programs.[74]

These lawyers were not sadists. They did not enter public service in order to torture captured members of al-Qaeda and the Taliban. Rather, these were men who had several beliefs in common: a theory that 9/11 constituted an act of war; an unswerving belief in a strong, unitary executive; and a suspicion of international law as binding upon U.S. actions. These beliefs—combined with their ability to implement them thanks to their access and influence—would challenge the existing norm framework and ultimately lead to the authorization of torture as official U.S. policy.

9/11 AS AN ACT OF WAR

The central argument driving the lawyers' contestation was the view that 9/11 constituted an act of war. Viewing 9/11 through the lens of war both triggered the president's commander-in-chief powers and departed from the precedent of treating terrorism foremost as a criminal act. In his memoirs about his tenure at the OLC, John Yoo clearly lays out this line of argumentation:

> Here is how we at the Justice Department sat down to think about September 11. On that clear, sunny day, four coordinated attacks had taken place in rapid succession, aimed at critical buildings at the heart of our national financial system and our nation's capital. The terrorists who hijacked these airplanes in some ways had conventional military objectives—to decapitate America's political, military, and economic headquarters.[75]

To treat such an attack as a criminal act "would be a huge mistake," according to Yoo.[76] "Applying criminal justice rules to al-Qaeda terrorists would gravely impede the killing or capture of the enemy, as well as compromise the secrecy of the United States' military efforts," he writes.[77] This legal delineation between war and crime set the stage for the entire strategy against al-Qaeda and the Taliban. Approaching 9/11 as an act of war rather than as a crime opened the toolbox for what means were acceptable—and legal—to combat al-Qaeda and the Taliban. Jack Goldsmith summarizes the importance of this conceptual shift:

> Our government chose to use the legal framework of war because after 9/11 it believed that military force would be necessary to defeat al-Qaeda—not as a complete solution, or even the primary solution, but as a necessary part of the solution. The eight-year law enforcement approach to Islamist terrorism—which began with the 1993 World Trade Center bombings, which ignored Bin Laden's 1996 declaration of war, and which persisted even though the United States suffered many vicious blows from al-Qaeda around the globe, and knew of plots to commit even more spectacular attacks inside the United States—failed.[78]

Viewing the struggle with al-Qaeda and the Taliban as a war provided the strongest possible foundation for all of the other arguments the lawyers would make about executive power and international law. War is anathema to the status quo—a fact that the lawyers would point out time and again in their efforts to contest the post-Vietnam normative regime.

EXECUTIVE POWER

Following Watergate, the balance of power in the U.S. government seemed to swing away from 1600 Pennsylvania Avenue and toward Capitol Hill. The lawyers in the executive branch sought to correct this swing during the war on terror. Building on the views expressed in the Iran-Contra minority report, the lawyers argued that neither Congress, the courts, nor the American public could unduly limit the powers of the unitary executive in general and especially during wartime, when the president's commander-in-chief powers granted him wide prerogative. This view was clearly laid out in a key passage of the first Bybee memo, which claimed, in the words of Barton Gellman:

> That the president may authorize any interrogation method, even if it indisputably constitutes torture. U.S. and treaty laws forbidding "any" person to commit torture, that passage stated, "do not apply" to the commander-in-chief, because Congress "may no more regulate the President's ability to detain and interrogate enemy combatants than it may regulate his ability to direct troop movements on the battlefield."[79]

The same argument would be made throughout the administration's legal battles over its detention and interrogation policies. For example, in a famous presidential signing statement drafted by administration lawyers[80] and attached to the 2005 Detainee Treatment Act, President Bush declared he would interpret the bill's limitation on his interrogation power

> in a manner consistent with the constitutional authority of the President to supervise the unitary executive and as Commander-in-Chief and consistent with the constitutional limitations on the judicial power, which will assist in achieving the shared objective of the Congress and the President . . . of protecting the American people from further terrorist attacks.[81]

The extent of authority claimed in these statements represents an extreme belief in the power of the executive during wartime, eclipsing even Alexis de Tocqueville's centuries-old claim that "it is chiefly in foreign relations that the executive power of a nation, finds occasion to exert skill and strength."[82] While many scholars and policy makers had previously pointed to the advantages possessed by the president in foreign affairs—a first-mover advantage; an information advantage; the ability to act quickly, secretly, and decisively—this articulation of an executive seemingly without any checks was radical even by the standards of those sympathetic to the argument. Upon becoming head of the OLC in 2003, Jack Goldsmith reviewed the Bybee memos and concluded that they were "deeply flawed" in part because they were "incautious in asserting extraordinary constitutional authorities on behalf of the President."[83]

The constitutional rationale behind this view of executive power was laid out succinctly in Yoo's book *The Powers of War and Peace*, his first book written after leaving the OLC. Here, Yoo lays out a vision for the constitutional distribution of foreign affairs powers that directly challenges the view put forth by Henkin and other influential legal academics in the post-Vietnam era. He argues that

> the Constitution depends less on fixed legal processes for decisionmaking and more on the political interaction of the executive and legislative branches. It allocated different powers to the president, Senate, and Congress that allow them to shape different processes depending on the contemporary demands of the international system and their relative political position. The constitution does not require a single, correct method for making war or peace, for making international agreements or breaking them, or for interpreting and enforcing international law. Rather, it allows the branches to cooperate or compete in the foreign affairs field by relying on their unique constitutional powers.[84]

Yoo comes to this conclusion because the Constitution, as addressed previously, is relatively silent on the distribution of foreign affairs powers. The theories put forward by scholars like Koh and Henkin, he declares, assume this silence means the text is incomplete and rely on extraconstitutional sources to fill in the gap.[85] In contrast, Yoo sees the Constitution's silence on foreign affairs as deliberate. "The conflict among the branches of government over foreign affairs," he contends,

> is not a flaw in the constitutional design, but is instead its conscious product. . . . This not only gives the nation more flexibility in reaching foreign affairs decisions, it gives each of the three branches of government the ability to check the initiatives of the others in foreign affairs. The deepest questions of American foreign relations law remain open because the Constitution wants it that way.[86]

The result of this constitutional design, according to Yoo, is a presidency vested with wide-ranging foreign affairs powers. For example, Yoo compares the wording of Article I, which grants only the powers listed within to Congress, to the wording of Article II, which vests an undefined and unlimited executive authority in the president. Given that the Constitutional Convention was called largely to address the incompetence of the Articles of Confederation with regard to foreign affairs, and given that foreign affairs has always been seen as an executive function, Yoo believes this framework is intentional and indicates the framers wanted a presidency with strong foreign affairs prerogatives.[87] As a result, not only does wartime "naturally enhance presidential power,"[88] but also a president would be derelict in his duty if he did not take advantage of the full scope of his authorities.[89]

Yoo buttresses his argument by claiming that the views put forth by Henkin, Schlesinger, and Koh were the product of a specific era of international affairs, one where it was hoped that the incidence of conflict, which was primarily seen as state based, was in decline because of the collapse of the Soviet Union. Consequently, "an understanding of the Constitution that was very strict and legalistic would support such an end by making it harder for the use of American force."[90] September 11 "made this mode of thinking outdated and dangerous," according to Yoo. "The international system no longer places a premium on a warmaking system that relies on consensus, time, deliberation, and the approval of multiple institutions."[91] Ultimately, 9/11 proved that living in a dangerous world requires a strong presidency for safety, which, according to Yoo and his fellow lawyers inside the administration, was exactly what the framers wanted and the Constitution provides for.

RESTORE THE UNITARY EXECUTIVE

In addition to making the academic arguments for a strong executive, the lawyers inside the Bush administration worked hard to implement their vision. The central goal of this effort was to reduce resistance to the president's initiatives from Congress, the courts, and the independent lawyers inside executive branch departments. In framing this objective, Goldsmith presented the view common inside the administration that these constraints were suffocating the presidency. "Many people think the Bush administration has been indifferent to wartime legal constraints," he writes. "But the opposite is true: the administration has been strangled by law, and since September 11, 2001, this war has been lawyered to death."[92] Lawyers inside the White House sought to end this legacy of the post-Vietnam normative consensus.[93]

Despite being controlled by Republicans, Congress was a constant target of the lawyers' ire. Goldsmith once asked Addington why the administration did not just go to Congress to get its approval for the entire detention program. "Why are you trying to give away the President's power?" he responded. According to Goldsmith, Addington "believed that the very act of asking for Congress's help would imply, contrary to the White House line, that the President needed legislative approval and could not act on his own."[94] As the chief legal enforcer of this ideological pursuit, Addington made it a habit to ask two questions whenever someone proposed working with Congress to achieve some policy goal: "Do we have the legal power to do it ourselves?" and "Might Congress limit our options in ways that jeopardize American lives?"[95]

This confrontational approach carried over into the administration's dealing with the courts. In his book covering the Cheney vice presidency, Barton Gellman recounts how Addington successfully pushed for Ted Olson, the administration's solicitor general, to argue before the Supreme Court in the *Rasul v. Bush* and *Hamdi v. Rumsfeld* cases that the president had absolute discretion to detain any combatant without access to a lawyer or habeas corpus rights.[96] This was the most extreme of the available arguments, and the Supreme Court rejected it in both cases. Several years later, in the aftermath of the *Hamdan v. Rumsfeld* case, Addington drafted a one-page bill, "which amounted to asking Congress to reverse the outcome in *Hamdan*. By this proposal, Bush would not ask Congress for authority to hold military tribunals. He would ask Congress to affirm that Bush did not need its permission, and to strip the Court of jurisdiction over the matter."[97] While the administration this time did not take Addington's advice, it shows just how far he was willing to go to assert his vision of executive power.

Top administration lawyers also took direct action to reduce the independence of the JAGs in the DoD as well as lawyers at the Department of

State. For instance, when drafting an OLC opinion, it is standard procedure for the Justice Department lawyers to reach out to other lawyers in the executive branch that may have experience with the issue being reviewed. In the case of the Bybee memos, the exact opposite happened: lawyers at the Department of State were kept out of the process at the direction of the White House.[98] Likewise, in the DoD, General Counsel William Haynes worked to reduce the ability of the JAGs to challenge White House authority. According to Philippe Sands, Haynes and Addington "had a principled commitment to reducing JAG independence based on notions of civilian control of the military" and "principled views about the non-applicability of the UCMJ and the Geneva Conventions to certain aspects of the war on terrorism, and about vindicating these views—which were, after all, the views of the President—throughout the military."[99] To this end, Haynes initiated an effort to streamline legal advice within the DoD so that the general counsel would speak for the entire Pentagon. He wanted to bring the service lawyers, the legal staff of the Joint Chiefs, and the other military JAGs under the official control of the general counsel, which would have centralized all legal decision making in his office and ended the tradition of independent legal advice within the department.[100]

While ultimately not successful, a preview of what such a system would have looked like can be seen in the legal-review process given to the interrogation techniques requested from Guantánamo Bay. Despite the seriousness of the issues being considered, the memo from Guantánamo bypassed the normal review process because of Haynes's intervention. For example, Haynes never let the lawyers from the staff of the Joint Chiefs finish their review of the proposal. According to Jane Dalton, counsel to then-chairman of the Joint Chiefs Richard Myers, "[Haynes] pulled this away; we never had a chance to complete the assessment."[101] Furthermore, the memo that Haynes ultimately presented to Rumsfeld for his approval had no "buckslip," which is the routine routing slip that shows a document's circulation and on which everyone usually signs off. The entire process by which EITs were approved for use at Guantánamo was manipulated by Haynes in conjunction with senior White House lawyers such as Addington. As Sands notes, the service lawyers were silent in October and November 2002, as the eighteen techniques were being considered. They were silent because they had no idea what Rumsfeld and Haynes were doing; they had no idea about the eighteen techniques. "They just cut the Services out," Romig [a former Army JAG] told me. "Someone overheard Addington say 'Don't bring the JAGs into the process, they aren't reliable.'"[102]

For the top lawyers in the Bush administration, the law, like everything else within the executive branch's domain, should be subservient to the needs of the president. As advocates of the unitary executive, independent legal advice was not a virtue to be promoted but rather a danger to be extinguished.

DANGERS OF INTERNATIONAL LAW

Closely related to the issue of executive power was the relevance of international law. For administration lawyers, international law was seen as both threatening and irrelevant at the same time. Before being tapped to lead the OLC, Goldsmith worked as a lawyer inside the DoD tasked with analyzing the risk posed by "lawfare" to the United States. In a memo to Secretary Rumsfeld assessing the newborn ICC, Goldsmith declared, "The ICC is at bottom an attempt by militarily weak nations that dominated ICC negotiations to restrain militarily powerful nations."[103] Likewise, key lawyers inside the White House saw international law as being insufficient to handle the terrorist threat. According to one participant in a White House Situation Room meeting a few days after 9/11, "if you favored international law, you were in danger of being called 'soft on terrorism' by Addington."[104]

In addition to seeing international law as a threat to the United States' freedom of action, lawyers in the executive branch claimed that international law simply did not apply to the United States. Ignoring decades of precedent—and centuries of tradition—the lawyers in the OLC concluded that "the Geneva Conventions had not assumed the status of customary international law that bound the United States, nor, for that matter, all the nations in the world."[105] As such, the president was free to interpret the conventions as he saw fit. In a public debate with the international legal scholar Philippe Sands, Yoo confirmed this position, declaring: "Even if international law requires the United States not to engage in inhumane or degrading treatment the U.S. view is that that rule does not apply in the war against terrorism and against members of al-Qaeda."[106]

Administration lawyers even expressed strong opinions on how international law forms or should be formed. Echoing a refrain popularized by the political scientist John Mearsheimer, Goldsmith and Judge Eric Posner argued in a 2005 book that states comply with international law out of a coincidence between that law and self-interest, not because the law has become embedded in state practice or out of a sense of moral obligation.[107] Yoo went even further in his memoirs, claiming that given its preponderance of power, the United States should be the definer of customary international law:

> At this moment in world history the United States' conduct should bear the most weight in defining the customs of war. Our defense budget is greater than the defense spending of the next fifteen nations combined. We are the only nation that consistently fights wars around the world to protect its interests, maintain peace in unstable regions, and to prevent human rights catastrophes. . . . U.S. practice in its wars—to maintain global peace and stability—have primary authority in setting international law on the rules of warfare.[108]

For the lawyers inside the Bush White House, the prevailing normative regime on international law was nothing but a menace to be ignored or reshaped in the United States' likeness.

CONCLUSION

The controversy that ensued over the Bush administration's detainee policies is a reflection of the level of normative contestation in which the

lawyers were engaged. The lawyers themselves seem to recognize this, offering as a defense the argument that they were simply providing legal advice,
not making policy decisions. Yoo makes this argument in his memoirs in
regard to the decision not to grant Geneva protections to al-Qaeda and the
Taliban:

> OLC wanted to make clear that we were discussing only issues of law,
> not policy. Even if al-Qaeda or Taliban fighters did not deserve the legal
> protections of the Geneva Conventions, the President could still extend
> those rights as a matter of policy and goodwill. . . . Our point was that the
> United States could find it advantageous to follow the Geneva Conven-
> tions, even if not legally bound to, but that then again it might not. That
> would be a question for the policy makers—Powell, Rumsfeld, Ashcroft,
> Tenet, and Rice—to decide, not OLC.[109]

Yoo's claim of only offering legal advice is disingenuous if one looks
closely at the language used in the legal memos presented to the White
House. Administration lawyers were not simply laying out a disinterested
argument for why Geneva did not apply: they were saying that the conflict
with al-Qaeda rendered its provisions "quaint" and "obsolete."[110] Such language cast the argument in moral and political tones, telling the president,
essentially, that he would be naïve and foolish to extend Geneva protections to the unconventional enemy now facing the country. Moreover, the
evidence of the lawyers' involvement effectively negates any claim that only
a few "bad apples" are to blame for the implementation of the EITs. Laced
through the 2014 SSCI Report are mentions of the role of the lawyers, particularly the lawyers in the OLC, who concluded, inter alia, that the president's commander-in-chief powers gave him the legal authority to do as he
pleased with captured enemy combatants.[111]

In sum, lawyers such as Yoo, Addington, and Haynes used their influence
to challenge the pre-9/11 normative consensus on executive power, the role
of international law, and the authority and independence of other lawyers
inside the executive branch. In the process, they became key players in the
push for using EITs, functioning simultaneously as policy advocates and

facilitators of the argument. While these men uniformly believed the interrogation techniques were useful and necessary, this conviction was an ancillary component of their larger ideological and political goals: increasing the power of the unitary executive and reducing the influence of international law in U.S. policy. As the subsequent chapter will show, the lawyers' arguments found a receptive audience in a group of policy makers that, scarred by the attacks of 9/11, vowed never again to let the United States be victimized like it was that day.

5

POW TREATMENT
AND POLICY MAKERS

What was the alternative—letting them go and then hoping to catch
them as they were committing their next terrorist attack against the
American people?

—DONALD RUMSFELD, KNOWN AND UNKNOWN: A MEMOIR

A T THE END of the Vietnam War, POW handling and treatment
occupied an important and significant place in the minds of U.S.
policy makers. In large part, this was a response to concerns about
the morally degrading effects the war had inflicted on domestic society.
By the mid-1970s, Vietnam, in conjunction with national scandals such
as Watergate, the release of the Pentagon Papers, and revelations of secret
domestic surveillance programs, had severely undermined public faith in
the government and led to widespread doubt that the United States was
living up to its ideals.

To that end, policy makers' concern with the treatment of POWs was
part of a larger reevaluation of how U.S. values aligned with U.S. foreign policy actions. As highlighted in chapter 3, accounts of torture and
noncombatant deaths in Vietnam led the Pentagon to implement extensive changes to its doctrine and training and education programs. These
changes, however, represented only the tip of the iceberg. Between the end
of the Vietnam War and 9/11, policy makers in each presidential administration implemented changes and gave speeches that slowly affirmed the
internalization of the norms of humane treatment. These efforts reached
their peak in the 1991 Persian Gulf War, after which a representative of the
ICRC declared, "The treatment of Iraqi prisoners of war by U.S. forces was

the best compliance with the Geneva Convention by any nation in any conflict in history."[1]

While U.S. actions in this period never perfectly matched Washington's rhetoric on humane treatment and the importance of international humanitarian law, these deviations from the norm were motivated by opportunism rather than an underlying desire to alter the normative framework. As this chapter will show, the attacks of 9/11 provided the shock necessary to make altering the normative consensus possible. Responding to the attack, policy makers inside the Bush administration used their access and influence to support the embedding of a new normative understanding of detainee treatment and international humanitarian law.

EMBEDDED NORM: NORM CONTEXT BEFORE 9/11

The existing norm framework for policy makers emerged out of twin stimuli from the Vietnam War: concern over the treatment and repatriation of U.S. POWs and concern over allegations of U.S. abuse of POWs and noncombatants during Vietnam. Together, these two concerns drove policy makers to take a variety of actions that solidly embedded the norm of humane treatment.

CONCERN ABOUT TREATMENT OF U.S. POWS

Imagine you're imprisoned in a cage; imagine the cage surrounded by the smell of feces; imagine the rotted food you eat is so infested with insects that to eat only a few is a blessing; imagine knowing your life could be taken by one of your captors on a whim at any moment; imagine you are subjected to mental and physical torture designed to break not bones but instead spirit on a daily basis. That was being a prisoner of North Vietnam.[2]

Unlike the indifferent reception many returning Vietnam veterans received, the concern for the returning—and still held—POWs from Vietnam occupied a large place in the emotional psyches of the American public and U.S. policy makers during and following the war. The physical and psychological abuse leveled against the young men held by North Vietnam included torture, humiliation, and coercion. Concerns about their reintegration into society and their seen and unseen scars dominated many of the policy makers' statements about resolving the war and, ultimately, restoring normal relations with Vietnam. Despite wide variations in how each policy maker processed the Vietnam experience as a whole for the United States, both Republicans and Democrats affirmed the importance of the return and repatriation of U.S. POWs. Presidents Reagan, George H. W. Bush, and Clinton, for example, all called the return of POWs an "issue of the highest national priority."[3]

Beginning with President Nixon, the importance of caring for and treating former U.S. POWs from Vietnam would command policy makers' attention over the next three decades. By publicizing the stories of U.S. POWs—their experiences, for example, in solitary confinement, in enduring severe torture, in being denied basic medical care and clean food and water—policy makers reinforced the notion that those in the custody of belligerents during war still deserved basic humane treatment. Moreover, by linking these standards for humane treatment to larger policy objectives, U.S. policy makers underscored their significance. In his speech announcing the signing of the Paris Peace Accords in January 1973, President Nixon listed the return of U.S. POWs as the first obligation of the North Vietnamese government after abiding by the cease-fire. Later in the speech, Nixon took a special moment to "say a word to some of the bravest people I have ever met—the wives, the children, the families of our prisoners of war and the missing in action."[4] In this way, the rights of and obligations to U.S. POWs were not an afterthought of the U.S. war effort or cease-fire but a central component.

More than a decade later, in a 1987 speech before the POW/MIA National League of Families, Secretary of State George Shultz stated that the POW/MIA issue with Vietnam must be resolved before a normalization of relations between the states could be possible.[5] Five years later, standing before the same organization, President George H. W. Bush stated unequivocally that "without further positive movement on the POWs and MIAs, we cannot and will not continue to move forward with Hanoi."[6] The consistency and endurance of this theme—that POWs were essential to the baseline of relations between the United States and Vietnam—signaled that this issue was not merely a rhetorical exercise for the policy makers. As Michael J. Allen notes in *Until the Last Man Comes Home: POWs, MIAs, and the Unending Vietnam War*, relatively few Americans went missing in Vietnam compared to previous wars, yet the United States spent far more time and money on finding those missing persons than it did in other previous conflicts.[7]

Concern about the treatment of U.S. POWs in Vietnamese hands spilled over into concerns about the treatment of U.S. POWs in other conflicts, notably the Iran hostage crisis, the Gulf War, and Kosovo. Though the hostages taken in Iran were not technically POWs since they were neither combatants nor taken during a time of war, the language used by President Carter to discuss their plight mimics the language used by other policy makers to refer to the importance of returning U.S. POWs. For example, in his 1980 State of the Union Address, Carter spent considerable time on the hostage crisis in Iran, stating, "If the American hostages are harmed, a severe price will be paid. We will never rest until every one of the American hostages are released."[8] Similarly, nine years later, Manuel Noriega's treatment of U.S. captives in Panama constituted an important reason for President Bush's invasion of the small Latin American country. In his address to the public explaining the rationale for the invasion, the treatment of detained U.S. citizens seemed to be the tipping point. He stated:

> Last Friday, Noriega declared his military dictatorship to be in a state of war with the United States and publicly threatened the lives of Americans in Panama. The very next day forces under his command shot and killed an unarmed American serviceman, wounded another, arrested and brutally beat a third American serviceman and then brutally interrogated his wife, threatening her with sexual abuse. That was enough.[9]

These were not casual side thoughts or musings; they were an expression of a deeply held belief and representative of official U.S. policy. Treating captives humanely was an obligation of every government, and Washington would not tolerate the abuse of captured U.S. citizens.

This position would continue through the 1991 Persian Gulf War with Secretary of Defense Dick Cheney arguing on a network television news program that Iraq had a "solemn legal obligation to abide by the Geneva Conventions in terms of treatment of prisoners. To do anything else would in fact constitute a war crime."[10] Then, in 1999, President Clinton gave a speech about NATO action in Kosovo at the Norfolk Naval Station that included a warning to Serbian president Slobodan Milošević regarding the fate of three captured American servicemen. "President Milošević should make no mistake," he declared. "We will hold him and his Government responsible for their safety and for their well-being."[11]

Taken together, these statements of concern from major U.S. policy makers provided a framework in which POW issues were central both to leaders' decisions about U.S. actions in war and to decisions regarding issues such as the normalization of relations with another country and the determination to use force in the first place.

CONCERN ABOUT U.S. TREATMENT OF ENEMY POWS

Policy makers after the end of the Vietnam War took tangible steps to align the United States more closely with its values and its domestic and international legal commitments. For example, President Ford took many steps to restore the credibility of U.S. leadership, both domestically and internationally. In the wake of the Church Committee and Pike Committee findings, Ford issued Executive Order 11905, which, among other things, banned U.S. participation in assassinations, created the Intelligence Oversight Board, and mandated the NSC to conduct semiannual evaluations of the nation's intelligence operations, including the continued "appropriateness of special activities in support of national foreign policy objectives."[12] President Ford also used his authority to create the position of coordinator for human rights and humanitarian affairs within the Department of State.[13] Located within a separate office in the Deputy Secretary of State's Office, the coordinator was accompanied by a deputy coordinator for human rights and humanitarian affairs as well as coordinators for refugee and migration affairs and POW/MIA affairs.[14] Overall, in conjunction with congressional actions taken during the same period, Ford's efforts during his brief time in office signaled that no U.S. government agency would be above the law and that the promotion of human rights would again occupy an important place in U.S. foreign policy. As Rebecca Gordon notes in *Mainstreaming Torture*, "After the Church Committee's well-publicized deliberations, a national consensus about torture reigned; U.S. torture was incompatible with U.S. 'decency, fair dealing, and moral leadership.'"[15] President Jimmy Carter not only continued with this theme but also expanded upon it; for Carter, U.S. foreign policy must be just and moral. This theme was evident in his inaugural address, where he declared, "To be true to ourselves, we must be true to others. We will not behave in foreign places so as to violate our rules and standards here at home, for we know that the trust which our Nation earns is essential to our strength."[16]

The importance of moral leadership would be a theme that Carter referred to consistently over the course of his presidency, especially with regard to how the United States had erred in its past actions in foreign policy and leadership. In his commencement address at the University of Notre Dame in 1977, he advanced the notion that a commitment to human rights is compatible with U.S. foreign policy goals:

> I believe we can have a foreign policy that is democratic, that is based on fundamental values, and that uses power and influence, which we have, for humane purposes. We can also have a foreign policy that the American people both support and, for a change, know about and understand. . . . For too many years, we've been willing to adopt the flawed and erroneous principles and tactics of our adversaries, sometimes abandoning our own values for theirs. We've fought fire with fire, never thinking that fire is better quenched with water. This approach failed, with Vietnam the best example of its intellectual and moral poverty. But through failure we have now found our way back to our own principles and values, and we have regained our lost confidence.[17]

In this speech, Carter sought to separate the United States and its adversaries not on the basis of their foreign policy goals but instead on the basis of values, methods, and principles. Carter also continued the bureaucratic work of his predecessor by converting the Office of the Coordinator for Human Rights and Humanitarian Affairs into a full-fledged Bureau of Human Rights and Humanitarian Affairs and by explicitly tasking other Department of State bureaus to include human rights in their portfolios. To that end, Secretary of State Cyrus Vance assigned Deputy Secretary of State Warren Christopher the responsibility of creating a Human Rights Coordinating Group of State Department officials at the deputy assistant secretary level to "serve as an 'internal mechanism' for decision-making."[18] Moreover, the Carter administration submitted numerous human rights treaties to the Senate for its advice and consent.[19] While none of them were ratified during Carter's presidency, the move was still important as a symbol of the president's determination to set the country on a new course. In this way, Carter's legacy outlasted his single term in office. Carter "set a new course for American foreign policy. It was an effort to bring our foreign policy into line with our domestic values. It was a policy that grew out of a decade of rising disillusionment with the war in Viet Nam."[20]

His successor, President Reagan, also highlighted the importance of human rights in foreign policy, in particular by using the issue as a moral distinction between the United States and the Soviet Union. Reagan's rhetoric was especially important in this effort, carefully choosing his words to bolster the image of the United States as a "shining city on hill" while denouncing the USSR as an "evil empire."[21] Even when discussing specific policies or actions, Reagan often highlighted the importance of human rights. For example, in his speech on the invasion of Grenada, Reagan made a special effort to address the fair and just treatment given to the Cubans found on the island: "At the moment of our landing, we communicated with the Governments of Cuba and the Soviet Union and told them we would offer shelter and security to their people on Grenada. Regrettably, Castro ordered his men to fight to the death, and some did. The others will be sent to their homelands."[22]

As detailed in chapter 3, under President George H. W. Bush, U.S. treatment of POWs was outstanding, with U.S. servicemen and women complying with the Geneva Conventions in U.S. operations in Panama[23] and the Persian Gulf. Bush even justified U.S. action against Iraq in 1991 using just-war terminology, stating, "From the very first day of the war, the allies have waged war against Saddam's military. We are doing everything possible, believe me, to avoid hurting the innocent. Saddam's response: wanton, barbaric bombing of civilian areas. America and her allies value life."[24] With U.S. behavior abroad reflecting Washington's rhetoric, President Bush further confirmed human rights as a national priority, legitimizing U.S. leadership on the world stage.

Soon to follow, President Clinton occupied the presidency during a watershed period for human rights in the international system. Clinton's tenure overlapped with a geopolitical moment in which transnational groups, individuals, and governments were taking human rights seriously as ends unto themselves and in which the collapse of the USSR created the space for states and nonstate actors to address the importance of human dignity in the international system. Clinton's term included the fiftieth anniversaries of the trials at Nuremberg, the promulgation of the UDHR, the creation of the United Nations, and the creation of the 1949 Geneva Conventions. In a speech marking the anniversary of the decisions at Nuremburg, Clinton stated, "With our purpose and with our position comes the responsibility to help shine the light of justice on those who would deny to others their most basic human rights. We have an obligation to carry forward the lessons of Nuremberg."[25] Moreover, Clinton declared it to be official U.S. policy to support the establishment of "a permanent international court to prosecute, with the support of the United Nations Security Council, serious violations of humanitarian law." This, he said, "would be the ultimate tribute to the people who did such important work at Nuremberg."[26]

Later in his presidency, Clinton followed his predecessor's decision to couch the actions of the United States in just-war language by relying on *jus ad bellum* tenets to address the decision to use force in Kosovo. In his speech to the nation announcing the beginning of air strikes, Clinton railed against the abuses being perpetrated by Serbian forces:

We've seen innocent people taken from their homes, forced to kneel in the dirt, and sprayed with bullets; Kosovar men dragged from their families, fathers and sons together, lined up and shot in cold blood. This is not war in the traditional sense. It is an attack by tanks and artillery on a largely defenseless people whose leaders already have agreed to peace.[27]

Clinton also issued an apology to Guatemala for U.S. support of human rights–abusing regimes there during the Cold War,[28] and he created the position of U.S. ambassador at large for war crimes in 1997 within the Department of State. In May of that year, the inaugural ambassador, David Scheffer, addressed the U.S. Army First Corps at Fort Lewis, Washington, on the importance of U.S. adherence to international humanitarian law. He claimed:

> The U.S. military leads the world in the art of integrating legal advice into the process of planning and executing operations. When you train at any of the Combat Training Centers today, you will find Army lawyers whose function is to challenge your state of training and compliance with the laws of armed conflict in a tactical environment, not in some sterile lecture. The Army leadership is committed to reinforcing legal principles in the real world of military practice because the laws of armed conflict do not simply exist as some ethereal smoke in the ozone. They are not some rigid code of unrealistic regulation imposed upon you by a disinterested chain of command.[29]

These statements—by past presidents and their subordinates—represented the existing norm framework on the eve of 9/11. The concern over the fate of U.S. POWs and shame over U.S. behavior during Vietnam together formed a narrative for U.S. policy makers that would endure across administrations and partisan lines. During this time, opinion was widespread that U.S. compliance with international humanitarian law was critical for both the expression of values as ends in themselves and the promotion of foreign policy prerogatives. This is not to imply that U.S. behavior was without stain. For example, evidence exists to confirm that the United States taught torture as a technique to many foreign military students at training programs such as the School of the Americas and in the course of international conflicts did engage in practices that dehumanized captives.[30] However, none of these activities truly constituted a challenge to the normative regime. There was no attempt by policy makers inside or outside the government to rewrite domestic norms on torture or to question the importance of the human rights regime. On the eve of 9/11, policy makers viewed humane treatment of those in U.S. custody in wartime as lawful, just, and essential.

AMBIGUITY/SHOCK: WHAT WAS THE ACTION OR INACTION THAT CAUSED ARGUMENTS?

It is difficult to overstate the impact of the attacks of 9/11 on the norm behavior of the policy makers. It "changed the way we view foreign policy," declared former national security advisor and secretary of state Condoleezza Rice.[31] Three days after 9/11, President Bush proclaimed a national emergency, which he renewed every year he was in office.[32] In his speech to a joint session of Congress on September 20, 2001, Bush stated:

> Americans have known wars, but for the past 136 years they have been wars on foreign soil, except for one Sunday in 1941. Americans have known the casualties of war, but not at the center of a great city on a peaceful morning. Americans have known surprise attacks, but never before on thousands of civilians. All of this was brought upon us in a single day, and night fell on a different world, a world where freedom itself is under attack.[33]

Terrorist groups had attacked the United States previously. In 1983, elements that would become Lebanese Hizballah attacked the U.S. embassy in Beirut, and six months later, a suicide bomber drove a truck laden with explosives into the U.S. Marine barracks at the Beirut airport.[34] These two attacks resulted in the deaths of 258 Americans and represented—until

9/11—the deadliest terror attacks against U.S. citizens in history. The U.S. response to these attacks was not to declare war on Hizballah but rather ultimately to pull U.S. troops from Lebanon and target the group by targeting its sponsors—Iran and Syria—through tough sanctions.

But the attacks of 9/11 were different. While the attacks in Beirut certainly alerted the U.S. government to the willingness of terror organizations to use violence against Westerners to achieve their goals, they did not result in a widespread and fundamental reexamination of U.S. policy toward terrorism. The attack on the U.S. homeland by a terrorist organization most Americans had never heard of catalyzed an urgency among the policy makers to do everything in their power and authority to ensure that the U.S. public never had to endure that type of vulnerability again. The goal among all policy makers was to "prevent another attack on our people"[35] and "to put pressure on terrorists around the world and make everything they do harder."[36] Rice admits that "we were in an environment in which saving America from the next attack was a paramount concern."[37] Having failed to stop the 9/11 attacks, the pressure on the Bush administration to prevent another terror attack was critical. Not helping the matter was the seriousness of the threats. "It is hard to overstate the impact that the incessant waves of threat reports have on the judgment of people inside the executive branch who are responsible for protecting American lives," writes Jack Goldsmith in his account of his time inside the Bush White House.[38] Writing in his memoirs, former director of central intelligence George Tenet concurs with this statement: "You simply could not sit where I did and read what passed across my desk on a daily basis and be anything other than scared to death about what it portended."[39]

Thus, 9/11 presented a perfect storm of shock, fear, and ambiguity that would allow for the contestation of the existing norm framework. In his 1998 fatwa against Jews and Crusaders, Osama bin Laden had issued a call to arms for all Muslims, declaring: "The ruling to kill the Americans and their allies—civilians and military—is an individual duty for every Muslim who can do it in any country in which it is possible to do it."[40] This echoed his earlier 1996 fatwa: "The walls of oppression and humiliation cannot be demolished except in a rain of bullets. The freeman does not surrender leadership to infidels and sinners."[41] The challenge was unambiguous: al-Qaeda had attacked America on land, in the air, and at sea.[42] And they would not hesitate to strike again. For the policy makers, this was a threat that could not be ignored.

Confronted by the pressure to head off increasingly dangerous threats, a mindset emerged that extraordinary methods were necessary to ensure success; the existing tools relied upon by previous administrations would not be sufficient. President Bush captured this mood in his address to the Pentagon a week after 9/11:

> But I know that this is a different type of enemy than we're used to. It's an enemy that likes to hide and burrow in, and their network is extensive. There are no rules. It's barbaric behavior. They slit throats of women on airplanes in order to achieve an objective that is beyond comprehension. And they like to hit, and then they like to hide out. But we're going to smoke them out. And we're adjusting our thinking to the new type of enemy.[43]

Vice President Dick Cheney reiterated this message in his famous exhortation to work through the "dark side":

> We also have to work, though, sort of the dark side, if you will. We've got to spend time in the shadows in the intelligence world. A lot of what needs to be done here will have to be done quietly, without any discussion, using sources and methods that are available to our intelligence agencies, if we're going to be successful. That's the world these folks operate in, and so it's going to be vital for us to use any means at our disposal, basically, to achieve our objectives.[44]

The move toward extraordinary policies would be widespread. The decision to frame the U.S. response as a War on Terror meant that everything from intelligence collection and interrogation methods to military posture and domestic budgets would be significantly altered. In a memo titled "We're at War" on September 16, 2001, Tenet captured the scope of the transformation about to occur within the U.S. government when he unequivocally stated: "all of the rules have changed."[45]

Much was made of the "new type" of warfare 9/11 seemed to usher into play. A common refrain in speeches and memos was the extent to which the unconventional type of warfare typified by terrorist acts challenged existing modes of thinking. Responding to terrorism required a nimbler, faster response than the United States had previously relied upon in other engagements. For policy makers, the unconventional methods of the terrorists required unconventional responses. In this view, the United States could not afford to be bound by norms and treaties designed for a different type of warfare.

CONTESTATION: WHAT ARGUMENTS WERE MADE?

To implement this new normative paradigm, administration policy makers used their positions of power to put in place new policies and legitimize them through public discourse. With regard to detainee treatment, these efforts manifested themselves in efforts to revise what were considered acceptable means to collect intelligence and to expand executive authority.

INTELLIGENCE COLLECTION

The most important changes sought by the Bush administration involved access to intelligence. The new type of warfare envisioned by the White House required faster intelligence collection to reveal operational planning and ultimately prevent future attacks. Fighting terrorists required a new appreciation for the relationship between intelligence and military force. In the Cold War, the difficult task was not finding Russian battalions but figuring out how to defeat them with military force. As such, the U.S. government invested copious resources in building a modern and capable DoD. In the GWOT, this relationship was entirely reversed; the hardest part was simply finding the terrorists. In this new war, information—rather than military capability—was paramount.

The major policy makers within the administration echoed this view. In the words of Cheney:

> I recalled the days after 9/11 and the absolute determination of the Bush administration to make sure our nation never again faced such a day of horror. The key to ensuring that was intelligence, and we gave our intelligence officers the tools and lawful authority they needed to gain information . . . through tough interrogation, if need be.[46]

This determination, driven by the fear of another attack on the U.S. homeland, reverberated throughout the U.S. government. In her memoirs, former U.S. national security advisor Condoleezza Rice agreed that intelligence collection was critical to avoiding another 9/11. "If you don't learn what terrorists are planning, thousands of innocent people die," she argued. "This isn't like law enforcement, where you punish the crime after the fact."[47]

The leaders of the two organizations tasked with detainee handling—the DoD and CIA—concurred. According to former secretary of defense Donald Rumsfeld,

> Because of the urgency and importance of obtaining information from detainees to help us prevent future 9/11s, the task was to develop interrogation guidelines, clarify rules and regulations, and improve our human intelligence-gathering capabilities to fit the unconventional and protracted first war of the twenty-first century.[48]

With regard to the CIA, one week after the attacks President Bush granted the agency "broad operational authority."[49] In the words of Tenet, this meant, "We were accelerating intelligence-gathering and doing our best to turn the screws on al-Qa'ida and the Taliban, we [the CIA] were also loosening constraints on our own people and their imaginations."[50] In sum, the guiding belief was that information was desperately needed to save innocent lives, and it would need to be obtained at any cost.

The frenzy to acquire intelligence assets and information was exacerbated by the weak state of the intelligence community following severe cutbacks, which left it unprepared for the new and increased demands placed on it following 9/11. After the collapse of the Soviet Union, the IC saw a twenty-three percent budget cut during the 1990s.[51] As funding for intelligence activities declined, manpower losses occurred across the IC. The CIA activities that suffered the most significantly were human source collection and all-source analysis.[52] According to DNI Clapper:

> During the mid to late 1990s, we closed many CIA stations, reduced HUMINT [human intelligence] collectors, cut analysts, allowed our overhead architecture to atrophy, and we neglected basic infrastructure needs, such as power, space, and cooling, and we let our facilities decay. And most damaging, most devastatingly, we badly distorted the workforce.[53]

With no new immediate threat on the horizon, the CIA did not recruit new case officers or analysts, the NSA did not hire new steganalysts or cryptanalysts, and the DoD reduced its funding for tactical intelligence capabilities.[54]

Not only was the IC underfunded and understaffed, but many within the government believed it was too risk averse. Following the end of the Cold War, a general sense of scaling back reigned across the IC. For example, DCI John Deutch, who was appointed by President Clinton in 1995, arrived at Langley with a mandate to "improve the oversight of clandestine operatives after evidence surfaced that an agent in Guatemala had covered up two murders."[55] As part of this effort, Deutch ordered a scrub of all HUMINT assets, examining in particular any assets who had records of human rights violations or other criminal activity. He then put in place the so-called Deutch rules of HUMINT recruitment, requiring that CIA case officers receive approval from CIA headquarters to recruit known human rights abusers as sources. While no valuable relationship was squandered because of the Deutch rules, and no evidence exists that they actually constrained the recruitment of sources, these guidelines were heavily scrutinized after 9/11.[56] Restrictions such as these were criticized for creating a culture of risk aversion that caused the CIA to miss key intelligence opportunities. Confronted by these inherited constraints, officials inside and outside the Bush administration pushed back. Tenet, Deutch's successor, rescinded the restriction on source recruitment in 2002. "I'm not going to succeed against terrorism unless I recruit terrorists," said James Pavitt, then–CIA deputy director for operations, in an April 30, 2004, interview. "I'm not going to succeed in terms of the tough issues in this business unless I'm right in the middle of it."[57] President Bush's father, former president and former DCI George H. W. Bush, came out in support of efforts to free the IC from its 1990s-era shackles. "If we're going to provide the president with the best possible intelligence," he argued, "we have to free up the intelligence system from some of its constraints."[58] In total, following 9/11, policy makers inside the Bush White House convinced themselves of the pressing need for broader, deeper, and enhanced intelligence-gathering methods, including the torture of detainees. This normative argument, stoked by the fear of another 9/11, quickly translated into policy action with regard to the detainees captured in Afghanistan and other theaters of the nascent GWOT.

The first significant detainee decision the Bush administration took was that the Geneva Conventions would not apply. As covered in chapter 4, this decision was framed partially in the language of executive power; as head of the unitary executive, Bush had the exclusive right to interpret the United States' treaty obligations. However, the policy makers inside the Pentagon and White House (as well as other lawyers in the executive branch) added their own normative argument to the decision. Previous administrations had decided, as a matter of policy, to extend Geneva protections to unlawful combatants—most notably in Vietnam, where the Johnson administration decided to treat the Viet Cong as POWs. The Bush administration broke with this precedent, deciding instead that members of al-Qaeda and the Taliban did not qualify for Geneva protections because al-Qaeda did not constitute a state signatory to the conventions and that both they and the Taliban failed to wear fixed insignia, carry arms openly, and abide by the laws of war. Furthermore, the president accepted the position presented by the Department of Justice that even Common Article 3 protections were inadmissible because they apply only in "armed conflict not of an international character."[59] These decisions represented enormous normative changes. As covered in chapters 2 and 3, in previous conflicts facing unconventional opponents the United States had always extended Geneva protections to its enemies. Now, faced with a similar enemy, the U.S. government had decided to shift course on this decades-old tradition.

The impetus to shift course was to gain access to information the policy makers believed resided inside captured detainees. The discovery of the al-Qaeda Handbook (also known as the Manchester Manual) in 2000 revealed that the terrorists were training to resist interrogation. In particular, one of the first high-level detainees captured in March 2002—Abu Zubaydah—was alleged to have written al-Qaeda's resistance manual and lectured on the topic as well.[60] As such, methods that would normally be proscribed by Geneva were deemed necessary to break these defenses. This intention has been confirmed not just in the paper trail from that time period but also in interviews conducted years later. As the SSCI Report noted, "A letter drafted for DCI Tenet to the President urged that the CIA be exempt from any application of these protections, arguing that application of Geneva would 'significantly hamper the ability of CIA to obtain critical threat information necessary to save American lives.'"[61]

In a January 2003 memo, John Yoo reassured CIA General Counsel Scott Muller "that the language of the [February 2002] memorandum had been deliberately limited to be binding only on 'the Armed Forces' which did not include the CIA."[62] Likewise, in an interview with the international legal expert Philippe Sands, Doug Feith, who was the DoD undersecretary of defense for policy from 2001 to 2005, boasted that it was "absolutely" the intention of the administration to ensure none of Geneva's constraints on interrogation applied.[63]

With Geneva relegated to the sidelines, the two agencies tasked with detainee interrogation—the DoD and CIA—could begin pursuing new methods. The best-documented example of this is the process by which

Rumsfeld approved eighteen new techniques for use at the Guantánamo Bay detention facility, documented by an approval memo dated December 2, 2002.[64] While there is disagreement about whether the request for these techniques originated from interrogators on the ground in Cuba or whether they were simply responding to pressure from top administration officials, what is clear is that the thirst for information from the detainees was unquenchable.[65] As General Myers, then-chairman of the Joint Chiefs of Staff said, "There was a sense of urgency that in my forty years of military experience hadn't existed in other contingencies."[66] The development of the techniques approved by Rumsfeld began with a memo from General Michael Dunlavey, the commander of Joint Task Force 170 (JTF-170) in Guantánamo Bay, to the head of U.S. Southern Command requesting approval for additional, harsh interrogation techniques. The techniques approved and subsequently used on detainees included the removal of clothing, twenty-hour interrogations, poking and pushing, and stress positions.[67] It was an extraordinary response to a perceived extraordinary necessity.

The methods requested by the CIA were equally extraordinary. In 2002, the CIA requested OLC approval for the use of ten specific EITs on Abu Zubaydah. The techniques requested by the CIA largely mirrored those requested for use at Guantánamo. The memo produced by the OLC—known as the second Bybee memo—applied the redefinition of torture, which was stipulated in the first Bybee memo, also published on August 1, 2002, to the legality of techniques requested by the CIA.[68] Through this opinion, the limitations on interrogation were sharply reduced. The techniques, including waterboarding, were used by CIA interrogators at newly opened black sites around the world. And while the DoD enhanced interrogation program lasted only a few months because of pushback within the department, the CIA program continued, in some form or another, until President Obama's inauguration in January 2009. This was attributable, almost solely, to the continued support for the CIA EIT program from top administration policy makers. Upon vetoing the 2008 Intelligence Authorization Act, which would have ended the CIA program, President Bush stated:

The bill Congress sent me would take away one of the most valuable tools in the war on terror: the CIA program to detain and question key terrorist leaders and operatives. This program has produced critical intelligence that has helped us prevent a number of attacks. . . . The main reason this program has been effective is that it allows the CIA to use specialized interrogation procedures to question a small number of the most dangerous terrorists under careful supervision.[69]

In conjunction with these newly approved techniques, the Bush administration accelerated the use of extraordinary rendition, whereby captured suspects would be transferred to a third-party country for questioning using tactics that would be illegal for U.S. officials to use. The rendition program began under the Clinton administration to combat the threat of al-Qaeda. It was significantly changed and dramatically expanded under the Bush administration. Under Clinton, the goal was not to interrogate the detainees but rather simply to prevent them from belligerency. In contrast, under President Bush, instead of having third parties conduct the interrogations, CIA officials would conduct the interrogations, and then rendered al-Qaeda operatives were most often kept in U.S. custody.[70] After 9/11, each extraordinary rendition no longer required presidential approval, subjecting terror suspects to a program that used both outsourced and internal CIA interrogations.[71] There is no doubt that information collection became the primary purpose of the rendition program.

Looking back on her time in office, Rice believes: "Three pressing issues arose in the post-9/11 period that challenged traditional notions of security: the classification and treatment of detainees; how to try terrorism suspects; and how to gain access to information that they might hold through interrogation and electronic surveillance."[72] The methods and policies mentioned above represented an attempt to address these issues through a new normative framework on the value and role of humane treatment in official U.S. government policy. This effort, however, was not the only front in the normative battle being waged by the policy makers within the Bush administration. The push for new approaches to intelligence gathering was accompanied by an equally forceful campaign for expanded power for the executive branch. The nation was at war, and the Bush White House believed it needed all the authority it could muster to wage it effectively.

NEW AUTHORITIES

The second refrain that emerged as a result of 9/11 was a demand to expand the authorities available to the executive branch to fight the GWOT. As covered in chapter 4, administration lawyers played a large role in this normative argument. However, they were not alone—key policy makers inside the White House shared their passion. Sitting inside the presidential bunker beneath the White House on the morning of September 11, one of the first acts Cheney took while trying to coordinate the federal response was to summon his lawyer, David Addington, who had fled from the Eisenhower Executive Building along with the rest of the staff inside. Once inside the bunker, Cheney tasked Addington with developing a legal framework for the coming war. As Barton Gellman notes, "The question that Cheney asked Addington in the bunker—what new authority will the president need?—was nothing new to either man."[73]

Cheney came to the vice presidency with a long history of government service. As chief of staff to President Ford and a U.S. congressman during the 1980s, Cheney witnessed the gradual diminishing of the presidency from its pre-Watergate high. For Cheney this was not so much a personal issue as a practical one; he firmly believed that a strong unitary executive was not only necessary but also the original intent of the founding fathers. Cheney drew his inspiration from Federalist No. 70, which was written by Alexander Hamilton. In it, Hamilton declares:

> Energy in the Executive is a leading character in the definition of good government. It is essential to the protection of the community against foreign attacks; it is not less essential to the steady administration of the laws; to the protection of property against those irregular and high-handed combinations which sometimes interrupt the ordinary course of justice; to the security of liberty against the enterprises and assaults of ambition, of faction, and of anarchy.[74]

Key to a strong and energetic executive was first and foremost unity. "That unity is conducive to energy will not be disputed," writes Hamilton. "Decision, activity, secrecy, and dispatch will generally characterize the proceedings of one man in a much more eminent degree than the proceedings of any greater number; and in proportion as the number is increased, these qualities will be diminished."[75] Consequently, those who argue for a weak and divided executive are arguing in favor of "a feeble execution of the government," which is just "another phrase for a bad execution" that "must be, in practice, a bad government."[76]

For Cheney, this was a longstanding passion. In a 1989 essay titled "Congressional Overreaching in Foreign Policy" Cheney elaborated on how Congress had overstepped its boundaries and infringed on executive power to the detriment of the nation. He writes:

I am convinced that the history of the past few years once again confirms the Framers' wisdom. When Congress stays within its capacities, it can be a helpful participant in formulating policy. In a wide range of recent disagreements with the President, however, the Congress has used policy levers that go well beyond the ones the Constitution intended for the legislative branch. The issue is not limited to a formal violation of a parchment document. When Congress steps beyond its capacities, it takes traits that can be helpful to collective deliberation and turns them into a harmful blend of vacillation, credit-claiming, blame avoidance and indecision. The real world effect often turns out, as Caspar Weinberger has said, not to be *transfer* of power from the President to the Congress, but a *denial* of power to the government as a whole.[77]

Given this background, it is not surprising that as vice president "Cheney's overriding goal was the enlargement of presidential authority."[78] In fact, Cheney told his authorized biographer that the first order he gave to Addington as vice president was "to restore the powers of the presidency."[79] For Cheney, the issue of enhanced interrogation would become a primary battleground in this struggle. For example, after the Abu Ghraib scandal leaked, Cheney convinced Bush to ride out the storm and neither explain nor release anything.[80] In his testimony before the U.S. Senate, Attorney General John Ashcroft explained the administration's position: "I am refusing to disclose these memos because I believe it is essential to the operation of the executive branch that the president have the opportunity to get information from his attorney general that is confidential."[81] In other words, for the Bush administration, the executive branch is unitary and has an unlimited right to secrecy.

Tenet also reacted strongly to the attacks of 9/11 with a sense of enlarged authority. In his memoirs he characterized his position at the time as: "We're going to run these bastards down no matter where they are, we told ourselves. We're going to lead and everyone else is going to follow. And that's what we set out to do."[82] He continued: "For us at CIA, the new doctrine meant that the restraints were finally off. We already had on our shelves the game plan for going after both al-Qa'ida and its protectors, the Taliban, in Afghanistan."[83] Tenet was determined to shed the risk-averse culture he had inherited at the CIA and worked hard to augment its authority and operational leeway. However, Tenet knew he was treading a thin line and sought buy-in, cover, and approval as much as possible. According to Gellman,

> Tenet was convinced that he and his people would one day be hung out to dry. He insisted on political as well as legal backing. Tenet told Dick Cheney and Condi Rice, in separate meetings, that he needed approval from the top for the new "enhanced interrogation" techniques. If he went down, the rest of them were going with him.[84]

Even the responsibilities of the DoD expanded. As Rumsfeld noted, "Bush was delegating wartime responsibilities to the Department of Defense that had not been used by our government in more than half a century."[85] For Rumsfeld, this push for additional authority was actually quite worrisome. In his memoirs, he articulated that he "questioned whether our military was the appropriate institution to hold captured enemy combatants." He continued:

From World War II through Korea and Vietnam to the first Gulf War, it was true that the military had shouldered the responsibility for the detention of captured enemy forces. But as I saw it, this unconventional conflict—against an amorphous enemy and with no finite duration—did not fit neatly within the laws of war pertaining to conventional conflicts. When it came to detention, our military had been schooled in holding enemies of regular armed forces—that is, lawful combatants entitled to prisoner of war (POW) status. Our armed forces did not have experience or established procedures for dealing with captured terrorists who, under the laws of war, were not entitled to the privileges of POWs.[86]

Yet Rumsfeld's peers in the administration had no interest in asking Congress to legislate a different route. In this new paradigm, the executive had the exclusive right to determine detainee policy during wartime.[87]

CONCLUSION

For the policy makers in the Bush White House, the attacks of 9/11 produced a dual shock that enabled the norm of humane treatment to be disputed. First, it provided an argument for necessity to trump all other concerns. In this new war, gathering and accessing intelligence were seen as vital to preventing another attack. Given these new requirements, the policy makers agreed with the lawyers' argument that the old prohibitions on cruel and inhumane methods appeared "quaint" and "obsolete."[88] Second, 9/11 provided an opportunity for supporters of a strong, unitary executive to accrue powers they believed rightfully belonged to the president. In this context, the fight to implement EITs was not so much about the necessity of the methods but rather the righteousness of the political argument behind them. The White House's efforts to impose interrogation policy were simply one part of a broader war with Congress and the judicial branch over what it saw as the proper separation of powers in the aftermath of 9/11.

Previous presidents had rendered terrorists to other countries. Additionally, as U.S. history shows, compliance with the norms of humane treatment within the military was never perfect. However, in none of these instances did government officials argue publicly that these practices should constitute the new, overarching policy of the United States. Nor had previous administrations argued that they alone had the power to dictate detention policy for the country. The decision to torture after 9/11 was remarkable not simply because detainees were abused but because top policy makers within the government fervently believed that the policies they were approving—and the methods used to implement them—should become a new and accepted status quo.

6

POW TREATMENT AND
INTERROGATORS

Marines are taught and ordered to treat prisoners of war humanely.
In practice, however, there are human failings. One does not hit a foe in
the face with a shovel to prevent him from killing you and then pick up
his injured body, offer him a cigarette, and show each other pictures of the
family. That's the fiction of which movies are made.

—LEE BALLENGER, *THE OUTPOST WAR: THE U.S. MARINE CORPS IN KOREA, VOL. 1: 1952*

ANY ACCOUNTS OF the torture debate would likely answer the question of *how* this happened by pinpointing the role of the interrogators. In fact, this has been the claim frequently repeated by many senior policy makers. In the immediate aftermath of the revelations of Abu Ghraib, members of the Bush administration sought to portray the activities there, in the words of Donald Rumsfeld, as "exceptional, isolated."[1] His then deputy, Paul Wolfowitz, agreed, stating that the events at Abu Ghraib were perpetrated by "a few bad apples" that consequently "create[d] some large problems for everybody."[2] In a May 2004 speech—weeks after the revelation by CBS's *60 Minutes*—President Bush echoed this same refrain. He claimed that the actions at Abu Ghraib represented "disgraceful conduct by a few American troops who dishonored our country and disregarded our values."[3] Despite the frequency with which the Bush administration made its claim, this argument has been disputed consistently in the last decade, most notably by the 2008 Senate Armed Services Committee (SASC) Inquiry Into the Treatment of Detainees in U.S. Custody. The SASC report refuted the idea that a few lone actors caused the abuse. The report, which examined only military interrogations and not those conducted by the CIA, traced the line of abuse from Secretary Rumsfeld to Guantánamo Bay to the Middle East. The report's introduction plainly claims: "The abuse of detainees in U.S. custody cannot simply be attributed to the actions of 'a few bad apples' acting on their own."[4]

However, the military interrogators stand as the group of individuals often blamed for these acts. More than a decade later, names such as Lynndie England, Sabrina Harman, and Charles Graner are synonymous with abuse, cruelty, and maltreatment. In the case of Abu Ghraib, the highest-ranked individual charged with criminal responsibility was Staff Sergeant Ivan L. Frederick of the 372nd Military Police Company. He ultimately served three years of his eight-year sentence, having been convicted of dereliction of duty, conspiracy, maltreatment of detainees, assault, and indecent acts.[5] In addition to Frederick, eight other U.S. Army soldiers were court-martialed and ultimately convicted for the crimes committed at Abu Ghraib. The only officer court-martialed, Lieutenant Colonel Steve Jordan, was cleared of any wrongdoing in 2008.[6] Other officers, such as Brigadier General Janis Karpinski and Colonel Thomas M. Pappas, received non-judicial punishments for their roles in the activities. In addition to those convicted for the Abu Ghraib abuses, "bad apples" were also identified at Guantánamo Bay; the 2005 U.S. Report to the United Nations Committee Against Torture listed ten substantiated claims of misconduct committed at Guantánamo.[7] Soldiers were also prosecuted for abuses in Afghanistan, including the army interrogators who caused the deaths of two detainees by, among other abuses, beating them so hard and often in the legs "that a coroner compared the injuries to being run over by a bus."[8] The CIA also convened six accountability proceedings from 2003 to 2012 in order to determine the extent of improper actions. The proceedings ultimately investigated thirty individuals, of which sixteen were sanctioned for their actions.[9]

While the abuses committed by the interrogators were real, horrific, and deserving of punishment, this chapter shows how the interrogators were disproportionately blamed, as they lacked the access and influence to alter the normative framework around detainee treatment. As such, they could not be the architects of post-9/11 U.S. detainee policy. The chapter supports this argument by examining the numerous explanations for the actions of the interrogators before delving into the historical precedents for these activities. The chapter then concludes by applying the life-cycle theory of normative change to the interrogators and examining how we should assess their role.

INTERROGATION EXPLANATIONS

Much has been made about the "new" form of warfare that 9/11 ushered in and the effect this had on interrogation practices. Even official reports, such as the 2004 Schlesinger Report, highlighted the causal connection between this "new" type of warfare and interrogations:

> Military interrogators and military police, assisted by front-line tactical units, found themselves engaged in detention operations with detention procedures still steeped in the methods of World War II and the Cold War, when those we expected to capture on the battlefield were generally a homogeneous group of enemy soldiers. Yet, this is a new form of war, not at all like Desert Storm nor even analogous to Vietnam or Korea.[10]

To what extent is this true? And how does this illuminate the role played by the interrogators?

Assessing the role of interrogators is a complex one, complicated by the two categories of interrogators operating during the GWOT: those in the DoD and those in the CIA. More public information exists about the experiences of the military interrogators than those of the CIA, thanks to the availability of interview transcripts, trial proceedings, and investigation reports. The DoD interrogators comprised both trained military intelligence officials and military police, the latter of whom were charged with detainee handling and security, not questioning. Little is known about the experience of CIA interrogators outside of the SSCI Report, the CIA comments on the report,[11] and similar congressional testimonies that reveal methods and practices.[12] Thus, because of a paucity of information about the motivations of the CIA interrogators, it is difficult to compare these two groups broadly. Based on the available evidence, however, a few general conclusions can be drawn.

Both the CIA and DoD interrogators operated from a climate of fear, anger, and—in some cases—a desire for retribution. The CIA officers strongly believed that actionable intelligence was needed in order to prevent, deter, or defuse the next attack.[13] Interrogations thus comprised an essential aspect of the intelligence cycle, driving collection, analysis, and further covert action. For some military interrogators, the sense of mission importance and resentment fueled frustration at the detainees.[14] In the words of Mike Gelles, a clinical forensic psychologist with the Naval Criminal Investigative Service (NCIS) who was stationed at Guantánamo during this time, the military interrogators identified themselves as "the tip of the spear in the struggle against an existential threat to the United States."[15] Despite this sense of urgency in the GWOT, it is uncontroversial to claim that the interrogators committed criminal acts.

The following section outlines the four major themes that emerge from the internal DoD reports and the recent SSCI Report to explain interrogation practices. The themes include relying on past guidance or popular influences, abusing detainees out of the belief that higher authorities approved it, maltreatment because of the absence of direction, and retribution for 9/11.

KNOWN PRACTICES

The first theme given for CIA and military abuse is that their personnel resorted to methods they already knew, whether from training modules on "Survival, Evasion, Resistance, and Escape" (SERE) methods or from popular influences such as television shows and movies.

In examining the development of the CIA's interrogation practices, the SSCI Report references the work of two contractor psychologists, Dr. James E. Mitchell and Dr. Bruce Jessen, identified in the report by the pseudonyms Dr. Grayson Swigert and Dr. Hammond Dunbar. Mitchell and Jessen had previously worked in the U.S. Air Force's SERE School, which instructs soldiers and sailors to develop immunities to harsh techniques if they are captured. These techniques can include face and body slaps, extreme temperatures, sleep deprivation, hooding, stress positions, subjection to loud music and disruptive light, and waterboarding.[16] In devising the CIA interrogation program, Mitchell and Jessen relied on their SERE experience because, as the SSCI Report states, "Neither psychologist had experience as an interrogator, nor did either have specialized knowledge of al-Qa'ida, a background in terrorism, or any relevant regional, cultural, or linguistic expertise."[17] Their use of SERE training as a model for their interrogation program is significant because SERE methods were designed specifically to counter the actions the Chinese communist regime used against prisoners in the Korean War. Many of these techniques would find their way into Mitchell and Jessen's enhanced interrogation model.

It is not imminently clear from the SSCI Report or other declassified government documents how precisely Mitchell and Jessen came to be employed by the CIA. However, NBC reported that their eponymous company Mitchell, Jessen and Associates was paid $81 million for their services to the CIA before their contract was terminated in 2009.[18] The 2008 report by the Senate Armed Services Committee outlines that DoD lawyers in December 2001 asked the Joint Personnel Recovery Agency (JPRA), Jessen's supervising command, for advice on interrogations. According to the report, the JPRA instructor Joseph Witsch wrote:

I believe our niche lies in the fact that we can provide the ability to exploit personnel based on how our enemies have done this type of thing over the last five decades. Our enemies have had limited success with this methodology due to the extreme dedication of [American] personnel and their harsh and mismanaged application of technique. The potential exists that we could refine the process to achieve effective manipulation/exploitation. We must have a process that goes beyond the old paradigm of military interrogation for tactical information or criminal investigation for legal proceedings. These methods are far too limited in scope to deal with the new war on global terrorism.[19]

According to one article in the *New York Times*, Mitchell attracted the CIA's attention in December 2001 for his theories on how learned helplessness might assist enemy interrogation.[20] He was consequently asked to review the Manchester Manual, a captured al-Qaeda manual on resisting interrogations; at that point, Mitchell contacted Jessen, and the two began work on a proposal to implement enhanced interrogation techniques. John Rizzo, however, offers a different version of the story. He claims that the CIA initially interrogated Abu Zubaydah with noncoercive measures. After these methods stopped working, agency interrogators were convinced Zubaydah still had pertinent information he was withholding. It was at this point, according to Rizzo, that Mitchell and Jessen suggested developing new techniques to "shift the dynamics of the interrogation." Tenet gave the approval, in Rizzo's account, but he did not specify that the new techniques be harsh. In Rizzo's words, "no one in the room, including me, had any inkling what they were going to come back with."[21] The SSCI Report, which offers a recent take on the issue, claims that the CIA did not seek Mitchell and Jessen out "after a decision was made to use coercive interrogation techniques." On the contrary, they "played a role in convincing the CIA to adopt such a policy."[22] For example, with regards to the interrogation of Abu Zubaydah, Mitchell and Jessen described waterboarding as an "absolutely convincing technique" to overwhelm Zubaydah's resistance.[23] While the timeline of events remains unclear, what is obvious is that in devising its EIT program, the CIA ultimately relied upon practices that were reverse engineered from SERE training. All told, the SERE-derived practices were used on thirty-eight detainees at black sites around the world.[24]

Second, the role popular culture played in affecting interrogation practices on both the military and CIA sides has been well documented. While the geopolitical consequences of television shows like *24* and video games like *Call of Duty* are outside the scope of this book, the social impact of graphic and brutal interrogations in popular culture cannot be underestimated. In one of the interviews conducted by Lieutenant General Paul T. Mikolashek, the army inspector general charged with reviewing detainee operations in the aftermath of Abu Ghraib, an unidentified platoon leader from Fourth Infantry Division at Ft. Hood, Texas, provided his assessment of the climate in Iraq: "officers and NCOs at the point of capture engaged in interrogations using techniques they literally remembered from movies."[25] In describing Abu Ghraib, Sgt. Javal Davis of the 372nd Military Police Company (among the soldiers taken to court for the abuses committed there) said, "Like something from a Mad Max movie. Just like that—like, medieval."[26] Similarly, in December 2006, the Intelligence Science Board, which was chartered to advise the director of national intelligence and senior members of the intelligence community on emerging scientific and technical issues, produced a report that stated that

> most observers, even those within professional circles, have unfortunately been influenced by the media's colorful (and artificial) view of interrogation as almost always involving hostility and the employment of force—be it physical or psychological—by the interrogator against the hapless, often slow-witted subject.[27]

Unfortunately, the lesson learned from popular media is that violence compels confessions and that these confessions save lives and prevent future attacks. With these frames comprising an interrogator's cognitive map, it is easy to see how they could believe actionable intelligence in the GWOT would be gleaned through abuse.

APPROVED BY AUTHORITY

The second theme that emerges is the idea that senior leaders authorized coercive behavior and also that these harsh techniques had been successfully employed in other areas of operations. This argument, however, is in no way a justification for the interrogators' actions: this Nuremberg defense remains unacceptable. Multiple sections of the SSCI Report bear evidence that dissent on the ground was silenced in favor of command authority. One passage notes that "At times, CIA officers were instructed by supervisors not to put their concerns or observations in written communications."[28]

This theme has often been repeated in the context of the military interrogations. For example, Colonel Thomas M. Pappas, the commander of the 205th Military Intelligence Brigade and the senior military intelligence officer at Abu Ghraib, repeatedly has argued that the techniques used against detainees—such as using guard dogs in interrogation rooms—emerged from "orders, pressure and encouragement" from his superiors.[29] Non-commissioned officers at Abu Ghraib have put forth this argument as well. In the case of Sgt. Ivan Frederick II, one of the defenses that emerged during his trial was that the chain of command was to blame for the abuses that occurred. During his court-martial, one witness referred to an e-mail from the U.S. command in Baghdad ordering the interrogators to be tough on prisoners. According to the witness, the e-mail read: "The gloves are coming off, gentlemen, regarding these detainees."[30]

DoD personnel have also argued that pressure emerged from senior leaders to use coercive techniques because of their success elsewhere. Army reservist Brigadier General Janis Karpinski, who commanded the 800th Military Police Brigade, was responsible for all of the military prisons and detainees in Iraq. Though Abu Ghraib was more heavily populated with criminals than "high value detainees,"[31] attempts were made to extract more actionable intelligence from the prisoners. In August 2003, Major General Geoffrey Miller, then commander of U.S. detention facilities at Guantánamo, traveled to Iraq in order to instruct Lieutenant General Ricardo Sanchez, the senior commander of U.S. forces in Iraq, on how to glean better intelligence from detainees. Karpinski claims that General Miller pressured her to incorporate lessons learned at Guantánamo in Iraq. She argues:

> We had a myriad of problems in our—in the prison system, not with detainees who were undergoing interrogations, but with Iraqi criminal prisoners. And instead of coming to give us support, he [Miller] was sent specifically to work with the military intelligence interrogators to teach them the harsher techniques that were being used down in Guantánamo.[32]

The timeline of abuse supports Karpinski's narrative; harsher tactics began to be included in prisoner interrogations at Abu Ghraib during the fall of 2003. In fact, according to the Fay-Jones report, an internal Pentagon investigation into the actions at Abu Ghraib, "Abusing detainees with dogs started almost immediately after the dogs arrived at Abu Ghraib on November 20, 2003."[33]

Some DoD reports, notably the Church Report, written by Vice Admiral Albert Church, inspector general of the navy, contend that service members in Afghanistan developed a system of interrogation methods independently from other areas of operation.[34] This system, while not born from the secretary of defense's December 2002 authorization of new interrogation methods for detainees at Guantánamo, included similar (and similarly controversial) counterresistance techniques. According to the Church Report, the basis for these new techniques was that inadequacies with FM 34-52, *Intelligence and Interrogation,* led "commanders, working with policy makers to search for new interrogation techniques."[35]

Despite the findings of the Church Report, other internal DoD reports add credence to the claim that abuse emanated from the Pentagon's senior leadership and migrated from Guantánamo to Iraq. The 2004 Schlesinger Report, the product of an independent four-member panel led by former secretary of defense James Schlesinger, contends that Secretary Rumsfeld's December 2002 interrogation technique authorization memo was the source of mistreatment in the field. In its words: "Although specifically limited by the Secretary of Defense to Guantánamo, and requiring his personal approval (given only in two cases), the augmented techniques for Guantánamo migrated to Afghanistan and Iraq where they were neither limited nor safeguarded."[36]

NO DIRECTION

In contrast to the argument that abuse resulted from direct senior guidance, the third theme asserts the exact opposite explanation: that a *lack* of direction fostered abuse. The perception that the rules of engagement were in flux was pervasive. The SSCI Report claims that before December 2002, CIA interrogators, "some with little or no training, were 'left to their own devices in working with detainees.'"[37] In his memoirs, John Rizzo paints a picture of an agency given zero guidance on the detention and interrogation of prisoners. In the days after 9/11, President Bush signed a Memorandum of Notification (MON) that greatly expanded the CIA's covert authorities for going after al-Qaeda. According to Rizzo, this MON "authorized the capture, detention, and questioning of al-Qaeda leaders, but was silent about the means by which any of it could be carried out."[38] It was left to the CIA to determine the details. The CIA first confronted this problem, according to Rizzo, with the interrogation of Abu Zubaydah. In Rizzo's version of the story, Zubaydah initially cooperated with CIA interrogators because he feared they were going to let him die (Zubaydah had been gravely wounded during his capture). When it became apparent that the CIA was not going to let him die, Rizzo posits that Zubaydah not only stopped cooperating but became sneering and mocking. This change of attitude is what prompted the decision to seek new interrogation methods. Rizzo writes:

> But the more he became convinced he was not going to die, the more confident, the more arrogant, he was becoming. He kept talking, all right, but now Zubaydah, feeling his oats, took to taunting our people. He was proving to be a twisted, smug little creep, offering up little tidbits that were either old news or outright lies, all the while taking care to torment his questioners by making clear that lies were his specialty and that he knew far more about ongoing al-Qaeda plots than he was ever going to tell us. The Agency shrinks, working with the CTC [Counterterrorism Center] experts, were busily putting together a psychological profile of Zubaydah. This guy is a cold-blooded psychopath, they concluded. They told George [Tenet] at one of the five o'clock sessions in early March that the Agency needed to do something to change the equation with Zubaydah, shift the dynamics of the interrogation. The "Joe Friday" approach was never going to work. Come up with something, and come up with it fast, George instructed them. As they were dispatched, no one in the room, including me, had any inkling what they were going to come back with.[39]

Therefore, in this narrative, the CIA's EIT program was the product of no guidance and the ignorance of an agency with no experience holding terrorist detainees.[40]

The narrative of no guidance is echoed in the DoD context and featured in multiple reports. Dave Becker, the head of the Interrogation Control Element of the Defense Intelligence Agency, told an army investigation that many of the aggressive techniques requested in October 2002 were "a direct result of the pressure we felt from Washington to obtain intelligence and the lack of policy guidance being issued by Washington."[41] The Church Report corroborates this story, stating, "dissemination of interrogation policy was generally poor,"[42] and "no specific guidance on interrogation techniques was provided to the commanders responsible for Afghanistan."[43] Similarly, the Schlesinger Report also notes that "changes in DoD interrogation policies . . . were an element contributing to uncertainties in the field."[44] Lastly, the 2004 Jacoby Report notes, "dissemination, implementation, and a corresponding appreciation for assignment responsibilities were inconsistent across the AO [area of operations]."[45] In fact, the Jacoby Report found that "there is a void in the availability of interrogations guidance in the field, and interrogation practice is as varied across the theater as are detention methods and procedures."[46] Taken together, these findings suggest that DoD detainee operations in the GWOT were defined by vague and ambiguous orders, which directly contributed to the grave instances of prisoner abuse that occurred.

FEAR OF ANOTHER 9/11 AND RETRIBUTION

The last theme that emerged is the role that 9/11—and fear of another 9/11—played in driving abusive behaviors. This was noted in the foreword to the SSCI Report, written by Senator Dianne Feinstein:

> It is easy to forget the context in which the program began—not that the context should serve as an excuse, but rather as a warning for the future. It is worth remembering the pervasive fear in late 2001 and how immediate the threat felt. Just a week after the September 11 attacks, powdered anthrax was sent to various news organizations and to two U.S. Senators. The American public was shocked by news of new terrorist plots and elevations of the color-coded threat level of the Homeland Security

Advisory System. We expected further attacks against the nation. I have attempted throughout to remember the impact on the nation and to the CIA workforce from the attacks of September 11, 2001. I can understand the CIA's impulse to consider the use of every possible tool to gather intelligence and remove terrorists from the battlefield, and CIA was encouraged by political leaders and the public to do whatever it could to prevent another attack.[47]

In his memoirs too, John Rizzo explains why he did not veto the EIT program before it began, when he had the power to do so. He writes:

> I couldn't shake the ultimate nightmare scenario: Another attack happens, and Zubaydah gleefully tells his CIA handlers he knew all about it and boasts that we never got him to tell us about it in time. All because at the moment of reckoning, the Agency had shied away from doing what it knew was unavoidable, what was essential, to extract that information from him. And with hundreds and perhaps thousands of Americans again lying dead on the streets or in rubble somewhere, I would know, deep down, that I was at least in part responsible. In the final analysis, I could not countenance the thought of having to live with that.[48]

Fear and revenge also motivated the actions of the personnel on the ground. When asked why the abuse of detainees occurred, Spc. Jeremy Callaway, who admitted to hitting twelve detainees at the Bagram Air Force Base in Afghanistan, answered plainly: "Retribution for September 11, 2001."[49] In his book *None of Us Were Like This Before*, Joshua Phillips investigates the 2002 abuse of two Afghan prisoners, Dilawar and Habibullah. After conducting extensive personal interviews with soldiers, military officials, and victims of U.S. torture, Phillips concludes that "senior government officials and low-ranking troops at Guantánamo had much in common. Everyone feared terrorist threats—the interrogators and their officers, the psychologists and clinicians, SERE trainers, and Ivy League–educated government lawyers."[50]

Ultimately, despite all the reports, courts-martial, accountability proceedings, and prosecutions to which the interrogators have been subjected, this group bears the least responsibility in answering the *how* of the torture question. The four narratives offered here as competing explanations for the interrogators' behavior are proof of this. With none of these narratives more compelling than the others, it is clear the interrogators were not motivated by a single issue. In other words, the interrogators were not a monolithic group seeking to disseminate a specific view of how detainees should be treated throughout the U.S. government. They were individuals who responded to their environment often at a personal level. Some were motivated by fear and retribution, others by vague orders. Still others believed they had official backing for their actions, while some reached into their memories of movies and television shows for inspiration. Such diversity in motivation contrasts with the unity of purpose exhibited by the lawyers and policy makers. Consequently, the interrogators could not be involved in normative contestation because they could not even agree on how to do so. The following section contributes to this finding by outlining how the DoD and CIA had vastly different historical precedents for their actions.

HISTORICAL PRECEDENTS

When examining the role of the interrogators, it is crucial to ask: where did these practices originate? For the CIA, many of these practices had been known for decades, and their use was encouraged by the Bush administration out of a desire for actionable intelligence. For the military, as discussed in previous chapters, decades of training and education—as well as manuals and doctrine—supported the notion that individuals in U.S. custody during wartime were required to be treated humanely. The historical precedents for these two institutions are worth addressing so as to compare their different cultures. The DoD adhered to the Geneva Conventions and the CAT because of their inclusion in domestic military law and because of their embeddedness in military identity. In contrast, the CIA did not share this institutional culture.

CENTRAL INTELLIGENCE AGENCY

The CIA possessed an institutional history of coercive programs implemented throughout the Cold War and then exported in the 1980s to Central American and South American countries. One example of these practices was the KUBARK Counterintelligence Interrogation program, designed to elicit information from a number of clandestine communist organizations.[51] Concerns about illegal activity, including bodily harm to subjects, is expressed in the KUBARK manual but is mitigated by encouraging interrogators to obtain approval from superiors if the tactics are needed for intelligence-gathering purposes.[52] In this way, loopholes exist that allow for torturelike techniques to be used. The manual contains an entire section on coercive methods, stating: "Control of the source's environment permits the interrogator to determine his diet, sleep pattern, and other fundamentals. Manipulating these into irregularities, so that the subject becomes disoriented, is very likely to create feelings of fear and helplessness."[53]

KUBARK methods were used, for example, against the Soviet defector Yuri Nosenko, a former KGB officer who endured "hostile interrogation" and confinement for more than two years at the hands of his CIA handlers.[54] Following Congress's investigations of the intelligence community in the 1970s, the KUBARK training manual was abandoned. In 1983, it was reissued as the Human Resource Exploitation (HRE) Training Manual in order to assist covert activities in El Salvador and Nicaragua.[55] A starred passage in the HRE Training Manual provides justification for coercive techniques, stating: "These techniques should be reserved for those subjects who have been trained or who have developed the ability to resist non-coercive techniques."[56] This suggests that even in the wake of the post-Vietnam congressional investigations, coercive interrogation techniques were deemed legitimate against noncompliant subjects in the fight against communism.

In her book *Truth, Torture, and the American Way*, the American lawyer and activist Jennifer Harbury recounts in detail how the CIA put its familiarity with coercive techniques to use in the Latin American "dirty wars" of the 1980s. She shows how the CIA engaged in "torture by proxy" by contracting out the dirty work to local intelligence and military officers. In one such example, Harbury explores how the CIA paid Argentinean intelligence officials to train other Latin American personnel in the use of cruel and inhumane techniques, thereby allowing the agency to hide its involvement.[57] The most moving moments in Harbury's book, however, come from the twenty-plus individual narratives she provides from torture survivors. In each of these stories, Harbury illustrates how "an obvious North American was present in their torture cells."[58] Ultimately, Harbury concludes that "the evidence suggests that [CIA] agents not only kept known torturers on agency payroll, but were often physically present in the torture cells as well. Sometimes the agents merely observed, sometimes they did the questioning, sometimes they advised, and sometimes they supervised. But they were there. Often."[59]

Despite the inclusion of coercive techniques in training manuals and their use in overseas operations, other official documents dispute the efficacy of this method to extract confessions. For example, one agency document written in 1958 and entitled "The Interrogation of Suspects Under Arrest" states:

> The question of torture should be disposed of at once. Quite apart from moral and legal considerations, physical torture or extreme mental torture is not an expedient device. Maltreating the subject is from a strictly practical point of view as short-sighted as whipping a horse to his knees before a thirty-mile ride. It is true that almost anyone will eventually talk when subjected to enough physical pressures, but the information obtained in this way is likely to be of little intelligence value and the subject himself rendered unfit for further exploitation. Physical pressure will often yield a confession, true or false, but what an intelligence interrogation seeks is a continuing flow of information.[60]

Thus, the CIA possessed knowledge of and experience using coercive means to extract information prior to the GWOT. Even more significant, despite documents such as the one above saying torture should not be used, CIA leadership refused to enforce the policy. According to the SSCI Report, the CIA officer that compiled the KUBARK methods into the

HRE manual in 1983 used the manual to provide interrogation training in Latin America in the 1980s. Though the CIA inspector general (IG) later recommended that this officer be orally admonished for using such interrogation techniques, it is unclear whether this happened. The SSCI Report does note that the IG's recommendation seems to have had no impact on this officer's career, as he was named the CIA's chief of interrogations in the CIA's renditions group in the fall of 2002.[61] Thus, despite official documents saying that coercive measures were not an effective means to obtain intelligence, the CIA promoted rather than punished the officer who employed these techniques.

DEPARTMENT OF DEFENSE

The norm context before 9/11 for the military indicates a consistent arc toward compliance with the standard of humane treatment of detainees, as demonstrated in chapters 2 and 3. After the Vietnam War, military doctrine regarding prisoner handling and treatment primarily rested upon field manuals that consistently reinforced the applicability of the Geneva Conventions. FM 19-40, entitled "Handling of Prisoners of War," originally issued in 1952 and reissued in 1976, reinforced the notion that the objectives of the detainee program were to implement the Geneva Conventions with full accountability.[62] The Field Manual on Military Intelligence, FM 34-52, and Army Regulation (AR) 190-8 left no doubt that zero tolerance exists for coercive methods in the course of interrogations. AR 190-8 explicitly states that inhumane treatment "is not justified by the stress of combat or with deep provocation. Inhumane treatment is a serious and punishable violation under international law and the Uniform Code of Military Justice."[63] The embedding of the norm of humane treatment also occurred through other initiatives. As detailed in chapter 3, Directive 5100.77—which established the DoD's law-of-war program and was reissued in 1979 and 1998—mandated robust training and education programs for both troops and officers in each service component on the laws of war. The directive also dramatically increased the role of the JAGs in advising and promoting compliance with the Geneva Conventions.

Yet, as previously discussed, despite the embeddedness of these norms, incidents of inhumane treatment by U.S. soldiers were not new. For example, in World War II, U.S. Army officials engaged in the widespread reeducation of captured Nazi soldiers, an effort that violated the spirit if not the letter of the 1929 Geneva Conventions.[64] Likewise, there is evidence that U.S. troops engaged in extrajudicial killings in both World War II and the Korean War.[65] Even techniques like waterboarding were used by members of the U.S. military in the Philippines during efforts to combat the insurgency there following the Spanish–American War.[66] In all these instances, the abuses took place in an environment where military doctrine, training, and education supported the view that humane treatment of detainees constituted an integral component of U.S. military identity.

Tellingly, initial military behavior toward detainees in the GWOT bears evidence of the depth of this norm's embeddedness. Compliance with the third Geneva Convention was initially assumed in Afghanistan in 2001. According to the Schlesinger Report, the commander of U.S. Central Command issued an order on October 17, 2001, stating that the Geneva Conventions would be applied according to the letter of the law. As specified by this order,

> belligerents would be screened to determine whether or not they were entitled to prisoner of war status. If an individual was entitled to prisoner of war status, the protections of Geneva Convention III would apply. If armed forces personnel were in doubt as to a detained individual's status, Geneva Convention III rights would be accorded to the detainee until a Geneva Convention III Article 5 tribunal made a definitive status determination.[67]

This order is consistent with standard practice according to international law, which states that when POW status is in doubt, captured fighters shall benefit from Geneva protections until a determination is made about their status.[68]

Diane Beaver, the staff judge advocate at Guantánamo Bay, confirms that initially DoD interrogators followed the standards outlined in official army doctrine. When she arrived at Guantánamo, the military was follow-ing FM 34-52 even though President Bush had already waived Geneva's applicability.[69] Mike Gelles repeats this observation, telling Philippe Sands that alongside his effort to secure information that could be used in crimi-nal prosecutions, there was a parallel interrogation effort aimed at produc-ing intelligence using the FM 34-52 techniques. As retold by Sands, "For the most part the military interrogators seemed to be eighteen- and nineteen-year-old kids passing through on short rotations. They'd gone through a six-week training program and were mechanically following the techniques allowed by the Army manual."[70] It was only after these techniques failed to produce any useful information that pressure for new methods began.

The historical precedents detailed here outline the vastly different cul-tures of the DoD and CIA. That they are different is no surprise given their divergent missions and methods. The DoD and CIA's different cultures take on added significance, however, within the life-cycle theory of nor-mative change. Much as the four competing narratives serve as evidence of a diverse set of motivations for the interrogators' behavior, the distinct cultures of the CIA and DoD further indicate that the interrogators were not a monolithic group. They were not guided by a single set of historical precedents or a unified culture. Instead, they came from two institutions with largely separate histories regarding detainee treatment. In other words, the interrogators were simply too diverse to act with purpose as a group. The following section takes this fact and assesses it through the framework of access and influence to show how the interrogators lacked the ability to engage in normative contestation.

NO ACCESS AND INFLUENCE

The norm cycle as outlined in chapter 1 details a process by which ambi-guities and inconsistencies around an embedded norm trigger questioning and disputes. The outcome of the questioning is either consolidation around a new norm framework or affirmation of the existing framework. Yet the interrogators—those individuals in the CIA and the DoD who actually carried out the abuses—do not play a significant role in the norm cycle examined here.

The norm cycle provides an explanation for how norms change in the domestic context. International norms and laws become embedded in the domestic context through inclusion in laws, codes, and manuals. Over time, these rules become so deeply held that they constitute part of the state's identity. Yet, instead of being the end of the story, the embedding of a norm is simply the beginning of a new stage in the broader life cycle of norms, where gaps and ambiguities in the laws form the basis for domestic contestation around the norm. One of the goals of this book is to challenge the deterministic view that once a state has signed onto international law, compliance will be automatic and assumed. However, not everyone can contest a norm. Only those who have both access to decision makers and the influence to achieve a new normative interpretation can successfully challenge the norm.[71]

How do we know who has access and influence to contest a norm? Given that the United States uses a democratic system with relatively open decision-making structures and processes, individuals can "lobby elected representatives and members of the executive branch, make campaign contributions, vote in elections, try to mold public opinion etc." in order to access the government.[72] Accessing decision makers, however, does not guarantee influence over the eventual policy decision, so actors must also build positive relations with the media and foster relationships with other national and transnational actors who share the same view. Thus, a set of prerequisites for access and influence exists, including financial resources, information, personal connections, and constituency size.[73]

There is a differential of access and influence for the actors studied here. The policy makers, examined in chapter 5, maintain the highest level of access and influence: they represent the individuals actually making the decisions (in the case of the president and the Cabinet members) or the individuals directly advising those actors. This group possesses no barriers to contest a norm. The lawyers, studied in chapter 4, also maintain a high level of access and influence because many of them had a direct channel to the policy makers, such as David Addington in the Office of the Vice President or Alberto Gonzales in his role as White House counsel. Unlike these groups, however, the interrogators possessed no such opportunity for access and influence. They lacked the authority to challenge the norm themselves and did not have the financial resources, knowledge, and media connections to access authority figures who did possess the requisite power. Moreover, they were unable to overcome these barriers in part because, as previous sections in this chapter have shown, they were not a mobilized group with a singular, unified set of preferences and goals. As such, they were unable to access and influence the rungs of power.

The interrogators, thus, do not fit neatly into the cycle of norm change depicted here. They lacked the ability and the opportunity to challenge the normative consensus. In short, they are the least responsible for how the torture decisions came to fruition despite being the group most punished. They were the group that poured the water and held the leashes, but they were not responsible for challenging the normative consensus.

CONCLUSION

In light of the intense domestic and international scrutiny of U.S. detainee operations, several changes were made to interrogation processes and leadership. Under the leadership of DCI Mike Hayden, the CIA's enhanced interrogation program was reviewed and slimmed down to six techniques.[74] DCI Hayden also persuaded President Bush to give his September 6, 2006, speech on terrorism, in which he announced that "Khalid Sheikh Mohammed, Abu Zubaydah, Ramzi bin al-Shibh, and 11 other terrorists in CIA custody have been transferred [from agency black sites] to the United States Naval Base at Guantánamo Bay."[75] According to the SSCI Report, the CIA ceased the use of enhanced interrogations in November 2007 and did not hold detainees after April 2008.[76] Lastly, President Obama issued an executive order on January 22, 2009, that required all interrogators—both CIA and military—to comply with the techniques outlined in FM 2-22.3 (the successor to FM 34-52).[77]

With regards to military interrogations, General Karpinski was immediately removed from command in Iraq, and her successor, General Miller, was also removed after reports surfaced of harsh treatment under his watch during his previous command at Guantánamo. Eventually, DoD detainee operations in Iraq were led by Major General John Gardner. Cognizant of the stain of Abu Ghraib, Gardner sought to address the allegations of abuse and improve conditions.[78] He created a nuanced categorization system for detainees based on their disciplinary record, level of military training, explanations for detention, interactions with others, and activity with any vigilante sharia courts inside prison.[79] To prevent radicalization inside the prisons, Gardner advocated frequent and abrupt prisoner relocation and filling empty hours of detention with physical activity, civics classes, and vocational training.[80]

By January 2005, the military's interrogation policy for Iraq was codified, including only those techniques described in FM 34-52 and specifically excluding the use of military working dogs and the removal of clothing during interrogation.[81] In December 2005, the U.S. Congress passed the Detainee Treatment Act, which explicitly prohibits the "cruel, inhuman, or degrading treatment or punishment" of detainees and calls for the establishment of a uniform code of interrogation policy.[82] In addition, FM 34-52 was further revised in 2006 to provide greater specificity about detention processes and greater clarity on prohibited techniques. The new FM even includes an appendix listing the full texts of the Third and Fourth Geneva Conventions, something that was missing in FM 34-52 despite its frequent references to those treaties.

Gardner's successor in Iraq, Major General Douglas Stone, continued these efforts to improve detainee quality of life and minimize the possibility of prison radicalization. Stone's command coincided with the deployment of the surge and the application of counterinsurgency doctrine in Iraq. As such, the number of detainees held by the United States swelled from 13,000 in early 2006 to its peak of 25,000 in late 2007.[83] Stone—consistent with the counterinsurgency doctrine employed by General Petraeus—sought to "win in the battlefield of the brain" by encouraging detainees to read and interpret the Qur'an for themselves.[84] Under Stone, classes, vocational training, and

Islamic discussions continued, as did pay-for-work programs designed to prepare detainees to reenter Iraqi society and contribute to the reconstruction effort.[85] In addition, detainees in these programs were allowed to remit their salaries to their families. Review panels were also established to evaluate detentions and to determine when prisoners might be ready for release, and prisoners were provided access to good medical care. Stone also sought to change the public perception—both U.S. and Iraqi—of detainee operations by actively working on strategic communications. He participated in a bloggers' roundtable in 2007 in which he directly answered questions about detainee policies and practices,[86] in addition to engaging in press visits and interviews with Al-Iraqiya, Al Arabiya TV, Al Jazeera English, and Baghdad Satellite TV.[87]

Similar efforts were made in Afghanistan to improve detainee treatment policy. In 2009, Obama conducted a wide-ranging review of Afghan operations, policies, and requirements, including those for detainee treatment. Following this review—and incorporating lessons learned from the treatment of the tens of thousands of prisoners in Iraq—the detainees in Afghanistan were moved to a new facility with a larger holding capacity at Bagram Air Base. The new facility includes review boards, composed of three U.S. military officials advised by a military lawyer, where prisoners can question and challenge their internment.[88]

In addition, per a directive issued by former secretary of defense Robert Gates in June 2009, General Stanley McChrystal completed an overall assessment of the situation in Afghanistan against the backdrop of the rising insurgency and diminishing government legitimacy. McChrystal's classified report was leaked to the media, and a subsequent redacted report was released by the Obama administration. This assessment recommended a shift in strategy from offensive military operations to a comprehensive population-centric counterinsurgency, of which detainee operations were a critical component.[89] In the assessment, General McChrystal argued that the conditions in prisons and weak judicial system in Afghanistan were directly fostering the insurgency and created the possibility of turning detention operations into a strategic liability for U.S. and ISAF forces. In this assessment, McChrystal claimed that "there are more insurgents per square foot in corrections facilities than anywhere else in Afghanistan. Unchecked, Taliban / al-Qaeda leaders patiently co-ordinate and plan, unconcerned with interference from prison personnel or the military."[90] Detainee treatment, left unaltered, was a detriment to the overall U.S. war effort.

Ultimately, despite the interrogators' role on the ground, widespread abuse would not have occurred but for the lawyers and the policy makers. The theme that emerges from an examination of the interrogators is not one of challenging a normative consensus but rather the U.S. government using low-level military personnel as scapegoats for larger institutional failures. According to Spike Bowman, then–deputy general counsel of the FBI for National Security Law: "What you are doing is giving these techniques to a bunch of young soldiers who don't have a clue about interrogation, who are told this is OK, but not told why it's OK, or what they are going to get from it."[91] As this chapter has shown, no individual interrogator had the access or influence to implement such a large and rapid change in procedures. This was both because the interrogators lacked any role in the policy-making process and because the interrogators were driven to act by different moti-vations, making them too diverse to act as a coherent group. The fact that four competing explanations exist for the interrogators' behavior, with none more plausible than the others, is proof of this discord. Instead, the stan-dards for treatment eroded so quickly because of the normative contestation of the lawyers and policy makers who gutted the legal foundations and pro-tections for the standards of humane treatment.

PART THREE

CONCLUSION

7

IMPLICATIONS AND RECOMMENDATIONS

All I want to say is that there was before 9/11 and after 9/11. After 9/11 the gloves came off.

—JOSEPH COFER BLACK, "STATEMENT OF COFER BLACK: JOINT INVESTIGATION INTO SEPTEMBER 11"

D ESPITE THE SHOCK of 9/11, the decision to use torture as part of the official U.S. government counterterrorism response was not predetermined. As chapters 2 and 3 illustrated, previous shocks and conflicts often motivated compliance with international law and encouraged an expansive view of human rights. Across all types of conflicts and in a variety of geographic spaces, the United States sought to treat lawful combatants, rebel soldiers, and unlawful insurgents equally. As a result, the United States concluded each war with a greater appreciation for the humane treatment of detainees and endeavored to expand its doctrine, training, and education to match this view. This book has examined this process through the lens of normative change. U.S. history reveals a recurrent normative pattern: in the face of new and unexpected POW issues and legal ambiguities in conflict after conflict, the country sought to reinforce, rather than degrade, its founding principles and strove to match its practices with its values.

The GWOT fundamentally changed this narrative. Instead of seeking to improve U.S. compliance with the norm of humane treatment, policy makers and lawyers inside the Bush administration contested the longstanding normative framework that had been recently reinforced by the U.S. experience in Vietnam. For the first time in the history of the Geneva Conventions, the United States used the law to take away—rather than expand—human rights. Following September 11, the humane treatment of detainees was seen as unduly restrictive and incompatible with the necessity of gathering actionable intelligence. The issue of detainee treatment was further used as a vehicle in the broader battle over executive power and the role of international law in U.S. policy making. This debate had significant political, legal, and strategic consequences. In addition to examining these ramifications, this chapter explores what we can learn from the life cycle of norms and whether a new normative consensus has been reached on the issue of detainee treatment. It concludes by offering several policy recommendations and future avenues of research for scholarship.

EMPIRICAL HARMS

The policy makers and lawyers responsible for challenging the normative regime have argued that no significant harms resulted from the torture decisions. Rather, these individuals often point to the successful capture of high-value targets, such as Khalid Sheikh Mohammed, and the death of others, such as Osama bin Laden, as evidence that the program worked.[1] Not only have these claims been challenged multiple times—most recently by the SSCI Report—but the use of torture harmed a wide range of U.S. interests.[2] Legal, foreign policy, and operational harms call into question the narrative that the United States is better off as a result of inhumane detainee treatment. These are not obscure, nebulous disadvantages of the program: among other impacts, the torture decisions eroded legal regimes, weakened U.S. alliances, and damaged U.S. operational capability in the field.

LEGAL HARMS

Given that the majority of the normative contestation on the issue of torture occurred within the realm of legal scholarship and arguments, it is not surprising that the decision to use torture had numerous and wide-ranging consequences for the United States' relationship with domestic and international law. To begin with, the use of torture diminished the United States' ability to be a respected advocate for human rights around the globe. Even more significantly, the use of torture called into doubt the role of law in U.S. society and undermined the reputation of the government, thereby eroding public support for the war effort. As with all wars, the GWOT is a clash of wills, to paraphrase Clausewitz.[3] Therefore, any action that has a negative impact on the legitimacy of the war, or of the government fighting it, constitutes a significant concern. Unfortunately, the use of torture had such an effect.

There is no question that the United States' use of torture undermined its credibility as a promoter of international human rights and humanitarian law. In a 2006 editorial, the *Boston Globe* noted the charges of hypocrisy being leveled at Washington by countries such as China and NGOs such as Amnesty International for its yearly country human rights reports. Among other examples, the *Globe* cited the "painful irony" of the U.S. State Department criticizing Egypt and Jordan for using torture even though, at that time, the United States was rendering captives to those very states for the explicit purpose of them being interrogated via torture. "How seriously can the U.S. government's human rights scorecard be taken when U.S. authorities are asking the foreign torturers denounced in the report to torture people as a favor to America?" asks the *Globe*.[4] In light of the torture decisions and actions, U.S. authority in the realm of human rights was greatly diminished.[5] As William Schulz, the director of the U.S. section of Amnesty International at the time stated, "The United States government considers itself a moral leader on human rights issues, but its record of indefinite and arbitrary detentions, secret 'black sites,' and outsourced torture in the 'war on terror' turns it from leader to human rights violator."[6] The decision to use torture had even more profound effects on the role of law domestically. The law represents a society's expression of its values and, as such, its decency. This is especially true in the United States, whose constitution dedicates the country to the eternal pursuit of a "more perfect union." The resort to torture was anathema to this tradition and consequently undermined a core pillar of U.S. identity—the use of torture represented a regression in the Enlightenment-inspired quest to separate the application of the law from the routine exercise of cruelty.[7]

The use of torture also undermined the United States' quest for a rules-based international system by demonstrating that, as a powerful state, it could and would break widely held norms when it viewed it as necessary to do so.[8] In this sense, the actions of the Bush administration supported the arguments of realist international relations scholars who argue states comply with international law only when it serves their national interest. The United States' use of torture served as a stark reminder that no matter how universally accepted, international treaties such as the Geneva Conventions and the CAT will always be susceptible to brazen acts of noncompliance.

Lastly, using torture inflicted severe damage on the reputation of the U.S. legal and political system. Evidence for this can be found in the debate over whether Bush-era officials should be prosecuted for their actions in implementing the torture policy. The most recent chapter of this now long-running debate occurred in December 2014 after the release of the SSCI report. In a string of dueling op-eds and editorials, columnists debated whether the officials knowingly violated the law or whether they had correctly sought legal advice that simply turned out to be improper.[9] For some observers, torture will remain a black eye on the credibility of the U.S. legal system as long as former officials are able to escape criminal prosecution. According to Steven W. Hawkins, the executive director of Amnesty International USA, "If our laws have meaning, we can't accept that some of our country's most senior officials authorized criminal conduct and were never held accountable."[10] Others, however, have argued that the focus on criminal prosecution is misplaced. Jack Goldsmith, for example, believes that "accountability includes much more than criminal punishment and does not turn only on individual mistakes or wrongdoing. Accountability includes a whole array of sanctions, and an assessment of the proper sanction includes an assessment of the costs of various forms of accountability on the community or the nation."[11] In Goldsmith's eyes, therefore, the system has worked as intended. Officials involved in the torture program have been exposed to criminal investigations, professional inquiries, and public shaming; the focus on criminal prosecution is thus unnecessary. Overall, though, that this issue continues to be debated long after the Obama administration decided to forgo prosecution indicates the lack of political and legal unity on how best to move forward.[12] Thus, the U.S. reputation as a law-abiding state and U.S. laws were damaged by these decisions and actions.

FOREIGN POLICY HARMS

The impact of the torture decision extended beyond domestic and international legal harms. In fact, some of the largest consequences have played out in the realm of U.S. foreign policy. The use of torture ruined the careers of allied political leaders, negatively affected the United States' relationship with many allied governments, and led to a severe deterioration in the United States' reputation abroad—a change that inflicted and continues to inflict significant strategic consequences.

For many of the leaders of allied states who sided with the United States on detention issues, the use of cruel and inhumane treatment became politically catastrophic. Even some of the leaders who did not explicitly side with U.S. detainee policy but who had supported the U.S. war in Iraq faced serious domestic backlash from the revelations of abuse at places such as Abu Ghraib. For these leaders, it became impossible to separate support for one aspect of the GWOT from its association with torture, making cooperation with the United States politically toxic for many allied politicians. For example, revelations from Abu Ghraib intensified the British public's opposition to the war in Iraq, eventually forcing Prime Minister Tony Blair to resign in 2007. The perception of an exceptionally close relationship between Bush and Blair, on top of the already strong relationship between the United States and United Kingdom, meant the prime minister would share in all the successes, and failures, of the war.[13] Even though there is no evidence to suggest British involvement in devising or implementing U.S. torture policy, the policy's existence was so damaging that it even contributed to an effort to impeach Blair, which represented the first time impeachment of a government official had been attempted in the United Kingdom in over 150 years.[14]

The use of torture also affected the overall relationship between the United States and many of its key European allies. This was partly the result of a divergence of opinions on how to respond to terrorism in general. Most

European countries did not share the United States' view that the struggle against terrorism represented a military struggle rather than a criminal one. As a result, the wartime tools utilized by the United States, such as the unlimited detention of captured fighters and the use of military commissions, were controversial policies within many European capitals. These states' preferred policy—using the criminal justice system to prosecute terrorists—meant far stronger legal and humanitarian protections for captured suspects. Moreover, unlike the United States, most European states have ratified Additional Protocol I to the Geneva Conventions, which extends POW protections to guerrillas, insurgents, and other types of fighters traditionally classified as unlawful combatants. Overall, according to Jack Goldsmith, "These factors combined to give the Europeans a very different portrait of [U.S. detention policy] than the one administration lawyers had painted."[15] In this context, the decision to use torture, especially when some of the detainees were citizens of allied nations, was just another extreme, incomprehensible, and unacceptable U.S. policy choice.

The Bush administration belatedly recognized the negative impact of detainee policy on its relationships with allies. After Bush was reelected in late 2004, the administration began to pay more attention to assuaging allies' concerns. According to Barton Gellman, the issue of detainee handling and treatment became a "big foreign-policy problem. Chronic trouble with allies over Guantánamo became acute after Abu Ghraib and the torture memos. Rice succeeded Powell as secretary of state in January 2005. She made it a top priority to stop the diplomatic bleeding."[16]

Rice consequently directed her counselor Philip Zelikow to draft a new strategy for the detainee program.[17] Zelikow collaborated with a few like-minded colleagues inside the DoD to craft a plan that represented a sharp break with the prevailing practices of the administration. Zelikow proposed to reveal publicly the CIA black sites and sharply curtail their use, culminating in the eventual transfer of all prisoners to the regular detention system. The plan also provided for the closure of the prison at Guantánamo Bay and the transfer of its prisoners to facilities in the continental United States. As part of this plan, the administration would have voluntarily acknowledged and extended Common Article 3 protections to all captives, although it would maintain its argument that the prisoners were not *legally* entitled to them. This effort proved largely futile, however, as key figures in the administration—such as Rumsfeld and Cheney—objected to the proposal and had it scrapped.[18] Moreover, Bush continued to defend the use of enhanced interrogation techniques by the CIA and blocked any efforts to rescind them.[19] As a result, torture, and its impact on America's reputation and relationships, became a prominent issue in the 2008 campaign. In one debate with the Republican nominee John McCain, then-candidate Obama declared:

> One of the things I intend to do as president is to restore America's standing in the world. We are less respected now than we were eight years ago or even four years ago, and this is the greatest country on earth, but because of some of the mistakes that have been made, and I give Senator McCain great credit on the torture issue, for having identified that as something that undermines our long term security, because of those things, we, I think, are going to have a lot of work to do in the next administration to restore that sense that America is that shining beacon on a hill.[20]

By linking the United States' reputation to its security, Obama was recognizing a fundamental element of the GWOT: reputation has a causal impact on strategic outcomes. Specifically, the only way to achieve strategic victory against violent nonstate actors such as al-Qaeda was by winning hearts and minds, thereby reducing support for these extremists. General David Petraeus expressed this view when he stated: "Our values and the laws governing warfare teach us to respect human dignity, maintain our integrity, and do what is right. Adherence to our values distinguishes us from our enemy. This fight depends on securing the population, which must understand that we— not our enemies—occupy the moral high ground."[21] Given that the respect for law and human dignity are significant determinants of the United States' reputation abroad, it is no surprise that the decision to use torture tarnished the country's image and made "victory" that much more elusive.

OPERATIONAL HARMS

The decision to use torture most negatively influenced U.S. counterterrorism operations. Among other effects, torture served as a recruiting tool for U.S. adversaries, hampered operational cooperation with allies, and undermined the cohesion of the federal government. Ironically, the use of torture also negatively affected the United States' ability to collect intelligence. Therefore, the enhanced interrogation program represents a failure.

Among the most damaging operational impacts of the torture decision has been its use as a recruiting tool for terrorist organizations. This is particularly true with regards to the existence of Guantánamo Bay and the legacy of Abu Ghraib. According to then-senator Joe Biden, Guantánamo "has become the greatest propaganda tool that exists for [sic] recruiting of terrorists around the world."[22] General Petraeus reiterated this idea in 2010 when he stated, "Abu Ghraib and other situations like that are nonbiodegradables. They don't go away. The enemy continues to beat you with them like a stick in the Central Command area of responsibility."[23]

There is no shortage of evidence to support these claims. For example, in a 2006 audiotape, Osama bin Laden reminded his listeners of the perceived injustices occurring at Guantánamo:

> And then I call to memory my brothers the prisoners in Guantánamo—may Allah free them all—and I state the fact, about which I also am certain, that all the prisoners of Guantánamo, who were captured in 2001 and the first half of 2002 and who number in the hundreds, have no connection whatsoever to the events of September 11th, and even stranger is that many of them have no connection with al-Qaida in the first place, and even more amazing is that some of them oppose al-Qaida's methodology of calling for war with America. . . . My mentioning of these facts isn't out of hope that Bush and his party will treat our brothers fairly in their cases, because that is something no rational person expects, but rather it is meant to expose the oppression, injustice and arbitrariness of your administration in using force and the reactions that result from that.[24]

The theme has been echoed by other prominent terrorist leaders in their propaganda. For example, Anwar al-Awlaki, an al-Qaeda propaganda leader in Yemen who was killed by a U.S. drone strike in 2011, included supporting Muslim POWs as one of his "44 Ways to Support Jihad."[25] Likewise, in issue 9 of their glossy magazine *Dabiq*, ISIL issues this warning to those who refuse to fight against the West:

> As for those who continue to suffer from the disease of being indifferent towards the obligations of hijrah, jihād, and bay'ah, so much so that they see nothing wrong with residing amongst, and paying taxes to, the very crusaders who belittle the Sharī'ah on their news and entertainment programs, who arm the secularists and Rawāfid in Muslim lands, *who imprison and torture Muslim men and women*, and on top of all who burn the Qur'an and mock the Prophet (sallallāhu 'alayhi wa sallam), then let them prepare their flimsy excuses for the angels of death.[26]

In total, the frequency with which senior al-Qaeda leaders, ISIL propaganda, and other significant terrorist voices refer to U.S. mistreatment of captives indicates the power of the narrative. U.S. torture of prisoners has served as a rallying cry for terrorists around the world and serves as one of their key justifications for waging war against the United States.

The use of torture not only served as a recruiting tool for terrorists, but it also hampered operational cooperation with allied states. For instance, in the Obama administration's debate over whether to release several top-secret memos on the torture program, CIA officers "acknowledged that some foreign intelligence agencies had refused, for example, to share information about the location of terrorism suspects for fear of becoming implicated in any eventual torture of those suspects."[27] This information has been corroborated by David Kris, former assistant attorney general for national security, who wrote in a journal article that "many of our key allies around the world are not willing to cooperate with or support our efforts to hold suspected terrorists in law of war detention or to prosecute them in military commissions."[28] This discord even spilled over into allied decisions on troop contributions to the war in Iraq where, in mid-2004, "revelations about the

Abu Ghraib prison abuse led Hungary's opposition to call for a withdrawal despite originally supporting the deployment."[29] Just a few months later, the Hungarian government announced its decision to withdraw its three hundred troops by the beginning of 2005.[30]

Torture also proved divisive within the U.S. government and contributed to a crisis of legitimacy that prompted damaging leaks by disenchanted insiders. Writing about the Terrorist Surveillance Program—President Bush's secret domestic wiretapping initiative—Goldsmith posits that leaks about the program's existence didn't start occurring until broader doubts about the administration's legitimacy began to surface. In his opinion:

> The main cause of leaks was not the absence of sanctions [against leakers] but rather the perception within the government of illegitimate activity. Classified surveillance activities that began in 2001 did not leak until after a legitimacy crisis had developed, beginning in June 2004 around the time of the Abu Ghraib scandal and the leaked interrogation memos.[31]

Looking ahead, it is likely that the decision to use torture will continue to influence U.S. interests in the future. For example, it is possible that the legacy of torture will make it harder for the U.S. military to compel enemies to surrender on the battlefield since they may prefer to be killed fighting than be exposed to cruel treatment for an undetermined amount of time.[32] Such a situation would represent a terrible development for the United States because it would make the job of fighting future wars that much harder. It is instructive to contrast this possibility with the example of the 1991 Persian Gulf War. In that conflict, the allied coalition dropped more than 32,000,000 surrender leaflets promising soldiers who surrendered good treatment, food, and "Arabic hospitality."[33] Over eighty thousand Iraqi soldiers surrendered in the hundred hours of ground operations, with over 70 percent of them citing the leaflets as a factor in their decision.[34] It is unlikely that as many Iraqi soldiers would have surrendered if they had had a reason to doubt the United States' promise of good treatment. Such a situation may not be possible in the future.

Proof that the legacy of torture still haunts the United States can be found in the recent executions of U.S. and foreign hostages by members of ISIL. These hostages, including the U.S. journalist James Foley, were purposefully dressed in orange jumpsuits so as to draw a direct line between their execution and the U.S. treatment of detainees at Guantánamo Bay. In the words of Undersecretary of Defense for Policy Brian McKeon at a recent Senate Armed Services Committee hearing: "It is no coincidence that the recent ISIL videos showing the barbaric burning of a Jordanian pilot and the savage execution of a Japanese hostage each showed the victim clothed in an orange jumpsuit, believed by many to be the symbol of the Guantánamo detention facility."[35]

The greatest operational harm done by the decision to use torture was to the United States' ability to collect intelligence. According to a 2008 Senate Armed Services Report, U.S. detention policy "damaged our ability to collect accurate intelligence that could save lives, strengthened the hand of our enemies, and compromised our moral authority."[36] Six years later, in a speech on the Senate floor in the wake of the SSCI report's release, Senator John McCain asserted that the use of torture was "shameful and unnecessary; and, contrary to assertions made by some of its defenders and as the Committee's report makes clear, it produced little useful intelligence to help us track down the perpetrators of 9/11 or prevent new attacks and atrocities."[37]

These testimonies only serve to reinforce the principle that coercive methods do not produce accurate and actionable intelligence. As the history of U.S. detainee treatment illustrates (see chapters 2 and 3), this is not a new revelation. The 1992 revision to FM 34-52 captured this established wisdom when it stated:

Experience indicates that the use of prohibited techniques is not necessary to gain the cooperation of interrogation sources. Use of torture and other illegal methods is a poor technique that yields unreliable results, may damage subsequent collection efforts, and can induce the source to say whatever he thinks the interrogator wants to hear.[38]

Even after 9/11, the nation's experts in interrogation at the FBI had warned the DoD of these consequences, ultimately deciding to pull its interrogators from Guantánamo Bay in order to avoid being associated with them.[39]

LOSING AGAINST UNCONVENTIONAL WARFARE

The main takeaway from these legal, foreign policy, and operational harms is that the use of torture challenges the United States' ability to disrupt, degrade, and deny terrorist capabilities in the GWOT. Like all conflicts dominated by unconventional warfare, the GWOT can only be won by winning the public. Or as Colin Gray puts it, in unconventional warfare "the decisive combat occurs in and about the minds of civilians, not on the battlefield."[40] Winning the public in the targeted country, and therefore removing terrorists' sanctuary and access to weapons and recruits, is vital to sustainable victory. This is why the United States has reaped so little strategic benefit from its success in eliminating rank-and-file terrorists and their senior leaders. Killing terrorists can be useful to counter unconventional warfare, but only if more belligerents are not created in the process of doing so. The number that matters is not how many terrorists have been killed but rather how many are left.

The United States' use of torture has had a detrimental effect not only on its efforts to win the public overseas but also on maintaining domestic support for the war. In this regard, the U.S. experience in the GWOT largely parallels its experience in Vietnam, where overwhelming firepower could not compel a U.S. victory. In Vietnam, the Viet Cong and the North Vietnamese Army employed a strategy that prioritized undermining American support for the war effort rather than destroying U.S. military capabilities.[41] Along the way, the United States helped its adversaries' cause by committing abuses such as the My Lai massacre and by using indiscriminant tactics on the North Vietnamese people, such as the widespread dropping of conventional munitions, napalm, and Agent Orange. These tactics, which were designed to produce gains on the battlefield, ended up backfiring by reducing the legitimacy of the overall war effort. In the GWOT, torture has played largely the same role.

The consequences of the EIT program have been significant. While debates continue around whether the coerced interrogations did produce actionable information, it is undeniable that the program ruined relationships, reputations, and legacies.[42] While many changes and reforms have been enacted since the program started in 2002, a large number of these costs continue to affect the United States. Only time and further dedication to reform—to embracing a "never again" posture—will resolve these lingering wounds. The important question to answer now is whether the United States has reached a new normative consensus on the use of torture and what such a consensus, or lack of one, means for the future of U.S. detainee policy. To answer this question, however, we first need to examine what the life-cycle theory of normative change teaches us.

WHAT DOES UNDERSTANDING THE LIFE CYCLE OF NORMS TEACH US?

Norms are like any other institution—they are subject to the same inevitable process of decay if left unattended. The norm of humane treatment for detainees was a key component of U.S. identity during its revolutionary struggle against the British. But it was only because of the efforts of subsequent generations, who during conflict after conflict recommitted themselves to this norm, that it survived. Plenty of other states have been founded on noble ideals only to discard them as time moves on. The life cycle of norms teaches us that norms cannot be taken for granted. An embedded norm is not a perfect norm. It will eventually face challenges as questions regarding its applicability arise and new situations reveal unforeseen ambiguities in its composition. How society responds to this contestation is a choice that depends upon history, power, and the broader network of norms in which the debated norm resides.

According to Wayne Sandholtz, normative contestation is informed by more than just the issues of the moment. Arguments over norms rely heavily on past instances of dispute, and therefore one cannot understand present debates without understanding past debates. Sandholtz writes:

> The cases are linked forward and backward: each episode takes place in a context shaped by previous disputes, and each dispute modifies the normative context for subsequent controversies. The historical view helps us to see the connections between episodes, as disputants in one period invoke norms and precedents from prior disputes.[43]

Understanding the norm of humane treatment in U.S. society therefore requires understanding its complex history. To focus simply on the decisions of the Bush administration without examining their historical context would result in a starkly incomplete and insufficient analysis. More significantly, such an analysis would prove relatively useless as a predictor of future normative arguments. Norms evolve over time, with the arguments and decisions of the past directly influencing the arguments and decisions of today. Future periods of contestation will therefore refer back to current and past debates.

In addition to a broad historical analysis, one must appreciate the role of power in the development of norms. The ability to change and promulgate norms is directly proportional to the power an actor wields. Powerful actors have a far greater ability to shape norms than weaker ones. Access and influence gives actors the ability not only to challenge norms but to survive the backlash or escape blame if their challenge fails, making them more willing to launch a challenge in the first place. This fact is illustrated in the disproportionate punishment meted out to the interrogators in comparison to that received by the lawyers and policy makers. That said, powerful actors can find themselves successfully constrained by the normative arguments of weaker actors in certain circumstances. The success of the JAGs in pushing back against the advocates of torture inside the DoD is a good example of this. This experience suggests that while power is key, powerful actors can be constrained by others that wield significant legitimacy. The JAGs are a broad and diverse group of individuals that, in theory, should be subservient to the orders of the president. However, the JAGs' reputation for independence and honesty gave them a legitimacy that allowed them successfully to thwart the designs of more powerful actors inside the administration. Power and legitimacy, therefore, act as key independent variables throughout the history of a norm's development.

Lastly, norms do not exist in isolation. Cycles of norm change, and norms in general, are interconnected. In other words, norms exist within broader networks of norms, where each individual idea influences the others. The norm of humane treatment of detainees follows this pattern. Over the past several centuries, POW norms evolved in conjunction with broader norms about the sanctity of innocent life and the desirability of ameliorating the effects of war for the most vulnerable populations. While significant in its own right, the norm of humane treatment cannot be separated from this broader trend because it is the source of many of its most basic principles.

In total, the life cycle of norms teaches us to be aware of context. Norms do not exist as static entities in a vacuum, impervious to change. Instead, norms are a direct product of a long historical development among actors with the requisite power and legitimacy to shape them as well as related norms in their network. As such, the life cycle of norms should be seen as a heuristic tool allowing us to understand better the process by which norms change and reminding us that we can act to ensure they change in the way we desire. The embedding of a norm is not the end of its story but rather just one stage in an iterative and unending process.

THEORY OF NORMS AS IT APPLIES TO POLICY

So how could the antitorture stance of the United States prior to the 9/11 attacks be brushed aside so rapidly, in a manner contrary to constructivist predictions and the U.S. historical experience? The account offered in this book presents a theory of norms in which each circumstance of U.S. POW decision making and behavior changed the country's interpretation of the POW norms. Prior to the 9/11 attacks, conflicts clarified and reinforced the norm with additional domestic laws, training, education, and doctrine. While the norms had begun to unravel prior in the 1990s, they were significantly disputed after 9/11. As a result of the beliefs and arguments of some administration lawyers and policy makers, the most recent life cycle of the POW norm left the norm significantly weakened. The notion that the norms against torture and the humane treatment of those in U.S. custody are less salient as a result of the U.S. experience in the GWOT is supported by the U.S. public's evolution of views on torture.

A Pew poll from December 2011 revealed that 53 percent of Americans believe torture can be often or sometimes justified compared to 42 percent who say it can rarely or never be justified.[44] These results represent a reversal of opinion from the first time Pew polled on the subject in 2004. In that poll, 53 percent of respondents said that torture could rarely or never be justified versus 43 percent who said it could often or sometimes be a legitimate tool for the government.[45] An even more recent *Washington Post* poll from December 2014 confirms this change of opinion. In that poll, 58 percent of respondents declared torture could be often or sometimes justified compared to 39 percent who said it could be rarely or never justified.[46] As such, it is unrealistic to say that the use of torture will become a relic of the past. As long as the debates over international law and the balance between security and liberty remain lively, and as long as a significant portion of Americans believe torture can be justified, there will always remain the possibility that actors with access and influence will continue to contest the normative principle of humane treatment for detainees.

For decades, the United States embraced the Geneva Conventions and other human rights laws across a varied range of actors and in contradistinction to its enemies. Several iterations of the norm life cycle both illuminated gaps and subsequently strengthened the humanitarian norms. While the recent decisions and actions illustrate that these norms are embedded— since even in their violation, the lawyers and policy makers referenced these norms emphasizing humane POW treatment—they also illustrate the ease with which actors with access and influence can challenge and modify the norm. As it applies to policy, the experience of the U.S. detainee behavior in the GWOT has weakened the salience of this norm and called into question U.S. reputation and identity. Yet, though the norm has been weakened, another set of actors who are equally empowered to enhance the norm may emerge in a future U.S. conflict. The key is to learn from the normative experience of the GWOT in order to adapt and strengthen these humanitarian norms in the future.

WHERE DO WE GO FROM HERE?

The decision to use torture was highly controversial and triggered significant pushback from the courts, Congress, and the American people. As a result, by the end of the Bush administration, much of the interrogation program had changed. The DoD stopped its use of enhanced interrogation tactics only a few months after approving them in late 2002. Meanwhile, the CIA slimmed down the number of techniques it used from the initially approved ten to just six by September 2006.[47] But not everything changed. Up until the last day of Bush's presidency, legal loopholes remained that allowed for the use of harsh interrogation tactics against captured detainees. This was only put to an end after Obama's election, when, two days after his inauguration, he signed an executive order banning the use of torture.[48] The next president, however, could easily overturn this ban.

So where does this leave us? Taking everything into account, it is clear that the Bush administration failed in its efforts to establish a new normative consensus approving the use of torture. However, many of the ambiguities and flaws of the previous normative regime remain unresolved. Obama's Executive Order 13491 closed the legal loopholes that permitted torture, but the broader question of how to handle detainees in the GWOT continues to confound U.S. policy makers. Obama's failed effort to close the prison at Guantánamo Bay is a potent example of how the issue is far more complex than many of Bush's detractors wish to admit. Most significantly, the issues that spawned the contestation in the first place—the applicability of international humanitarian law that was written in the age of conventional warfare, the extent of executive power, and the proper balance between security and liberty—remain open to future disputes. All that is required is another group of actors with the access, power, and ideological drive to challenge these issues. U.S. society, therefore, is in an ambiguous place where (for now) the worst abuses of the Bush administration have been checked but where the issues underlying them remain open to reinterpretation.

A new normative consensus on detainee treatment has not been reached, but neither has the old consensus been fully restored.

PUSHBACK AGAINST THE BUSH ADMINISTRATION AND A NEW STATUS QUO

Pushback against the use of torture on captured detainees emerged almost immediately after its approval, but it played out differently across the sectors of the government. In the DoD, the lawyers that were silenced in the months leading up to the Haynes memo successfully reclaimed their access and influence by protesting the administration's policies inside and outside the courtroom, ultimately bringing the EIT program to a halt.[49] As a result, by January 2003, the techniques were no longer officially approved, and a new working group had been tasked with drafting a new list of acceptable interrogation procedures. The report, issued in April 2003, listed thirty-five techniques, of which twenty-five were purely verbal.[50] Upon receipt of this list, Rumsfeld approved twenty-four of the thirty-five techniques, of which seventeen were based on techniques listed in FM 34-52 and the remainder were intended to produce mild discomfort, such as switching hot, fresh food for Meals Ready-to-Eat, altering the temperature in the room in a nonhazardous way, and adjusting the sleep schedule of the detainee from regular patterns (not to be confused with sleep deprivation). The one exception was the approval of solitary confinement, but even this was recommended for no more than thirty days at a time.[51] Therefore, by mid-2003, the DoD had rescinded the use of techniques that could be considered torture. However, because of the confusing way in which detainee policy was handled and communicated, many of the old techniques would endure for some time after this and see use in the field, as the example of Abu Ghraib so clearly shows.

For the CIA, the restrictions grew more slowly. In the years following the initial authorization to use torture in 2002, the CIA routinely sought reconfirmation from the Justice Department and top White House officials that the EIT program was legal and authorized. In total, from 2002 to 2007 there would be a total of ten major OLC opinions issued to the agency confirming the legality the program.[52] Despite this continued support, the CIA was cautious about executing the program, suspending it numerous times in the wake of scandals such as Abu Ghraib or new pieces of legislation such as the Detainee Treatment Act of 2005.[53] According to David Cole, this history of caution reveals "an agency that is extremely sensitive to whether the program is legally authorized and approved by higher-ups—no doubt because it understood that what it was doing was at a minimum controversial, and very possibly illegal."[54] In 2006, this caution culminated in a self-imposed reduction in the number of approved techniques from ten to six and a push to get President Bush to acknowledge publicly the existence of the CIA's black-site prisons, which he did in a landmark speech in September that year.[55] President Obama ended the program when he signed Executive Order 13491 on January 22, 2009, which rescinded all the OLC memos approving the use of cruel and inhumane techniques and limited all U.S. personnel to interrogation methods found in the U.S. Army's interrogation field manual.[56] As of this writing, U.S. personnel no longer engage in the cruel and inhumane treatment of detainees.

This pushback and reevaluation was prompted by an emerging consensus between concerned lawyers inside and outside the administration and an unprecedented willingness from the courts to intervene in adjudicating national security law.[57] Lawyers inside the DoD, who had grown used to their independence and reputation as protectors of the military's honor, found common cause with civilian lawyers at NGOs such as the Center for Constitutional Rights (CCR).[58] When the CCR brought suit against the administration's detainee policies, the JAGs and other military lawyers supported its arguments with amici curiae briefs. According to Goldsmith, the message of these amici was clear: "The presidency was untrustworthy, out of control, and defying the rule of law and military traditions."[59] Over a period of several years, a regular back and forth emerged, whereby the lawyers would sue, the Supreme Court would rule in their favor, and the administration would attempt to rebuff their counterattacks. In an attempt to settle these disputes, Congress passed several pieces of legislation that aimed to bring greater clarity to the laws covering detainee policy and revise the process by which the judicial branch could exercise oversight. Consequently, by the time Bush left office, cases such as *Rasul v. Bush, Hamdan v. Rumsfeld*, and *Boumediene v. Bush*, in combination with legislation such as the 2005 Detainee Treatment Act and 2006 Military Commissions Act, had greatly restricted the executive's ability to manage detainees on its own.

Although the Court's decisions brought the detainees habeas corpus rights and Common Article 3 protections, President Bush used his executive authority to shield the CIA's interrogation program from these restrictions.[60] But Bush could not undo the damage to the powers of the presidency. According to Goldsmith, the "main effect" of the administration's commitment to expanding presidential power "was to cause the public, the press, the Congress, and the courts to view Bush's wartime practices in a suspicious light, especially as the 9/11 threat faded from view."[61] The back-and-forth battle in the courts and Congress over detainee policy ultimately left the presidency less powerful than when Bush inherited it. Rather than advancing the vision of the unitary executive, the battle over detainee policy resulted in greater restraints on the powers of the president and greater skepticism of unilateral executive power. By relying on executive power to the point of producing a backlash, the administration, in the words of Goldsmith, "borrowed against the power of future presidencies. Presidencies that, at least until the next attack, and probably even following one, will be viewed by Congress and the courts, whose assistance they need, with a harmful suspicion and mistrust because of the unnecessary unilateralism of the Bush years."[62]

The legal, operational, and political landscape surrounding the use of EITs looks remarkably different today than it did back in 2002. Torture is no longer employed, and the executive branch has seen its power to dictate war policy diminished not only thanks to the interventions of the courts and Congress but also because of the distrust the actions of the Bush administration fostered in the American people. The country seems to have reached a new status quo, but the stability is misleading. Some of the ambiguities that led to the decision to use torture remain unresolved and are simply waiting for the next crisis to be invoked once more.

At the most basic level, the arguments over the proper balance between security and liberty and the role of international law in U.S. society remain unresolved. Some scholars, such as Richard Posner, see the Constitution as a tool with two goals: to provide security and liberty. The Constitution's powers and protections then serve as the fulcrum that balances the two in accordance with the context of the time.[63] Others, however, see the Constitution as enshrining rigid protections for civil liberties that cannot be violated for any reason.[64] These opposing camps, not surprisingly, have different perspectives on the government's counterterror agenda. For Posner, the threat posed by terrorism justifies a greater emphasis on security than on liberty; as long as the threat remains, the efforts of the government are warranted. He notes: "The fact that a struggle is protracted is no reason to suspend security measures before it ends; as long as we are threatened, we must defend."[65] The ACLU, on the other hand, does not believe the terrorism threat justifies the government's security response. In testimony before the House Committee on Foreign Affairs in 2010, the ACLU declared: "We all acknowledge the government's legitimate interest in protecting the nation from terrorism and in stemming actions that further the unlawful, violent acts of terrorist groups. But just because a threat exists does not justify the erosion of principles that are at the core of our constitutional identity."[66]

FUTURE AREAS OF RESEARCH FOR SCHOLARS

Several avenues exist for future research for scholars interested in both the life cycle of norms and domestic contestation of these regimes. One avenue would be to examine the evolution and disputes of other norms apart from the norms governing the humane treatment of noncombatants and POWs in wartime, for example, the life cycle of norms governing U.S. hostage policy.

Researchers could also expand this theoretical model from simply an examination of the Third Geneva Convention to a study of the Fourth Geneva Convention, with a particular emphasis on recent U.S. military actions in Iraq and Afghanistan. In military operations during the last decade, for example, the United States was effective at avoiding the intentional targeting of civilians but was often less effective at avoiding military endeavors that knowingly placed civilians at risk or destroyed civilian infrastructure. U.S. military leaders and civilian policy makers repeatedly stressed the importance of minimizing civilian casualties both leading up to and during the U.S. engagements in Iraq and Afghanistan. Speaking about the U.S.-led conflict in Afghanistan, Gen. Tommy Franks stated, "I can't imagine there's been a conflict in history where there has been less collateral damage, less unintended consequences."[67] In addition, one of the findings from WikiLeaks in 2008 was the revelation of detailed guidelines in Iraq to protect civilians.[68] Prior to the invasion of Iraq in 2003, the DoD hosted reporters at a briefing to outline U.S. military targeting procedures and efforts to minimize casualties to noncombatants and prevent collateral damage. Sharp distinctions were drawn between the mandates of international law, which distinguishes between combatants and noncombatants, and the actions of Saddam Hussein. The briefing stated:

> He [Saddam Hussein] deliberately constructs mosques near military facilities, uses schools, hospitals, orphanages and cultural treasures to shield military forces, thereby exposing helpless men, women and children to danger. These are not tactics of war, they are crimes of war. Deploying human shields is not a military strategy, it's murder, it's a violation of the laws of armed conflict and a crime against humanity, and will be treated as such.[69]

Furthermore, the United States officially recognized that the Fourth Geneva Convention applied to occupied Iraq.

Despite this commitment, ambiguities exist in this norm regime. For example, drone strikes and the use of precision-guided weapons with global positioning systems are intended to increase accuracy and minimize collateral damage, but they can result in hundreds of unintentional civilian deaths.

Finally, detailed process training by future scholars can examine the steps by which the norm of noncombatant immunity was challenged during

Vietnam, reaffirmed through the DoD Law of War program, and then tested in Iraq and Afghanistan.

POLICY RECOMMENDATIONS

To ensure the gloves stay on with regard to detainee treatment, it is imperative that U.S. policy makers strengthen the norm of humane treatment and reduce the likelihood of future disputes. The following recommendations would help U.S. policy makers achieve these goals:

- *Recognize historical precedents and ambiguities.* As Sandholtz's work shows, norms evolve as part of a historical process. They evolve over time and in close relationships with other, similar norms. Strengthening the norm of humane treatment, therefore, requires grappling with this complex history and network of interlinked norms. Equally important is identifying the ambiguities in normative regimes and working to clarify them before they are tested. To this end, policy makers should highlight the United States' long history of humane POW treatment in speeches, interviews, and other forms of discourse. Emphasizing the historical nature of the issue would place POW treatment within its proper context and help combat the idea that POW policy is sui generis for each conflict. Furthermore, policy makers should note the connection between POW treatment and other norms that constitute important parts of U.S. identity, such as the rule of law and the value of individual life. In so doing, policy makers would reinforce the notion that noncompliance with the norm of humane treatment puts other important norms at risk.
- *Ensure accountability.* Examining how the United States abandoned its long tradition of abiding by human rights conventions is critical to understanding U.S. identity and how authority is wielded during wartime. Equally important is examining whether and how the nation will correct its course. At stake is not only U.S. domestic and international identity but the very rule of law and civilization upon which the United States was founded.

To that end, the U.S. public—and current policy makers—must grapple with the notion of what accountability regarding the torture question looks like. Advocates of pardoning claim that this act helps the United States move past these terrible decisions and actions in a nonpartisan way.[70] Advocates of prosecution counter that judicial action is needed to restore U.S. integrity and its position as a defender of human rights and international humanitarian law.[71] Ultimately—whether the answer is pardon, prosecution, disbarment, or doing nothing—the American public and policy makers need to engage in a national conversation about the accountability of policy makers and lawyers.

- *Emphasize POW handling.* In his book on the history of U.S. POW treatment from the Revolutionary War to the War on Terror, the historian Paul J. Springer shows how the United States has never entered a war prepared for the task of POW handling.[72] Part of this, Springer notes, is because of the improvisational nature of U.S. war fighting. However, the recurrent theme throughout his work is that even within this context of improvisation, POW handling has received a relatively low priority from military commanders and policy makers. As such, Springer notes the mismatch between U.S. rhetoric on the importance of humane treatment for POWs and the lack of actual preparation to ensure this ideal is put into practice once war starts. Closing this gap between rhetoric and practice should be a top priority of U.S. policy makers. Having strong legal, educational, and doctrinal guidelines for POW treatment is a good start, but these efforts will prove unsatisfactory if low-performing troops are assigned POW handling. Consequently, policy makers should act to ensure POW duty is a viable career within the military and assign highly competent personnel to the task.

CONCLUSION

Using the life-cycle theory of normative change, this book has attempted to answer the question of how the Bush administration succeeded in instituting the inhumane treatment of detainees as official U.S. policy. The theory reveals an unambiguous narrative where, despite centuries of compliance with the norm of humane treatment, top administration lawyers and policy makers were able to use their access and influence to contest the post-Vietnam normative consensus. In contrast with other explanations for the use of torture after 9/11, the life-cycle theory illustrates how the interrogators were incapable of being the ones responsible for such a significant departure from the status quo. Nevertheless, despite their limited responsibility, they have been the group most punished for the abuses of the past. This injustice would be less troubling if it was clear that the country's experience with using torture had made it resolved never again to use cruelty against captured fighters.

Unfortunately, this possibility remains open, as some of the ambiguities that led to the contestation of the norm in the first place remain unresolved. The gloves may be back on for now, but the possibility that they will be removed again in the future is still present. The United States' experience with torture after 9/11, therefore, is a reminder that the process of normative development and embedding is never over. Norms should never be taken for granted. Instead, they must be actively reinforced over time or face certain decay and obsolescence. Therefore, as the nation moves forward, future leaders will face an important decision: to use their access and influence to reinforce the normative prohibition on cruelty against detainees, or to undermine the longstanding consensus, thereby paving the way for the gradual removal of a core component of U.S. identity since the country's founding.

APPENDIX A

Who's Who

LAWYERS

David Addington	Counsel to the Vice President (2001–2005); Vice President's Chief of Staff (2005–2009)
John Ashcroft	Attorney General (2001–2005)
Lt. Col. Diane Beaver	Staff Judge Advocate, U.S. Army, stationed at JTF-170
Marion "Spike" Bowman	Deputy General Counsel for National Security Law, FBI (1995–2006)
Jay Bybee	Assistant Attorney General, OLC (2001–2003)
Maj. General Michael Dunlavey	Commander JTF-170 at Guantánamo Bay (2002)
Jack Goldsmith	Assistant Attorney General, OLC (2003–2004)
Alberto Gonzales	White House Counsel (2001–2005); Attorney General (2005–2007)
William Haynes	General Counsel, Department of Defense (2001–2008)
Alberto Mora	General Counsel, U.S. Navy (2001–2006)
John Rizzo	Deputy General Counsel/Acting General Counsel at CIA (2001–2009)
John Yoo	Deputy Assistant Attorney General, OLC (2001–2003)

POLICY MAKERS

George W. Bush — President of the United States (2001–2009)

Dick Cheney — Vice President of the United States (2001–2009)

Michael Hayden — Director of Central Intelligence (2006–2009)

Colin Powell — Secretary of State (2001–2005)

Condoleezza Rice — National Security Advisor (2001–2005); Secretary of State (2005–2009)

Donald Rumsfeld — Secretary of Defense (2001–2006)

George Tenet — Director of Central Intelligence (1997–2004)

INTERROGATORS

Dave Becker — Head of Interrogation Control Element, Defense Intelligence Agency

Spc. Jeremy Callaway — 377th Military Police Company

Sgt. Javal Davis — 372nd Military Police Company

Spc. Lynndie England — 372nd Military Police Company

Staff Sgt. Ivan L. Frederick — 372nd Military Police Company

Maj. General John Gardner — Deputy Commander for Detainee Operations/Commander of Task Force 134, Multinational Force Iraq (2005–2007)

Mike Gelles — Criminal forensic psychologist with NCIS

Spc. Charles Graner — 372nd Military Police Company

Spc. Sabrina Harman — 372nd Military Police Company

Dr. Bruce Jessen — CIA contract psychologist

Lt. Col. Steve Jordan — Commander, Joint Interrogation Debriefing Center at Abu Ghraib prison, 205th Military Intelligence Brigade

Brig. General Janis Karpinski — Commander, 800th Military Police Brigade

Maj. General Geoffrey Miller — Commander JTF-170 at Guantánamo Bay (replaced Dunlavey)

Dr. James E. Mitchell — CIA contract psychologist

Col. Thomas M. Pappas — Commander, 205th Military Intelligence Brigade

Maj. General Douglas Stone — Deputy Commander for Detainee Operations/Commander of Task Force 134, Multinational Force Iraq (2007–2008)

APPENDIX B

Timeline of Major Events

1949	Geneva Conventions I–IV (United States ratifies in 1955)
1966	International Covenant on Civil and Political Rights completed (United States ratifies in 1992)
1969	My Lai Massacre becomes public knowledge in the United States
8/9/1974	President Nixon resigns in the wake of Watergate
11/5/1974	DoD Law of War program initiated via DoD Directive 5100.77
12/30/1974	Hughes-Ryan Act becomes law
4/30/1975	Vietnam War ends
1975	Rockefeller Committee established and issues its report
1975–1976	Church Committee established and issues reports
1975–1976	Pike Committee established and issues reports
1976–1977	Congress establishes the SSCI and the HPSCI
2/18/1976	Gerald Ford issues Executive Order 11905
1977	Protocols I & II to Geneva Conventions completed (United States does not ratify)
1983	Invasion of Grenada
1984	Convention Against Torture completed (United States ratifies in 1994)
1989	Invasion of Panama
1991	Operation Desert Storm
1992	Army Interrogation Field Manual (FM 34-52) revised following Gulf War
1994	Federal Anti-Torture Statute becomes law
1995	DCI John Deutch issues new rules on source recruitment at CIA
1996	Federal War Crimes Act becomes law
1999	NATO Bombing of Kosovo

9/11/2001	Al-Qaeda attacks the United States using hijacked civilian aircraft
9/14/2001	Authorization for the Use of Military Force
9/14/2001	President Bush declares a national emergency
10/7/2001	Invasion of Afghanistan begins
11/13/2001	Bush issues Military Order authorizing military commissions
1/9/2002	OLC draft memo on Geneva applicability to captured detainees
2/7/2002	Bush issues memo declaring Geneva conventions will not apply to Taliban and al-Qaeda detainees
7/1/2002	ICC enters into force
8/1/2002	First and Second Bybee memos issued by OLC
10/11/2002	Diane Beaver memo (which eventually becomes the Haynes memo) on EITs leaves Guantánamo to begin review process up the chain of command
11/23/2002	Rumsfeld authorizes the use of EITs on Mohammed al-Qahtani at Guantánamo
12/2/2002	Rumsfeld approves Haynes memo and use of eighteen EITs at Guantánamo Bay
12/17/2002	Alberto Mora first hears about the DoD EIT program
1/12/2003	Rumsfeld suspends use of the EITs
1/15/2003	Rumsfeld rescinds the Haynes memo
3/20/2003	Invasion of Iraq begins
4/28/2004	Abu Ghraib photos published by *60 Minutes*, igniting scandal
6/28/2004	*Rasul v. Bush*
6/28/2004	*Hamdi v. Rumsfeld*
12/30/2005	Detainee Treatment Act signed into law
6/29/2006	*Hamdan v. Rumsfeld*
9/6/2006	Revision to FM 34-52; now known as FM 2-22.3
9/6/2006	Bush delivers speech on CIA program; he announces the move of high-value detainees from black sites to Guantánamo Bay
10/17/2006	Military Commissions Act of 2006 signed into law
7/20/2007	Bush issues Executive Order 13440
11/1/2007	CIA halts use of EITs
6/12/2008	*Boumediene v. Bush*
1/22/2009	Obama issues Executive Order 13491
5/2/2011	Osama bin Laden killed by U.S. forces in Abbottabad, Pakistan

APPENDIX C

Acronyms

AO	Area of Operations
AR	Army Regulation
AUMF	Authorization for the Use of Military Force
CAT	Convention Against Torture
CIA	Central Intelligence Agency
CCR	Center for Constitutional Rights
CTC	Counterterrorism Center
DCI	Director of Central Intelligence
DO	Directorate of Operations inside the CIA
DoD	Department of Defense
DOJ	Department of Justice
DRV	Democratic Republic of Vietnam
EITs	Enhanced Interrogation Techniques
EO	Executive Order
FBI	Federal Bureau of Investigation
FISA	Foreign Intelligence Surveillance Act
FM	Field Manual
FWMAF	Free World Military Assistance Force
GWOT	Global War on Terror
HPSCI	House Permanent Select Committee on Intelligence
HRE	Human Resource Exploitation training manual
HUMINT	Human Intelligence
IC	Intelligence Community
ICC	International Criminal Court

ICCPR	International Covenant on Civil and Political Rights
ICRC	International Committee of the Red Cross
IG	Inspector General
IR	International Relations
ISAF	International Security Assistance Force
JAG	Judge Advocate General
JPRA	Joint Personnel Recovery Agency
JTF-170	Joint Task Force 170
MACV	Military Assistance Command, Vietnam
MON	Memorandum of Notification
NATO	North Atlantic Treaty Organization
NCIS	Naval Criminal Investigative Service
NGO	Nongovernmental Organization
NSC	National Security Council
POW	Prisoner of War
OLC	Office of Legal Counsel
SASC	Senate Armed Services Committee
SERE	Survival, Evasion, Resistance, and Escape training
SJA	Staff Judge Advocate
SSCI	Senate Select Committee on Intelligence
UCMJ	Uniform Code of Military Justice
UDHR	Universal Declaration of Human Rights
VC	Viet Cong
WPR	War Powers Resolution

NOTES

1. INTRODUCTION

1. Jack L. Goldsmith, *The Terror Presidency: Law and Judgment Inside the Bush Administration* (New York: Norton, 2007).
2. "The Senate Intelligence Committee's Report on the CIA's Detention and Interrogation Program," *Washington Post*, December 9, 2014, http://www.washingtonpost.com/wp-srv /special/national/cia-interrogation-report/document/.
3. "Majority Says CIA's Harsh Interrogations Justified," *Washington Post*, http://www .washingtonpost.com/page/2010-2019/WashingtonPost/2014/12/16/National-Politics /Polling/release_376.xml.
4. Karen J. Greenberg and Joshua L. Dratel, eds., *The Torture Papers: The Road to Abu Ghraib* (New York: Cambridge University Press, 2005); Jane Mayer, *The Dark Side: The Inside Story of How the War on Terror Turned Into a War on American Ideals*, reprint ed. (New York: Anchor, 2009); Barton Gellman, *Angler: The Cheney Vice Presidency*, reprint ed. (New York: Penguin, 2009); David Cole, ed., *Torture Memos: Rationalizing the Unthinkable* (New York: The New Press, 2009); David Cole, "Taking Responsibility for Torture," *The New Yorker*, December 9, 2014, http://www.newyorker.com/news/news-desk/taking-responsibility -torture; John Yoo, *The Powers of War and Peace: The Constitution and Foreign Affairs After 9/11* (Chicago: University of Chicago Press, 2005); John Yoo, *War by Other Means: An Insider's Account of the War on Terror* (New York: Atlantic Monthly Press, 2006).
5. "Embedded norm" is the phrase first coined in Judith Goldstein and Robert Keohane, eds., *Ideas and Foreign Policy: Beliefs, Institutions, and Political Change* (Ithaca, N.Y.: Cornell University Press, 1993). The authors examine the relationship between norm embeddedness and foreign policy. They argue that ideas affect policy through three distinct causal pathways: by providing road maps that increase clarity about ends-means relationships, by

affecting outcomes of strategic importance in which there is no unique equilibrium, and by becoming embedded in political institutions.

6. Frank Schimmelfennig, "Strategic Calculation and International Socialization: Membership Incentives, Party Constellations, and Sustained Compliance in Central and Eastern Europe," *International Organization* 59, no. 4 (2005): 827–860.

7. Various scholars use different terminology to signify embeddedness. Andrew P. Cortell and James W. Davis Jr., in "How Do International Institutions Matter? The Domestic Impact of International Rules and Norms," *International Studies Quarterly* 40, no. 4 (December 1996): 451–478, use the term "salient"; Martha Finnemore and Kathryn Sikkink, in "International Norm Dynamics and Political Change," *International Organization* 52, no. 4 (October 1998): 887–917, use the terminology of "internalized norms"; and Jeffrey Checkel, in "Why Comply? Social Learning and European Identity Change," *International Organization* 55, no. 03 (June 2001): 553–588, prefers the use of the phrases "diffused norms" or "socialized norms." I will use the term "embedded norm" to capture all of these meanings.

8. Cortell and Davis, "How Do International Institutions Matter?"

9. Finnemore and Sikkink, "International Norm Dynamics and Political Change," 895.

10. Harold Hongju Koh, "Why Do Nations Obey International Law?" *Yale Law Journal*, Faculty Scholarship Series, 106 (1997): 2599–2659.

11. International Committee of the Red Cross, "South Sudan: World's Newest Country Signs up to the Geneva Conventions," news release, July 19, 2012, https://www.icrc.org/eng /resources/documents/news-release/2012/south-sudan-news-2012-07-09.htm.

12. United Nations, "Convention Against Torture and Other Cruel, Inhuman, or Degrading Treatment or Punishment," December 10, 1984, http://www.un.org/en/ga/search/view _doc.asp?symbol=A/RES/39/46.

13. Article 1: For the purposes of this convention, the term "torture" means any act by which severe pain or suffering, whether physical or mental, is intentionally inflicted on a person for such purposes as obtaining from him or a third person information or a confession, punishing him for an act he or a third person has committed or is suspected of having committed, or intimidating or coercing him or a third person, or for any reason based on discrimination of any kind, when such pain or suffering is inflicted by or at the instigation of or with the consent or acquiescence of a public official or other person acting in an official capacity. It does not include pain or suffering arising only from, inherent in, or incidental to lawful sanctions.

Article 2.2: No exceptional circumstances whatsoever, whether a state of war or a threat of war, internal political instability, or any other public emergency, may be invoked as a justification of torture.

14. Koh, "Why Do Nations Obey International Law?"

15. Theodor Meron, "The Time Has Come for the United States to Ratify Geneva Protocol I," *American Journal of International Law* 88, no. 4 (October 1994): 678–686.

16. United Nations International Criminal Tribunal for the Former Yugoslavia, "Final Report to the Prosecutor by the Committee Established to Review the NATO Bombing Campaign Against the Federal Republic of Yugoslavia," June 13, 2000, http://www.icty.org/sid/10052#IVA4c.

17. The term "new sovereigntists" is explained in greater detail in Peter J. Spiro, "The New Sovereigntists: American Exceptionalism and Its False Prophets," *Foreign Affairs*, December 2000, https://www.foreignaffairs.com/articles/united-states/2000-11-01/new-sovereigntists-american-exceptionalism-and-its-false-prophets.

18. International Court of Justice, *Military and Paramilitary Activities in and Against Nicaragua: Nicaragua v. United States of America* (The Hague, 1986), 98.

19. Alberto R. Gonzales, "Decision Re Application of the Geneva Convention on Prisoners of War to the Conflict with al-Qaeda and the Taliban," in *The Torture Papers*, ed. Greenberg and Dratel, 118–121.

20. George W. Bush, "Guard and Reserves 'Define Spirit of America': Remarks by the President to Employees at the Pentagon," September 17, 2001, http://georgewbush-whitehouse.archives.gov/news/releases/2001/09/20010917-3.html.

21. Dick Cheney, "Remarks at the 56th Annual Alfred E. Smith Memorial Foundation Dinner," Waldorf-Astoria Hotel, New York, October 18, 2001, http://georgewbush-whitehouse.archives.gov/vicepresident/news-speeches/speeches/vp20011018.html.

22. Ibid.

23. Bob Woodward, "CIA Told to Do 'Whatever Necessary' to Kill Bin Laden," *Washington Post*, October 21, 2001, http://www.washingtonpost.com/wp-dyn/content/article/2007/11/18/AR2007111800655.html.

24. George W. Bush, "Military Order of November 13, 2001: 'Detention, Treatment, and Trial of Certain Non-Citizens in the War Against Terrorism,'" 66 Federal Register 222, National Archives and Records Administration, November 16, 2001, http://www2.gwu.edu/~nsarchiv/torturingdemocracy/documents/20011113.pdf.

25. Ibid.

26. Elisabeth Bumiller and David Johnston, "Bush to Subject Terrorism Suspects to Military Trials," *New York Times*, November 14, 2001, http://www.nytimes.com/2001/11/14/national/14DETA.html.

27. Ibid.

28. Laura A. Dickinson, "Using Legal Process to Fight Terrorism: Detentions, Military Commissions, International Tribunals, and the Rule of Law," *Southern California Law Review* 75, no. 1 (2001–2002): 1416.

29. Ibid., 1415.

30. Ibid., 1417–1418. The author goes on to state: "The procedural rules offered in the regulations appear to be largely for show. Acquittals may mean nothing."

31. Ruth Wedgwood, "Al Qaeda, Terrorism, and Military Commissions," *American Journal of International Law* 96, no. 2 (April 2002): 329.

32. Ibid.

33. Bumiller and Johnston, "Bush to Subject Terrorism Suspects to Military Trials."

34. Ibid.

35. David Cole, "Enemy Aliens," *Georgetown Law Faculty Publications and Other Works*, January 1, 2002, http://scholarship.law.georgetown.edu/facpub/956.

36. John Yoo, "Application of Treaties and Laws to Al Qaeda and Taliban Detainees," in *The Torture Papers*, ed. Greenberg and Dratel, 38–79.

37. "A Guide to the Memos on Torture," *New York Times*, June 25, 2004, http://www.nytimes.com/ref/international/24MEMO-GUIDE.html.

38. Jay Bybee, "Standards of Conduct for Interrogation Under 18 U.S.C. §§ 2340–2340a," in *The Torture Papers*, ed. Greenberg and Dratel, 172.

39. Ibid.

40. Ibid. Individuals within the broader CIA community disagree with the characterization of techniques like waterboarding as torture. Former director Robert James Woolsey has claimed that waterboarding is "not as permanently damaging as other forms of torture" such as "pulling out fingernails." In 2002, the CIA lawyer Jonathan Fredman said that torture "is basically subject to perception," in a meeting at Guantánamo Bay, implying that techniques such as waterboarding would not constitute torture if executed correctly. He said, "If the detainee dies, you're doing it wrong." "Former CIA Directors Defend Waterboarding, Rectal Rehydration," *RT International*, December 12, 2014, https://www.rt.com/usa/214031-cia-directors-waterboarding-torture/; Joby Warrick, "CIA Played Larger Role in Advising Pentagon," *Washington Post*, June 18, 2008, http://www.washingtonpost.com/wp-dyn/content/article/2008/06/17/AR2008061702862.html.

41. See, for instance, the works of Kathleen Clark and David Cole.

42. Kathleen Clark, "Ethical Issues Raised by the OLC Torture Memorandum," *Journal of National Security Law and Policy* 1, no. 455 (2005): 460–461.

43. United Nations, "Convention Against Torture."

44. Central Intelligence Agency, "Central Intelligence Agency, Office of Inspector General Special Review: Counterterrorism Detention and Interrogation Activities," May 7, 2004, appendix B, http://www2.gwu.edu/~nsarchiv/torture_archive/20040507.pdf.

45. Jay Bybee, "Memorandum for John Rizzo, Acting General Counsel of the Central Intelligence Agency: Interrogation of Al Qaeda Operative," Department of Justice, August 1, 2002, http://www.washingtonpost.com/wp-srv/nation/pdf/OfficeofLegalCounsel_Aug2Memo_041609.pdf.

46. Ibid.

47. Central Intelligence Agency, "Central Intelligence Agency, Office of Inspector General Special Review," 20.

48. Joseph Russomanno, *Tortured Logic: A Verbatim Critique of the George W. Bush Presidency* (Dulles, Va.: Potomac Books, 2011).

49. Jeffrey Legro, *Rethinking the World: Great Power Strategies and International Order* (Ithaca, N.Y.: Cornell University Press, 2005).

50. Alexander L. George and Andrew Bennett, *Case Studies and Theory Development in the Social Science* (Cambridge, Mass.: MIT Press, 2005).

51. Emmanuel Adler, "Constructivism and International Relations," in *Handbook of International Relations*, ed. Walter Carlsnaes, Thomas Risse, and Beth A. Simmons (London: Sage, 2002), 102.

52. Vaughn P. Shannon, "Norms Are What States Make of Them: The Political Psychology of Norm Violation," *International Studies Quarterly* 44, no. 2 (June 1, 2000): 293–316.

53. Finnemore and Sikkink, "International Norm Dynamics and Political Change," 904.

54. Wayne Sandholtz, *Prohibiting Plunder: How Norms Change* (Oxford: Oxford University Press, 2007), 9.

55. Ibid., 10.

56. Mayer, *The Dark Side*.

57. Greenberg and Dratel, eds., *The Torture Papers*.

58. Cole, "Taking Responsibility for Torture"; Cole, "Enemy Aliens"; Cole, *Torture Memos*.

59. Yoo, "Application of Treaties and Laws to Al Qaeda and Taliban Detainees"; Yoo, *The Powers of War and Peace*; Yoo, *War by Other Means*.

60. Sandholtz, *Prohibiting Plunder*.

61. Martha Finnemore, *National Interests in International Society* (Ithaca, N.Y.: Cornell University Press, 1996), 2; emphasis added.

62. Jeffrey T. Checkel, "Why Comply? Social Learning and European Identity Change," *International Organization* 55, no. 3 (June 2001): 579.

63. John Yoo, "From Guantanamo to Abbottabad," *Wall Street Journal*, May 4, 2011, http://www.wsj.com/articles/SB10001424052748703834804576301032595527372.

64. Jarett Murphy, "Rumsfeld Visits Abu Ghraib," May 14, 2004, http://www.cbsnews.com/news/rumsfeld-visits-abu-ghraib/.

65. Karl Rove, Hardball with Chris Matthews: Karl Rove Q&A—In-Depth Discussion on Bolton, Iraq, and Downing St. Memo, interview by Chris Matthews, June 22, 2005, http://www.nbcnews.com/id/8306049/ns/msnbc-hardball_with_chris_matthews/t/karl-rove-q/.

66. Adam Goldman and Julie Tate, "Captives Held by Islamic State Were Waterboarded," *Washington Post*, August 28, 2014, http://www.washingtonpost.com/world/national-security/captives-held-by-islamic-state-were-waterboarded/2014/08/28/2b4e1962-2ec9-11e4-9b98-848790384093_story.html.

67. U.S. Department of State, "Foreign Relations of the United States, 1964–1968, Volume III, Vietnam," https://www.state.gov/www/about_state/history/vol_iii/109.html.

68. J. A. Koch, *The Chieu Hoi Program in South Vietnam, 1963–1971* (Washington, D.C.: RAND Corporation, 1973).

69. Seymour M. Hersh, "The My Lai Massacre," *St. Louis Post-Dispatch*, November 25, 1969.

70. James F. Gebhardt, "The Road to Abu Ghraib: U.S. Army Detainee Doctrine and Experience," *Military Review* 85, no. 1 (January 1, 2005), https://www.questia.com/library/journal/1G1-129813229/the-road-to-abu-ghraib-u-s-army-detainee-doctrine.

2. HISTORY OF POW TREATMENT IN THE UNITED STATES: FROM THE REVOLUTIONARY WAR TO THE KOREAN WAR

1. U.S. Catholic Bishops, "The Challenge of Peace: God's Promise and Our Response," May 3, 1983, http://www.osjspm.org/the_challenge_of_peace_1.aspx.

2. Oran R. Young, "Regime Dynamics: The Rise and Fall of International Regimes," in *International Cooperation: Building Regimes for Natural Resources and the Environment* (Ithaca, N.Y.: Cornell University Press, 1989).

3. John S. Cooke, "Introduction: Fiftieth Anniversary of the Uniform Code of Military Justice Symposium," *Military Law Review* 165 (September 2000), http://www.loc.gov/rr/frd /Military_Law/Military_Law_Review/pdf-files/276085~1.pdf.

4. Edmund M. Morgan, "The Background of the Uniform Code of Military Justice," *Military Law Review* 28 (April 1965), http://www.loc.gov/rr/frd/Military_Law/Military_Law _Review/pdf-files/277077~1.pdf.

5. Ibid.

6. Worthington Chauncey Ford, ed., *Journals of the Continental Congress, 1774–1789* (Washington, D.C.: Government Printing Office, 1906).

7. Alex Markels, "Will Terrorism Rewrite the Laws of War?" *NPR*, December 6, 2005, http:// www.npr.org/2005/12/06/5011464/will-terrorism-rewrite-the-laws-of-war; John C. Miller, *Triumph of Freedom, 1775–1783* (Boston: Little, Brown, 1948).

8. Ibid.

9. Armstrong Starkey, "Paoli to Stony Point: Military Ethics and Weaponry During the American Revolution," *Journal of Military History* 58, no. 1 (1994): 24.

10. "Treaty of Amity and Commerce Between His Majesty the King of Prussia, and the United States of America" (Avalon Project, Yale University, September 10, 1785), http://avalon .law.yale.edu/18th_century/prus1785.asp; Peter D. Trooboff, ed., "Introduction," in *Law and Responsibility in Warfare: The Vietnam Experience* (Chapel Hill: University of North Carolina Press, 1975).

11. "Treaty of Amity and Commerce, 1785."

12. "Punishment for War Crimes: Duty: Or Discretion?" *Michigan Law Review* 69, no. 7 (June 1, 1971): 1312–1346.

13. "Treaty with Morocco" (Avalon Project, Yale University, July 28, 1786), http://avalon.law .yale.edu/18th_century/bar1786t.asp.

14. Ralph Robinson, "Retaliation for the Treatment of Prisoners in the War of 1812," *American Historical Review* 49, no. 1 (October 1, 1943): 65–70.

15. Andrew Lambert, "A British Perspective on the War of 1812," *PBS*, http://www.pbs.org /wned/war-of-1812/essays/british-perspective/.

16. "Prisoners of War in 1812," *PBS*, http://www.pbs.org/wned/war-of-1812/essays/prisoners-war/.

17. Ibid.

18. George G. Lewis and John Mewha, *History of Prisoner of War Utilization by the United States Army, 1776–1945* (Washington, D.C.: Department of the Army, 1955).

19. Office of the District Marshal for Massachusetts, "Document Regarding the Parole of Captain Henry Nelles, Prisoner of War, August 10, 1814," August 10, 1814, Archives of Ontario, http://www.archives.gov.on.ca/en/explore/online/1812/big/big_073_parole_terms.aspx.

20. Catherine Prendergast, "Extract from an Original Letter from Catherine Prendergast (Mayville) to William Merritt (Greenbush)," September 7, 1814, Archives of Ontario, http://www.archives.gov.on.ca/en/explore/online/1812/prisoners.aspx#merritt.

21. Donald R. Hickey, *The War of 1812: A Short History* (Champaign: University of Illinois Press, 1995).

22. "Treaty of Peace and Amity Between His Britannic Majesty and the United States of America (Treaty of Ghent)" (Avalon Project, Yale University, 1814), http://avalon.law.yale.edu/19th_century/ghent.asp.

23. Paul J. Springer, *America's Captives: Treatment of POWs from the Revolutionary War to the War on Terror* (Lawrence: University Press of Kansas, 2010), 68.

24. Ibid.

25. Richard R. Flores, "Memory-Place, Meaning, and the Alamo," *American Literary History* 10, no. 3 (Autumn 1998): 428–445.

26. Springer, *America's Captives*, 72.

27. Waddy Thompson, *Recollections of Mexico* (New York: Wiley and Putnam, 1846).

28. Stephanie Carvin, *Prisoners of America's Wars: From the Early Republic to Guantanamo* (New York: Columbia University Press, 2010); Robert Doyle, *The Enemy in Our Hands: America's Treatment of Prisoners of War from the Revolution to the War on Terror*, repr. ed. (Lexington: University Press of Kentucky, 2011); ibid.

29. George S. Prugh, "The Code of Conduct for the Armed Forces," *Columbia Law Review* 56, no. 5 (May 1, 1956): 678–707.

30. Carvin, *Prisoners of America's Wars*.

31. Ibid., 54.

32. "A Philadelphia Quaker," *Anti-Slavery Bugle*, June 26, 1846.

33. "General Veja Taken Prisoner!" *Jeffersonian Republican*, May 28, 1846.

34. Carvin, *Prisoners of America's Wars*, 59–60.

35. Doyle, *The Enemy in Our Hands*, 87–88.

36. Richard Shelly Hartigan, *Lieber's Code and the Law of War* (Chicago: Precedent, 1983).

37. Markels, "Will Terrorism Rewrite the Laws of War?"

38. Gregory A. Raymond, "Lieber and the International Laws of War," in *Francis Lieber and the Culture of the Mind*, ed. Charles R. Mack and Henry H. Lesesne (Columbia: University of South Carolina Press, 2005).

39. Frank Friedel, *Francis Lieber: Nineteenth-Century Liberal* (Baton Rouge: Louisiana State University Press, 1947).

40. Bryan Whitman, W. Hays Parks, and Pierre-Richard Prosper, "Department of Defense Briefing on Humane Treatment of Iraqi and U.S. Prisoners of War under Geneva Convention" (International Information Programs, 2003), http://www.defense.gov/Transcripts/Transcript.aspx?TranscriptID=2281.

41. Burrus M. Carnahan, "Lincoln, Lieber, and the Laws of War: The Origins and Limits of the Principle of Military Necessity," *American Journal of International Law* 92, no. 2 (April 1, 1998): 213–231.

42. Hartigan, *Lieber's Code and the Law of War*.

43. Francis Lieber, "General Orders No. 100 : The Lieber Code—Instructions for the Government of Armies of the United States in the Field" (Avalon Project, Yale University, April 24, 1863), http://avalon.law.yale.edu/19th_century/lieber.asp.

44. Ibid.

45. Geoffrey Best, *Humanity in Warfare: The Modern History of the International Law of Armed Conflicts* (London: Methuen, 1983).

46. Carnahan, "Lincoln, Lieber, and the Laws of War"; Hartigan, *Lieber's Code and the Law of War.*

47. L. Lynn Hogue, "Lieber's Military Code and Its Legacy," in *Francis Lieber and the Culture of the Mind*, ed. Charles R. Mack and Henry H. Lesesne (Columbia: University of South Carolina Press, 2005).

48. Ibid.

49. Friedel, *Francis Lieber*; Hartigan, *Lieber's Code and the Law of War.*

50. Best, *Humanity in Warfare*, 155.

51. "Laws and Customs of War on Land (Hague II); July 29, 1899," http://avalon.law.yale.edu/19th_century/hague02.asp.

52. "Convention for the Amelioration of the Condition of the Wounded and Sick in Armies in the Field (The Convention of 1906)," July 6, 1906, https://www.icrc.org/ihl/INTRO/180?OpenDocument.

53. Carvin, *Prisoners of America's Wars*, 85.

54. "Hague Convention Respecting the Laws and Customs of War on Land and Its Annex: Regulations Concerning the Laws and Customs of War on Land (Hague IV)," October 18, 1907, https://www.icrc.org/applic/ihl/ihl.nsf/INTRO/195.

55. Carvin, *Prisoners of America's Wars*, 85; Springer, *America's Captives*, 122; Tracy Fisher, "At Risk in No-Man's Land: United States Peacekeepers, Prisoners of War, and the Convention on the Safety of United Nations and Associated Personnel," *Minnesota Law Review* 85 (2001–2000): 669.

56. "Rules of Land Warfare" (Government Printing Office, 1914), 7, http://www.loc.gov/rr/frd/Military_Law/pdf/rules_warfare-1914.pdf.

57. Carvin, *Prisoners of America's Wars*, 85; Springer, *America's Captives*, 122; Fisher, "At Risk in No-Man's Land," 669.

58. Article 24 of the Geneva Convention states: "The provisions of the present Convention are obligatory only on the Contracting Powers, in case of war between two or more of them. The said provisions shall cease to be obligatory if one of the belligerent Powers should not be signatory to the Convention." Similarly, Article 2 of the Hague Convention reads: "The provisions contained in the Regulations referred to in Article 1, as well as in the present Convention, do not apply except between Contracting powers, and then only if all the belligerents are parties to the Convention."

59. Carvin, *Prisoners of America's Wars*, 86.

60. U.S. Department of State, "Papers Relating to the Foreign Relations of the United States, 1918. Supplement 2, The World War," 7, http://digicoll.library.wisc.edu/cgi-bin/FRUS/FRUS-idx?type=article&did=FRUS.FRUS1918Supp02.i0007&id=FRUS.FRUS1918Supp02&isize=M.

61. Ibid.

62. Ibid.

63. Ibid., 48–49.
64. Ibid., 49–50.
65. James Wilford Garner, *International Law and the World War* (London: Longmans, Green, 1920), 1:21–22.
66. Doyle, *The Enemy in Our Hands*, 168.
67. General Orders No. 106, General Headquarters American Expeditionary Forces, France. Cited in Fisher, "At Risk in No-Man's Land."
68. Doyle, *The Enemy in Our Hands*, 176.
69. U.S. Department of State, "FRUS Supplement 2: The World War," 51–53; Carvin, *Prisoners of America's Wars*, 86. For more on reprisals, see the works of Daniel W. Hill and Michael D. Ward.
70. U.S. Department of State, "FRUS Supplement 2: The World War," 51–52.
71. Fisher, "At Risk in No-Man's Land," 669.
72. Springer, *America's Captives*, 121.
73. U.S. Department of State, "FRUS Supplement 2: The World War," 55–58.
74. Carvin, *Prisoners of America's Wars*, 87.
75. "Convention Relative to the Treatment of Prisoners of War," July 27, 1929, https://www.icrc.org/applic/ihl/ihl.nsf/INTRO/305?OpenDocument.
76. "Convention Between the United States of America and Other Powers, Relating to Prisoners of War" (Avalon Project, Yale University, July 27, 1929), http://avalon.law.yale.edu/20th_century/geneva02.asp.
77. Iris Chang, *The Rape of Nanking: The Forgotten Holocaust of World War II* (New York: Basic Books, 1997); John W. Dower, *War Without Mercy: Race and Power in the Pacific War* (New York: Pantheon, 1986); Ulrich Strauss, *The Anguish of Surrender: Japanese POWs of World War II* (Seattle: University of Washington Press, 2003).
78. U.S. Department of State, "Foreign Relations of the United States Diplomatic Papers, 1941. General, The Soviet Union," http://digicoll.library.wisc.edu/cgi-bin/FRUS/FRUS-idx?type=header&id=FRUS.FRUS1941v01.
79. Gerald I. A. D. Draper, *The Red Cross Conventions* (London: Stevens & Sons, 1958).
80. Springer, *America's Captives*, 144; Doyle, *The Enemy in Our Hands*, 182–184; S. P. MacKenzie, "The Treatment of Prisoners of War in World War II," *Journal of Modern History* 66, no. 3 (September 1, 1994): 512.
81. "'Coddling' of Italian Prisoners Denied; Citizens of U.S. Found Among Captives," *New York Times*, June 30, 1944; Springer, *America's Captives*, 142; Doyle, *The Enemy in Our Hands*, 190.
82. "'Coddling' of Italian Prisoners Denied."
83. Ibid., 153; "Captives Trained to Police Germany: Hand-Picked Group of Anti-Nazis in Rhode Island to Serve as Aides to AMG," *New York Times*, September 23, 1945.
84. "German Prisoners 74% 'Re-Educated,'" *New York Times*, July 29, 1946.
85. For a discussion of Greek and Uruguayan attempts to insert antipropaganda language into the Geneva Conventions and their being blocked by a British objection, see Dorothy Moulton Mayer, "Educate War Prisoners: Opportunity to Teach Democracy, Lies in Our Prison Camps," *New York Times*, June 18, 1944.

86. Springer, *America's Captives*, 154.

87. Cheryl Benard et al., *The Battle Behind the Wire: U.S. Prisoner and Detainee Operations from World War II to Iraq* (Santa Monica, Calif.: RAND Corporation, 2011).

88. See, for instance, H. Landsberg, "Education Against Fascism: Prison Camps Suggested as Places to Start Experiment," *New York Times*, April 17, 1943, which states in a letter to the editor that "a great deal of attention has recently been devoted by various private and government agencies to the question of re-education of the Fascist nations after the war."

89. "Stimpson Rejects Plan to Teach Nazi War Prisoners Democracy," *New York Times*, November 30, 1944.

90. Springer, *America's Captives*, 154–155.

91. Doyle, *The Enemy in Our Hands*, 194.

92. Former World War II war correspondent Denis Warner describes one particular instance in which a U.S. colonel was instructed by his superiors, "You heard me, Colonel. I want no prisoners. Shoot them all." Denis Warner and Peggy Warner, *The Sacred Warriors: Japan's Suicide Legions* (New York: Avon, 1984); Dower, *War Without Mercy*; MacKenzie, "The Treatment of Prisoners of War in World War II"; Carvin, *Prisoners of America's Wars*.

93. Doyle, *The Enemy in Our Hands*, 209; Joseph Robert White, "Review of Straus, Ulrich, The Anguish of Surrender: Japanese POWs of World War II" (H-War, H-Review, January 2007), http://www.h-net.org/reviews/showrev.php?id=12797.

94. Ibid., 149.

95. Doyle, *The Enemy in Our Hands*, 205.

96. Ibid., 208.

97. MacKenzie, "The Treatment of Prisoners of War in World War II," 517.

98. Doyle, *The Enemy in Our Hands*, 209.

99. Ibid., 206.

100. Carvin, *Prisoners of America's Wars*, 91.

101. "Italian Prisoners May Aid the Army: Chance to Volunteer for Special Non-Combatant Service Units Is Being Offered Them," *New York Times*, May 7, 1944.

102. Springer, *America's Captives*, 147.

103. "Convention Relative to the Treatment of Prisoners of War."

104. Tanya Long, "German War Prisoners Present Complex Issues," *New York Times*, March 9, 1947; MacKenzie, "The Treatment of Prisoners of War in World War II," 502.

105. "1,500,000 Germans Still in U.S. Hands," *New York Times*, December 2, 1945.

106. Long, "German War Prisoners Present Complex Issues"; "French Use of POWs Seen 'Breeding War,'" *New York Times*, January 22, 1947; MacKenzie, "The Treatment of Prisoners of War in World War II," 503; James Bacque, "The Last Dirty Secret of World War Two," *Saturday Night*, September 1989, 31–39.

107. Caroline Moorehead, *Dunant's Dream: War, Switzerland, and the History of the Red Cross* (New York: Carroll & Graf, 1999).

108. "Convention Relative to the Treatment of Prisoners of War (III)," August 12, 1949, https://www.icrc.org/ihl/INTRO/375?OpenDocument.

109. Ibid., Article 4.

110. Ibid.

111. "Convention Between the United States of America and Other Powers, Relating to Prisoners of War," Article 2.

112. "Convention Relative to the Treatment of Prisoners of War (III)," Article 13.

113. Springer, *America's Captives*, 165.

114. Raymond T. Yingling and Robert W. Ginnane, "The Geneva Conventions of 1949," *American Journal of International Law* 46, no. 3 (July 1, 1952): 407.

115. Carvin, *Prisoners of America's Wars*, 96–97.

116. Springer, *America's Captives*, 165.

117. See a list of U.S. legislation and military and executive orders at https://www.icrc.org/applic/ihl/ihl-nat.nsf/vwLawsByCategorySelected.xsp?xp_countrySelected=US.

118. Benard et al., *The Battle Behind the Wire*, 19–20.

119. U.S. Congress Senate Committee on Armed Services, *General Ridgway: Hearings Before the United States Senate Committee on Armed Services, Eighty-Second Congress, Second Session, on May 21, 1952* (U.S. Government Printing Office, 1952), 22.

120. William T. Bowers, William M. Hammond, and George L. MacGarrigle, *Black Soldier, White Army: The 24th Infantry Regiment in Korea* (Honolulu: University Press of the Pacific, 2005).

121. Ibid.

122. Springer, *America's Captives*, 167–168.

123. As quoted in Joseph P. Bialke, "United Nations Peace Operations: Applicable Norms and the Application of the Law of Armed Conflict," *Air Force Law Review* 50 (2001): 50.

124. "Convention Relative to the Treatment of Prisoners of War (III)," Article 16.

125. "Communist Prisoners Wage New Kind of War: Men in Korea Camps Are 'Expendable' and Are Ordered to Riot," *New York Times*, December 21, 1952; Springer, *America's Captives*, 172; Doyle, *The Enemy in Our Hands*, 262; "23 Red Captives Die in New Korean Riot, Quelled by Troops," *New York Times*, March 8, 1953.

126. Springer, *America's Captives*, 163.

127. Benard et al., *The Battle Behind the Wire*, 26; U.S. Congress Senate Committee on Armed Services, *General Ridgway: Hearings Before the Committee on Armed Services*, 9, 17.

128. Doyle, *The Enemy in Our Hands*, 259; Benard et al., *The Battle Behind the Wire*, 27.

129. U.S. Congress Senate Committee on Armed Services, *General Ridgway: Hearings Before the Committee on Armed Services*, 216; Doyle, *The Enemy in Our Hands*, 261; Springer, *America's Captives*, 175.

130. "Korea Foe Charges Allied 'Massacre' of War Prisoners," *New York Times*, March 16, 1952.

131. Doyle, *The Enemy in Our Hands*, 252; Benard et al., *The Battle Behind the Wire*, 24.

132. William Lindsay White, *The Captives of Korea: An Unofficial White Paper on the Treatment of War Prisoners* (New York: Scribner, 1957).

133. "Convention Relative to the Treatment of Prisoners of War (III)," Article 38.

134. White, *The Captives of Korea*, 112–113; Benard et al., *The Battle Behind the Wire*, 25.

135. White, *The Captives of Korea*, 100.

136. Prugh, "The Code of Conduct for the Armed Forces," 133.

137. Ibid., 136.

138. Benard et al., *The Battle Behind the Wire*, 24.

139. U.S. Department of State, "Foreign Relations of the United States, 1952–1954. Korea: Volume XV, Part 1. Document 554," May 26, 1953, http://history.state.gov/historical documents/frus1952–54v15p1/d554.

140. U.S. Department of State, "Foreign Relations of the United States, 1952–1954. Korea: Volume XV, Part 1. Document 30," February 8, 1952, http://history.state.gov/historical documents/frus1952–54v15p1/d30.

141. Jaro Mayda, "The Korean Repatriation Problem and International Law," *American Journal of International Law* 47, no. 3 (July 1, 1953): 417, 427; Springer, *America's Captives*, 174; U.S. Department of State, "Foreign Relations of the United States, 1952–1954. Korea: Volume XV, Part 1. Document 286," October 8, 1952, http://history.state.gov/historicaldocuments /frus1952-54v15p1/d286; U.S. Department of State, "Foreign Relations of the United States, 1952–1954. Korea: Volume XV, Part 1. Document 197," June 30, 1952, http://history.state.gov /historicaldocuments/frus1952-54v15p1/d197.

142. United Nations, "Resolutions Adopted on the Reports of the First Committee, United Nations General Assembly, 399th Plenary Meeting, 7th Session," December 3, 1952, http:// www.worldlii.org/int/other/UNGARsn/1952/101.pdf; Jean Pictet, *Humanitarian Law and the Protection of War Victims* (Geneva: Henry Dunant Institute, 1975), 113–114.

143. Doyle, *The Enemy in Our Hands*, 165–168.

144. Springer, *America's Captives*, 173.

145. U.S. Congress Senate Committee on Armed Services, *General Ridgway: Hearings Before the Committee on Armed Services*, 25.

3. MODERN POW TREATMENT IN THE UNITED STATES: THE VIETNAM WAR, THE GENEVA CONVENTIONS, AND THE PRE-9/11 ERA

1. U.S. Department of State, "Foreign Relations of the United States, 1964–1968, Volume III, Vietnam, June–December 1965, Document 117," August 10, 1965, https://history.state.gov /historicaldocuments/frus1964-68v03/d117.

2. Frederic L. Borch, *Judge Advocates in Combat: Army Lawyers in Military Operations from Vietnam to Haiti* (Washington, D.C.: Government Printing Office, 2001), 20.

3. U.S. Department of State, "Foreign Relations of the United States, 1964–1968, Volume III, Vietnam, June–December 1965, Document 172," October 20, 1965, https://history.state.gov /historicaldocuments/frus1964-68v03/d172. After Ngo Dinh Diem's execution in November 1963, South Vietnam struggled to secure a stable leader for the government. After several unsuccessful coups, the leaders of the military appointed Nguyen Cao Ky prime minister. Ky was prime minister from 1965 to 1967, the time period in which the critical decisions regarding POW treatment were made.

4. George S. Prugh, *Law at War: Vietnam, 1964–1973* (Washington, D.C.: Department of the Army, 1975), 62.

5. Roger H. Hull and John C. Novogrod, *Law and Vietnam: Roger H. Hull and John C. Novogrod* (New York: Oceana, 1968).

6. Jeffrey J. Clarke, *Advice and Support: The Final Years, 1965–1973* (Washington, D.C.: Government Printing Office, 1988).

7. U. Alexis Johnson, "A Plan for the Development of Procedures and Facilities for Handling Combat Captives," ed. U.S. Army (U.S. National Archives, Suitland, Md., 1965).

8. Prior to partition, Vietnam acceded to the Prisoners of War Convention on November 14, 1953. See 181 UN Treaty Series 351 (1953).

9. After partition, North Vietnam acceded separately to the Prisoners of War Convention on June 28, 1957. See 274 UN Treaty Series 339 (1957). Though the government in North Vietnam ratified the treaty, it registered several reservations. Notably, one reservation related to Article 85 of the Third Geneva Convention, under which POWs "prosecuted under the laws of the Detaining Power for acts committed prior to capture shall retain, even if convicted, the benefits of the present Convention." See "Convention Relative to the Treatment of Prisoners of War (III)," August 12, 1949, https://www.icrc.org/ihl /INTRO/375?OpenDocument. It was according to Article 85 that the government in Hanoi based their opposition to treating captured American pilots as POWs.

10. Prugh, *Law at War*, 62.

11. "Convention Relative to the Treatment of Prisoners of War (III)."

12. "The Geneva Convention and the Treatment of Prisoners of War in Vietnam," *Harvard Law Review* 80, no. 4 (February 1, 1967): 851–868.

13. Kristina Daugirdas and Julian Mortenson, "Contemporary Practice of the United States Relating to International Law," *American Society of International Law* 60, no. 1 (1966), http://repository.law.umich.edu/articles/948.

14. Howard S. Levie, "Maltreatment of Prisoners of War in Vietnam," in *The Vietnam War and International Law*, ed. Richard A. Falk (Princeton, N.J.: Princeton University Press, 1969), 2:95; U.S. Army Chief of Staff, "U.S. Actions to Prevent War Crimes by U.S. and Republic of Vietnam Armed Forces" (Suitland, Md.: U.S. National Archives, 1970).

15. Prugh, *Law at War*, 63.

16. U.S. Department of State, "Foreign Relations of the United States, 1964–1968, Volume V, Vietnam, 1967," https://history.state.gov/historicaldocuments/frus1964-68v05.

17. "Convention Relative to the Treatment of Prisoners of War (III)."

18. Levie, "Maltreatment of Prisoners of War in Vietnam," 95–96.

19. Vernon E. Davis, *The Long Road Home: U.S. Prisoner of War Policy and Planning in Southeast Asia* (Washington, D.C.: Office of the Secretary of Defense, 2000), 60.

20. "International Review of the Red Cross," 1965, 586, http://www.loc.gov/rr/frd/Military _Law/pdf/RC_Nov-1965.pdf.

21. U.S. Department of State, "Foreign Relations of the United States, 1964–1968, Volume III, Vietnam, June–December 1965, Document 167," October 13, 1965, 167, https://history.state .gov/historicaldocuments/frus1964-68v03/d167.

22. Clarke, *Advice and Support*, 167.

23. Ibid.

24. Ibid.
25. "War Department Basic Field Manual (FM 19-5): Military Police" (United States Government Printing Office, June 14, 1944), 161, http://www.ibiblio.org/hyperwar/USA/ref/FM/PDFs/FM19-5.PDF.
26. "Rules of Land Warfare" (Government Printing Office, 1914), http://www.loc.gov/rr/frd/Military_Law/pdf/rules_warfare-1914.pdf.
27. "Department of the Army Field Manual (FM 19-40): Enemy Prisoners of War and Civilian Interests" (United States Government Printing Office, August 1964), http://www.survivalebooks.com/free%20manuals/1964%20US%20Army%20Vietnam%20War%20Enemy%20Prisoners%20of%20War%20&%20Civilian%20Internees%2056p.pdf.
28. Karen J. Greenberg and Joshua L. Dratel, eds., *The Torture Papers: The Road to Abu Ghraib* (New York: Cambridge University Press, 2005), 283.
29. James F. Gebhardt, "The Road to Abu Ghraib: U.S. Army Detainee Doctrine and Experience," *Military Review* 85, no. 1 (January 1, 2005), https://www.questia.com/library/journal/1G1-129813229/the-road-to-abu-ghraib-u-s-army-detainee-doctrine.
30. Department of the Army, "Report of the Department of the Army Review of the Preliminary Investigations into the My Lai Incident (Volume III: Exhibits, Book I—Directives)," March 14, 1970, http://www.loc.gov/rr/frd/Military_Law/pdf/RDAR-Vol-IIIBook1.pdf.
31. Prugh, *Law at War*, 75.
32. Howard S. Levie, *Documents on Prisoners of War* (Newport, R.I.: Naval War College, 1979), http://archive.org/details/documentsonpriso6olevi.
33. Ibid.
34. Jack L. Goldsmith and Robert Chesney, "Terrorism and the Convergence of Criminal and Military Detention Models," *Stanford Law Review* 60, no. 4 (February 1, 2008): 1079.
35. Ibid.
36. Guenter Lewy, *America in Vietnam* (New York: Oxford University Press, 1980), 366.
37. "U.S. Actions to Prevent War Crimes by U.S. and Republic of Vietnam Armed Forces."
38. Prugh, *Law at War*.
39. "U.S. Actions to Prevent War Crimes by U.S. and Republic of Vietnam Armed Forces."
40. Ibid.
41. "Army Regulation (AR 350-216): Training in the Provisions of the Geneva Conventions for the Protection of War Victims of 1949," April 24, 1967, http://usahec.contentdm.oclc.org/cdm/ref/collection/p16635coll11/id/2587.
42. "U.S. Actions to Prevent War Crimes by U.S. and Republic of Vietnam Armed Forces."
43. Lewy, *America in Vietnam*, 328–329.
44. Frederic L. Borch, *Judge Advocates in Vietnam: Army Lawyers in Southeast Asia, 1959–1975* (Fort Leavenworth, Kan.: U.S. Army Command and General Staff College, 2003), http://www.loc.gov/rr/frd/Military_Law/pdf/JAs_Vietnam.pdf.
45. Seymour Melman, "Prisoners of War and the Wounded in the Field," in *In the Name of America* (Annandale, Md.: Turnpike, 1968), 66.
46. Gebhardt, "The Road to Abu Ghraib," 42.

47. U.S. Department of State, "Foreign Relations of the United States, 1964–1968 Volume III, Vietnam, June–December 1965, Document 182," October 25, 1965, https://history.state.gov /historicaldocuments/frus1964-68v03/d182.

48. Prugh, *Law at War*, 67.

49. Borch, *Judge Advocates in Combat*, 20.

50. Levie, "Maltreatment of Prisoners of War in Vietnam."

51. Prugh, *Law at War*.

52. ICRC, "Report on Visit Made to Phu Quoc Pw Camp" (Suitland, Md.: U.S. National Archives, 1968); ICRC, "Annex to Report on Visit to Phu Quoc Pw Camp" (Suitland, Md.: U.S. National Archives, 1968).

53. Borch, *Judge Advocates in Combat*, 51.

54. Army Concept Team in Vietnam, "Accountability, Classification, and Record/Reporting System for Captured Enemy Personnel" (Suitland, Md.: U.S. National Archives, 1970).

55. Nicole Barrett, "Holding Individual Leaders Responsible for Violations of Customary International Law: The U.S. Bombardment of Cambodia and Laos," *Columbia Human Rights Law Review* 32 (2001): 453–457.

56. Department of Defense, "Department of Defense Directive: DoD Law of War Program," February 22, 2011, http://www.dtic.mil/whs/directives/corres/pdf/231101e.pdf.

57. Mark J. Osiel, "Obeying Orders: Atrocity, Military Discipline, and the Law of War," *California Law Review* 86, no. 5 (October 1998): 943–1129.

58. "Department of Defense Directive: DoD Law of War Program."

59. Philippe Sands, *Torture Team: Rumsfeld's Memo and the Betrayal of American Values* (New York: St. Martin's Press, 2008), 72.

60. J. Hermann Burgers, *The United Nations Convention Against Torture: A Handbook on the Convention Against Torture and Other Cruel, Inhuman, or Degrading Treatment or Punishment* (Dordrecht: Martinus Nijhoff, 1988).

61. Ibid., 40.

62. Iveta Cherneva, "The Drafting History of Article 2 of the Convention Against Torture," *Essex Human Rights Review* 9, no. 1 (June 2012): 6, http://projects.essex.ac.uk/ehrr/V9N1 /CHERNEVA.pdf; United Nations, "UN Document E/CN.4/L.1470: Cruel, Inhuman, or Degrading Treatment or Punishment," March 11, 1979, para. 57.

63. Manfred Nowak and Elizabeth McArthur, *The United Nations Convention Against Torture: A Commentary* (New York: Oxford Commentaries on International Law, 2008); Cherneva, "The Drafting History of Article 2 of the Convention Against Torture," 6–7.

64. Burgers, *The United Nations Convention Against Torture*, 78–79.

65. Ibid., 80.

66. Ibid., 99.

67. Matthew Lippman, "The Development and Drafting of the United Nations Convention Against Torture and Other Cruel Inhuman or Degrading Treatment or Punishment," *Boston College International and Comparative Law Review* 17, no. 2 (August 1, 1994): 312; "Convention Against Torture."

68. Ibid.

69. Edgar F. Raines Jr., *The Rucksack War: U.S. Army Operational Logistics in Grenada, 1983* (Washington, D.C.: U.S. Army Center of Military History, 2010), 195.

70. Stephanie Carvin, *Prisoners of America's Wars: From the Early Republic to Guantanamo* (New York: Columbia University Press, 2010), 119.

71. Raines, *The Rucksack War*, 205.

72. Ibid.

73. Ibid., 356.

74. Carvin, *Prisoners of America's Wars*, 119. Carvin gives a few examples of such worries: There was some concern expressed in the media about POW treatment after a photo of two POWs emerged with their hands tied behind their backs. Amnesty International also sent a telegram to the U.S. mission chief in Grenada expressing concern about alleged camp conditions.

75. Raines, *The Rucksack War*, 484.

76. Ibid.

77. Borch, *Judge Advocates in Combat*, 66.

78. Raines, *The Rucksack War*, 485.

79. "Remember Grenada?" *New York Times*, December 15, 1983, http://www.nytimes.com/1983/12/15/opinion/remember-grenada.html.

80. Carvin, *Prisoners of America's Wars*, 120–121; "Remember Grenada?"

81. "Remember Grenada?"

82. Carvin, *Prisoners of America's Wars*, 121.

83. Ibid.

84. Ibid., 121–122.

85. Kevin H. Govern, "Sorting the Wolves from the Sheep (Military Police PB 19-04-2)," U.S. Army, October 2004, http://www.wood.army.mil/ENGRMAG/pdfs/Oct%2004%20pdfs/Govern.pdf.

86. Ibid.

87. Ibid.

88. Carvin, *Prisoners of America's Wars*, 122.

89. Borch, *Judge Advocates in Combat*, 105.

90. Carvin, *Prisoners of America's Wars*, 122.

91. Department of Defense, "Final Report to Congress: Conduct of the Persian Gulf War," April 1992, 704, http://www.globalsecurity.org/military/library/report/1992/cpgw.pdf.

92. Ibid.

93. Gebhardt, "The Road to Abu Ghraib," 83.

94. Department of Defense, "Final Report to Congress: Conduct of the Persian Gulf War," 662.

95. Ibid.

96. Borch, *Judge Advocates in Combat*.

97. John R. Brinkerhoff, Ted Silva, and John Seitz, "United States Army Reserve in Operation Desert Storm, Enemy Prisoner of War Operations: The 800th Military Police Brigade," ed. Army Reserve Chief (Department of the Army, 1992), 67.

98. Ibid., 67–68.

99. Steven Keeva, "Lawyers in the War Room," *American Bar Association Journal* 77, no. 12 (December 1, 1991): 52–59.

100. "Army Training Circular: Prisoners of War (TC 27-10-2)," Department of the Army, September 17, 1991, http://www.loc.gov/rr/frd/Military_Law/pdf/prisoners-of-war-1991.pdf.

101. Ibid.

102. "Department of the Army Field Manual (FM 34-52): Intelligence Interrogation," September 28, 1992, sec. 1–8, https://fas.org/irp/doddir/army/fm34-52.pdf.

103. William J. Clinton, "Remarks at the Legislative Convention of the American Federation of State, County, and Municipal Employees," March 23, 1999, http://www.presidency.ucsb.edu/ws/?pid=57294.

104. Wippman, "Kosovo and the Limits of International Law," 130.

105. "Crisis in Kosovo: The Prisoners; American Soldiers Were Beaten When Captured, the Pentagon Says," *New York Times*, May 7, 1999, http://www.nytimes.com/1999/05/07/world/crisis-kosovo-prisoners-american-soldiers-were-beaten-when-captured-pentagon.html.

106. "POW Left 'Thank You' Note for Serb Guards," *CNN*, May 4, 1999, http://edition.cnn.com/US/9905/04/prisoners.note/.

107. Susan Sachs, "Crisis in the Balkans: Prisoners; Serbs Release 3 Captured U.S. Soldiers," *New York Times*, May 2, 1999, http://www.nytimes.com/1999/05/02/world/crisis-in-the-balkans-prisoners-serbs-release-3-captured-us-soldiers.html.

4. POW TREATMENT AND LAWYERS

1. U.S. Senate, "Foreign and Military Intelligence: Final Report of the Select Committee to Study Governmental Operations with Respect to Intelligence Activities," Washington, D.C., April 26, 1976, 9, http://www.intelligence.senate.gov/sites/default/files/94755_I.pdf.

2. Frank J. Smist Jr., *Congress Oversees the United States Intelligence Community, 1947–1994*, 2nd ed. (Knoxville: University of Tennessee Press, 1994), 25–81.

3. Loch K. Johnson, *A Season of Inquiry: The Senate Intelligence Investigation* (Lexington: University Press of Kentucky, 1985), 262.

4. Louis Fisher discusses U.S. executive-legislative relations and power struggles in depth in *The Politics of Shared Power* (College Station: Texas A&M University Press, 1998).

5. William G. Howell and Jon C. Pevehouse, *While Dangers Gather: Congressional Checks on Presidential War Powers* (Princeton, N.J.: Princeton University Press, 2007).

6. "Joint Resolution Concerning the War Powers of Congress and the President" (Avalon Project, Yale University, now 1973), http://avalon.law.yale.edu/20th_century/warpower.asp.

7. Alexander Hamilton, "The Federalist No. 8: The Consequences of Hostilities Between the States," November 20, 1787, http://www.constitution.org/fed/federa08.htm.

8. James Madison, "James Madison to Thomas Jefferson," April 2, 1798, http://press-pubs.uchicago.edu/founders/documents/a1_8_11s8.html.

9. *Foreign Intelligence Surveillance Act of 1978, 92 Stat. 1783*, vol. 92, 1978, http://www.gpo.gov/fdsys/pkg/STATUTE-92/pdf/STATUTE-92-Pg1783.pdf.

10. John Rizzo, *Company Man: Thirty Years of Controversy and Crisis in the CIA*, repr. ed. (New York: Scribner, 2014), 47.

11. Gerald R. Ford, "Imperiled Not Imperial," *Time*, November 10, 1980.

12. Arthur M. Schlesinger Jr., *The Imperial Presidency*, repr. ed. (Boston: Mariner, 2004).

13. Ibid., x.

14. Louis Henkin, *Foreign Affairs and the United States Constitution*, 2nd ed. (Oxford: Clarendon, 1997), 27–28.

15. Harold Hongju Koh, *The National Security Constitution: Sharing Power After the Iran-Contra Affair* (New Haven, Conn.: Yale University Press, 1990), 4.

16. Harold Hongju Koh, "War and Responsibility in the Dole-Gingrich Congress," *University of Miami Law Review* 50, no. 1 (January 1996): 6–7.

17. Koh, *The National Security Constitution*, 216; Koh, "War and Responsibility in the Dole-Gingrich Congress," 7.

18. Koh, *The National Security Constitution*, 210–211; Koh, "War and Responsibility in the Dole-Gingrich Congress," 7.

19. Arthur M. Schlesinger Jr., *War and the American Presidency* (New York: Norton, 2005), 53.

20. Ibid., 54.

21. Harold Hongju Koh, "Statement of Harold Hongju Koh Before the Senate Judiciary Committee, Subcommittee on The Constitution on Restoring the Rule of Law," United States Senate, September 16, 2008, http://fas.org/irp/congress/2008_hr/091608koh.pdf.

22. Harold Hongju Koh, *Libya and War Powers* (Washington, D.C.: U.S. Department of State, 2011), http://www.state.gov/s/l/releases/remarks/167250.htm; Paul Starobin, "Harold Koh's Flip-Flop on the Libya Question," *New York Times*, August 6, 2011, http://www.nytimes.com/2011/08/07/opinion/sunday/harold-kohs-flip-flop-on-the-libya-question.html.

23. Starobin, "Harold Koh's Flip-Flop on the Libya Question."

24. Koh, *Libya and War Powers*.

25. Rizzo, *Company Man*, 44–45.

26. Ibid.

27. "In the 1970s the CIA had only a handful of lawyers. But as legal restrictions on CIA activities grew, and despite huge personnel cuts in the 1990s, the number of CIA lawyers rose and rose, and today stands at well over one hundred. The number of lawyers in the Defense Department grew even more steeply during this period, and today stands at over ten thousand, not including reservists." Jack L. Goldsmith, *Power and Constraint: The Accountable Presidency After 9/11* (New York: Norton, 2012), 91.

28. Rizzo, *Company Man*, 73.

29. Ibid., 84–85.

30. Stephanie Carvin, *Prisoners of America's Wars: From the Early Republic to Guantanamo* (New York: Columbia University Press, 2010), 101–102.

31. Goldsmith, *Power and Constraint*, 127.

32. Judge Advocate General's Corps, "The Corps at the End of the 20th Century," *The Judge Advocate General's Corps Regimental History*, https://www.jagcnet.army.mil/8525736A005B E1BE/0/05FE336414E1920D8525735C00642BC0?opendocument&noly=1.

33. Goldsmith, *Power and Constraint*, 126.

34. Ibid., 177.

35. Anthony Zinni, "The SJA in Future Operations," *Marine Corps Gazette* 80, no. 2 (February 1996): 15–17, https://www.mca-marines.org/gazette/1996/02/sja-future-operations.

36. Goldsmith, *Power and Constraint*, 130, 170–172.

37. Ibid., 129–130.

38. Ibid., 129.

39. Philippe Sands, *Torture Team: Rumsfeld's Memo and the Betrayal of American Values* (New York: St. Martin's Press, 2008), 9.

40. "Understanding the Iran-Contra Affair: The Minority Report," Brown University, 2010, http://www.brown.edu/Research/Understanding_the_Iran_Contra_Affair/h-thereport .php.

41. "Reports of the Iran-Contra Committees: Excerpts from the Minority View," *New York Times*, November 17, 1987, http://www.nytimes.com/1987/11/17/world/reports-of-the-iran -contra-committees-excerpts-from-the-minority-view.html.

42. Daniel K. Inouye and Lee H. Hamilton, "Report of the Congressional Committees Investigating the Iran-Contra Affair with Supplemental, Minority, and Additional Views" (Washington, D.C.: U.S. Government Printing Office, November 17, 1987), 20, https:// archive.org/stream/reportofcongress87unit#page/n7/mode/2up.

43. "Understanding the Iran-Contra Affair: The Minority Report."

44. "Cheney in His Own Words," *PBS Frontline*, June 20, 2006, http://www.pbs.org/wgbh /pages/frontline/darkside/themes/ownwords.html#1.

45. "Understanding the Iran-Contra Affair: The Minority Report."

46. Peter J. Spiro, "The New Sovereigntists: American Exceptionalism and Its False Prophets," *Foreign Affairs*, December 2000, https://www.foreignaffairs.com/articles/united-states /2000-11-01/new-sovereigntists-american-exceptionalism-and-its-false-prophets.

47. E. H. Carr, *The Twenty Years' Crisis, 1919–1939: An Introduction to the Study of International Relations* (New York: Harper Perennial, 1964).

48. Ibid., 10–11.

49. Spiro, "The New Sovereigntists," 10–11.

50. Richard K. Betts, "Compromised Command," *Foreign Affairs*, August 2001, https://www .foreignaffairs.com/reviews/review-essay/2001-07-01/compromised-command.

51. David B. Rivkin Jr. and Lee A. Casey, "The Rocky Shoals of International Law," *The National Interest* (Winter 2000–2001), http://nationalinterest.org/article/the-rocky-shoals -of-international-law-523.

52. Carvin, *Prisoners of America's Wars*, 146.

53. Ibid., 145.

54. 9/11 Commission, "Final Report of the National Commission on Terrorist Attacks Upon the United States (The 9/11 Commission Report)," July 22, 2004, 131–132, http://www.9 -11commission.gov/report/911Report.pdf.

55. Benjamin Wittes, *Law and the Long War: The Future of Justice in the Age of Terror* (New York: Penguin, 2009), 20.

56. Ibid., 24.

57. Ibid., 29.

58. Charles J. Dunlap Jr., "Law and Military Interventions: Preserving Humanitarian Values in 21st Conflicts," Humanitarian Challenges in Military Intervention Conference, Washington, D.C., Carr Center for Human Rights Policy, Kennedy School of Government, Harvard University, 2001, 1–2, http://people.duke.edu/~pfeaver/dunlap.pdf.

59. Ibid., 18.

60. Jack L. Goldsmith, *The Terror Presidency: Law and Judgment Inside the Bush Administration* (New York: Norton, 2007), 33.

61. Rizzo, *Company Man*, 190.

62. Department of Justice, "Office of Professional Responsibility's Report of Investigation: The Office of Legal Counsel's Memoranda on Issues Relating to the Central Intelligence Agency's Use of 'Enhanced Interrogation Techniques' on Suspected Terrorists," July 29, 2009, 26, http://fas.org:8080/irp/agency/doj/opr-2nddraft.pdf.

63. Ibid., vi.

64. Jane Mayer, *The Dark Side: The Inside Story of How the War on Terror Turned Into a War on American Ideals*, repr. ed. (New York: Anchor, 2009), 64.

65. Ibid., 67.

66. John C. Yoo and Robert J. Delahunty, "Authority for Use of Military Force to Combat Terrorist Activities Within the United States," U.S. Department of Justice, October 23, 2001, http://nsarchive.gwu.edu/torturingdemocracy/documents/20011023.pdf.

67. Department of Justice, "Office of Professional Responsibility's Report of Investigation," 26.

68. Ibid., 69.

69. Barton Gellman, *Angler: The Cheney Vice Presidency*, repr. ed. (New York: Penguin, 2009), 40–41.

70. "Gonzales wanted Addington in the room because Addington knew things that he didn't. Gonzales came to Washington after a career as a corporate lawyer and a state court judge in Texas. He had thought little about presidential war powers, or national security law, or international law, and he had no experience with Washington bureaucratic politics, or with White House relations with Congress. But these subjects were at the heart of Addington's expertise. In the twenty years between 1981 and 9/11, he had been a lawyer in the CIA, the chief counsel for House of Representative committees on intelligence and international relations, a special assistant in the Reagan White House, the Republican counsel on the Iran-Contra committee, and special assistant and later general counsel to Dick Cheney when he was the Secretary of Defense. These experiences gave Addington a more comprehensive knowledge of national security law than anyone in the executive branch, and made him one of the savviest manipulators of the byzantine executive branch bureaucracy. It also gave him clout with Gonzales, who turned to Addington first for answers to the hard legal questions that arose after the 9/11 attacks." Goldsmith, *The Terror Presidency*, 76–77.

71. Gellman, *Angler*, 136–137.

72. Ibid., 136.

73. Sands, *Torture Team*, 95.

74. In his memoirs, John Rizzo states that he did not cancel the proposed EIT program, even though he had the authority to do so, because he could not live with the guilt if another attack occurred and he had canceled a program that might have stopped it from happening. However, when DCI Tenet asked Rizzo if the EITs were legal, he was unsure of their legality and declared that he would take the techniques to the OLC for their opinion. According to Rizzo, the main reason for this measure was legal deniability for the CIA. He states: "Above all, I wanted a written OLC memo in order to give the Agency—for lack of a better term—legal cover. Something that we could keep, and wave around if necessary, in the months and years to come, when memories would fade or be conveniently altered to tack with the shifting political winds." This pattern—Rizzo seeking legal cover by going to the OLC—would repeat itself many more times in the years to come, with Rizzo consistently asking the OLC for refreshed or new opinions that supported the EIT program. In total, from 2002 to 2007, the OLC would issue ten major opinions to the CIA on the legality of the EIT program. Rizzo, *Company Man*, 188–189, 212–216.

75. John Yoo, *War by Other Means: An Insider's Account of the War on Terror* (New York: Atlantic Monthly Press, 2006), 3.

76. Ibid.

77. Ibid., 16.

78. Goldsmith, *The Terror Presidency*, 105.

79. Gellman, *Angler*, 292.

80. Goldsmith, *The Terror Presidency*, 85–86.

81. White House, "President's Statement on Signing of H.R. 2863, the 'Department of Defense, Emergency Supplemental Appropriations to Address Hurricanes in the Gulf of Mexico, and Pandemic Influenza Act, 2006,'" December 30, 2005, http://georgewbush -whitehouse.archives.gov/news/releases/2005/12/20051230-8.html.

82. Alexis de Tocqueville, "The Federal Constitution (Chapter VIII)," in *Democracy in America*, ed. Isaac Kramnick, trans. Gerald Bevan, vol. 1 (London: Penguin, 2003).

83. Goldsmith, *The Terror Presidency*, 10.

84. Yoo, *The Powers of War and Peace*, viii.

85. Ibid., 17–18.

86. Ibid., 11–12.

87. Ibid., 18–19, 24–27.

88. Yoo, *War by Other Means*, 234.

89. Ibid., 180.

90. Yoo, *The Powers of War and Peace*, ix.

91. Ibid., x.

92. Goldsmith, *The Terror Presidency*, 69.

93. The White House lawyers had support from some international relations scholars as well, such as Richard Betts. In his 2007 book *The Enemies of Intelligence*, Betts argues that inflexible civil-liberties lawyers place "dangerous constraints on the government's ability to gather intelligence, especially the type that offers the best hope of foiling terrorist plots." In Betts's mind, the lawyers' unwillingness to admit any tradeoff between security

and liberty makes them an implacable foe. "Libertarian absolutists mimic the National Rifle Association," he states. "Like ardent proponents of the right to bear arms, they see even a limited concession as the first step in the unraveling of all privacy rights." Richard K. Betts, *The Enemies of Intelligence* (New York: Columbia University Press, 2007), 162–163.

94. Ibid., 124.
95. Ibid.
96. Gellman, *Angler*, 345.
97. Ibid., 355.
98. Sands, *Torture Team*, 73.
99. Goldsmith, *Power and Constraint*, 176.
100. Sands, *Torture Team*, 91.
101. Ibid., 134.
102. Ibid., 175–176.
103. Goldsmith, *The Terror Presidency*, 63.
104. Sands, *Torture Team*, 213.
105. Yoo, *War by Other Means*, 36.
106. Sands, *Torture Team*, 185.
107. Jack L. Goldsmith and Eric A. Posner, *The Limits of International Law* (Oxford: Oxford University Press, 2006), 225.
108. Yoo, *War by Other Means*, 37.
109. Ibid., 29–30.
110. The full quote from Gonzales's memo to Bush states: "This new paradigm renders obsolete Geneva's strict limitations on questioning of enemy prisoners and renders quaint some of its provisions requiring that captured enemy be afforded such things as commissary privileges." Alberto R. Gonzales, "Decision Re Application of the Geneva Convention on Prisoners of War to the Conflict with al-Qaeda and the Taliban," in *The Torture Papers: The Road to Abu Ghraib*, ed. Karen J. Greenberg and Joshua L. Dratel (New York: Cambridge University Press, 2005).
111. "The Senate Intelligence Committee's Report on the CIA's Detention and Interrogation Program," *Washington Post*, December 9, 2014, http://www.washingtonpost.com/wp-srv/special/national/cia-interrogation-report/document/.

5. POW TREATMENT AND POLICY MAKERS

1. Robert Doyle, *The Enemy in Our Hands: America's Treatment of Prisoners of War from the Revolution to the War on Terror*, repr. ed. (Lexington: University Press of Kentucky, 2011), 298.
2. Donna Miles, "Operation Homecoming for Vietnam POWs Marks 40 Years," *American Forces Press Service*, February 12, 2013, http://www.defense.gov/news/newsarticle.aspx?id=119272.

3. Michael J. Allen, *Until the Last Man Comes Home: POWs, MIAs, and the Unending Vietnam War* (Chapel Hill: University of North Carolina Press, 2012), 2–3.

4. Richard Nixon, "Address to the Nation Announcing Conclusion of an Agreement on Ending the War and Restoring Peace in Vietnam," January 23, 1973, http://www.presidency.ucsb.edu/ws/?pid=3808.

5. Norman Kempster, "Shultz Pessimistic on MIA Progress: Warns Families to Brace for Disappointment in New Talks," *Los Angeles Times*, July 19, 1987, http://articles.latimes.com/1987-07-19/news/mn-5056_1_mia-issue.

6. George H. W. Bush, "Remarks to the National League of Families of American Prisoners and Missing in Southeast Asia in Arlington, Virginia," July 24, 1992, http://www.presidency.ucsb.edu/ws/?pid=21263.

7. Allen, *Until the Last Man Comes Home*, 2–3.

8. Jimmy Carter, "State of the Union Address," January 23, 1980, http://www.jimmycarterlibrary.gov/documents/speeches/su80jec.phtml.

9. "Fighting in Panama: The President; A Transcript of Bush's Address on the Decision to Use Force in Panama," *New York Times*, December 21, 1989, http://www.nytimes.com/1989/12/21/world/fighting-panama-president-transcript-bush-s-address-decision-use-force-panama.html.

10. Mark Fineman and James Gerstenzang, "POWs to Be Shields, Iraq Says: Bush Expresses Anger," *Los Angeles Times*, January 22, 1991, http://articles.latimes.com/1991-01-22/news/mn-646_1_gulf-war/2.

11. "Crisis in the Balkans: Clinton's Speech on Kosovo: 'We Also Act to Prevent a Wider War,'" *New York Times*, April 2, 1999, http://www.nytimes.com/1999/04/02/world/crisis-balkans-clinton-s-speech-kosovo-we-also-act-prevent-wider-war.html.

12. Gerald R. Ford, "Executive Order 11905: United States Foreign Intelligence Activities," White House, February 18, 1976, http://fas.org/irp/offdocs/eo11905.htm.

13. Office of the Historian, "Carter and Human Rights, 1977–1981," U.S. Department of State, October 31, 2013, https://history.state.gov/milestones/1977–1980/human-rights.

14. Ibid.

15. Rebecca Gordon, *Mainstreaming Torture: Ethical Approaches in the Post-9/11 United States* (New York: Oxford University Press, 2014), 2–3.

16. Jimmy Carter, "Inaugural Address," January 20, 1977, http://www.presidency.ucsb.edu/ws/?pid=6575.

17. Jimmy Carter, "University of Notre Dame—Address at Commencement Exercises at the University," May 22, 1977, http://www.presidency.ucsb.edu/ws/?pid=7552.

18. Office of the Historian, "Carter and Human Rights, 1977–1981."

19. Prominent examples include the International Convention on the Elimination of All Forms of Racial Discrimination (1994); the International Covenant on Civil and Political Rights (1992); the International Covenant on Economic, Social, and Cultural Rights (never); and the American Convention on Human Rights (never). Date in parenthesis is date of ratification by U.S. Senate.

20. Mark L. Schneider, "Human Rights Policy Under the Carter Administration," *Law and Contemporary Problems* 43 (Spring 1979): 261–267.

21. "Reagan Quotes," *PBS American Experience*, http://www.pbs.org/wgbh/americanexperience/features/general-article/reagan-quotes/.

22. Ronald Reagan, "Address to the Nation on Events in Lebanon and Grenada," October 27, 1983, http://www.reagan.utexas.edu/archives/speeches/1983/102783b.htm.

23. Kevin H. Govern, "Sorting the Wolves from the Sheep (Military Police PB 19-04-2)," U.S. Army, October 2004, http://www.wood.army.mil/ENGRMAG/pdfs/Oct%2004%20pdfs/Govern.pdf.

24. George H. W. Bush, "Remarks at the Annual Convention of the National Religious Broadcasters," January 28, 1991, http://www.presidency.ucsb.edu/ws/?pid=19250.

25. William J. Clinton, "Remarks at the University of Connecticut in Storrs," October 15, 1995, http://www.presidency.ucsb.edu/ws/?pid=50655.

26. Ibid.

27. William J. Clinton, "Statement on Kosovo," March 24, 1999, http://millercenter.org/president/speeches/speech-3932.

28. John M. Broder, "Clinton Offers His Apologies to Guatemala," *New York Times*, March 11, 1999, http://www.nytimes.com/1999/03/11/world/clinton-offers-his-apologies-to-guatemala.html.

29. Sean D. Murphy, *United States Practice in International Law*: Vol. 1, *1999–2001* (Cambridge: Cambridge University Press, 2003), 369.

30. Jennifer K. Harbury, *Truth, Torture, and the American Way: The History and Consequences of U.S. Involvement in Torture* (Boston: Beacon, 2005).

31. Charles Wolfson, "The Legacy of Condoleezza Rice," *CBS News*, December 19, 2008, http://www.cbsnews.com/news/the-legacy-of-condoleezza-rice/.

32. Jack L. Goldsmith, *Power and Constraint: The Accountable Presidency After 9/11* (New York: Norton, 2012), ix.

33. "Text: President Bush Addresses the Nation," *Washington Post*, September 20, 2001, http://www.washingtonpost.com/wp-srv/nation/specials/attacked/transcripts/bushaddress_092001.html.

34. Matthew Levitt, "The Origins of Hezbollah," *The Atlantic*, October 23, 2013, http://www.theatlantic.com/international/archive/2013/10/the-origins-of-hezbollah/280809/.

35. Donald Rumsfeld, *Known and Unknown: A Memoir* (New York: Sentinel, 2012), 555.

36. John Brennan et al., *Face the Nation* transcript, September 11, 2011, interview by Bob Schieffer, http://www.cbsnews.com/news/face-the-nation-transcript-september-11-2011/3/.

37. Department of State, "Remarks with UK Foreign Secretary David Miliband and Google Senior Vice President David Drummond," May 22, 2008, http://2001-2009.state.gov/secretary/rm/2008/05/105182.htm.

38. Jack L. Goldsmith, *The Terror Presidency: Law and Judgment Inside the Bush Administration* (New York: Norton, 2007), 72.

39. George Tenet, *At the Center of the Storm: The CIA During America's Time of Crisis*, repr. ed. (New York: Harper Perennial, 2008).

40. Shaykh Usamah Bin-Mohammed Bin-Ladin et al., "Jihad Against Jews and Crusaders: World Islamic Front Statement," February 23, 1998, http://fas.org/irp/world/para/docs/980223-fatwa.htm.

41. "Bin Laden's Fatwa," *PBS NewsHour*, December 1996, http://www.pbs.org/newshour/updates/military-july-dec96-fatwa_1996/.

42. The 2000 attacks against the USS *Cole* off of the coast of the Aden Harbor in Yemen and the 1998 U.S. embassy attacks in Kenya and Tanzania were both attributed to al-Qaeda.

43. George W. Bush, "Guard and Reserves 'Define Spirit of America': Remarks by the President to Employees at the Pentagon," September 17, 2001, http://georgewbush-whitehouse.archives.gov/news/releases/2001/09/20010917-3.html.

44. Barton Gellman, *Angler: The Cheney Vice Presidency*, repr. ed. (New York: Penguin, 2009), 160.

45. George Tenet, "We're At War," Central Intelligence Agency, September 16, 2001, http://nsarchive.gwu.edu/news/20051209/at_war.pdf.

46. Dick Cheney, *In My Time: A Personal and Political Memoir*, repr. ed. (New York: Threshold Editions, 2012), 522–523.

47. Condoleezza Rice, *No Higher Honor: A Memoir of My Years in Washington* (New York: Broadway Paperbacks, 2012), 500.

48. Rumsfeld, *Known and Unknown*, 576.

49. Tenet, *At the Center of the Storm*, 179.

50. Ibid., 183.

51. Marshall C. Erwin and Amy Belasco, "Intelligence Spending and Appropriations: Issues for Congress," Congressional Research Service, September 18, 2013, http://fas.org/sgp/crs/intel/R42061.pdf.

52. George Tenet, "Written Statement for the Record of the Director of Central Intelligence Before the National Commission on Terrorist Attacks Upon the United States," Central Intelligence Agency, March 24, 2004, https://www.cia.gov/news-information/speeches-testimony/2004/tenet_testimony_03242004.html#Role.

53. James R. Clapper et al., *Current and Projected National Security Threats to the United States* (United States Senate, 2013), http://fas.org/irp/congress/2013_hr/threat.pdf.

54. Tenet, "Written Statement for the Record."

55. "The Secret History," *The New Yorker*, June 22, 2009, http://www.newyorker.com/magazine/2009/06/22/the-secret-history.

56. Loch K. Johnson, *The Threat on the Horizon: An Inside Account of America's Search for Security After the Cold War* (New York: Oxford University Press, 2011), 450–451; Barbara Belejack, "Editorial: Back to Guatemala," *Texas Observer*, June 7, 2002, http://www.texasobserver.org/751-editorial-back-to-guatemala/.

57. Douglas Jehl, "Abundance of Caution and Years of Budget Cuts Are Seen to Limit CIA," *New York Times*, May 11, 2004, http://www.nytimes.com/2004/05/11/us/abundance-of-caution-and-years-of-budget-cuts-are-seen-to-limit-cia.html.

58. Belejack, "Editorial: Back to Guatemala."

59. Bush Memo, "Humane Treatment of al Qaeda and Taliban Detainees," February 7, 2002, http://www.pegc.us/archive/White_House/bush_memo_20020207_ed.pdf.

60. "Psychological Assessment of Zain Al-'Abedin-Al-Abideen Muhammad Hassan a.k.a. Abu Zubaydah," July 24, 2002, https://www.aclu.org/sites/default/files/torturefoia/released /082409/olcremand/20040lc4.pdf.

61. "The Senate Intelligence Committee's Report on the CIA's Detention and Interrogation Program," *Washington Post*, December 9, 2014, http://www.washingtonpost.com/wp-srv /special/national/cia-interrogation-report/document/.

62. David Cole, "'New Torture Files': Declassified Memos Detail Roles of Bush White House and DOJ Officials Who Conspired to Approve Torture," *Just Security*, March 2, 2015, https://www.justsecurity.org/20553/new-torture-files-declassified-memos-detail-roles -bush-wh-doj-officials-conspired-approve-torture/.

63. Philippe Sands, *Torture Team: Rumsfeld's Memo and the Betrayal of American Values* (New York: St. Martin's Press, 2008), 35.

64. Department of Defense, "Memoranda: Counter-Resistance Techniques," 2002, http:// nsarchive.gwu.edu/NSAEBB/NSAEBB127/02.12.02.pdf.

65. The full history and content of the Haynes memo is difficult to cover for several reasons. To begin, as mentioned here, disagreement exists over whether the techniques requested originated from interrogators on the ground in Cuba or whether they were simply responding to pressure from top administration officials. Officials involved in the drafting of the techniques and the accompanying memo—such as Diane Beaver and General Dunlavey—claim they had been urged repeatedly by top administration officials inside the White House and Pentagon to seek new methods for gathering information from the detainees at Guantánamo Bay. This debate is covered in depth in Philippe Sands's book *Torture Team*. After reviewing the available documents and interviewing most of the main actors involved, Sands concludes that it is likely the interrogators at Guantánamo were responding to pressure from the top. But he cannot definitively prove this because of a lack of written records on the communication between administration officials and officials such as Dunlavey. Instead, he must infer and use deductive reasoning to make his case.

The second reason the Haynes memo is difficult to examine is because it is clear that it was relatively insignificant with regard to the actual application of torture to the detainees. The memo was approved in December 2002—yet enhanced interrogation of detainees at Guantánamo had already started by November of that same year. Moreover, the two Bybee memos were published in August 2002, which meant that any further legal review on the permissibility of enhanced interrogation was at that point unnecessary. With the OLC memos in hand, there was no need for the legal opinion of a staff judge advocate such as Diane Beaver.

As a result of these two challenges, the process by which the Haynes memo was *created* is difficult to use as proof of the contestation of the norm of humane treatment. However, the process by which it was *reviewed and approved*—which was largely orchestrated by Haynes himself—serves as a powerful representation of not only the pressing demand for intelligence but also the broader efforts to contest the norms of independent legal analysis within the DoD. Thanks to Sands, this process is well documented and understood. Not only does it reveal Haynes's efforts to minimize the role of the JAGs, but it also helps us understand how the pushback from the JAGs and civilian lawyers inside the DoD, such as Alberto Mora, occurred.

66. Sands, *Torture Team*, 88.

67. Department of Defense, "Memoranda: Counter-Resistance Techniques."

68. Ibid.

69. George W. Bush, "The President's Radio Address," March 8, 2008, http://www.gpo.gov /fdsys/pkg/PPP-2008-book1/pdf/PPP-2008-book1-doc-pg336.pdf.

70. Michael F. Scheuer, Bill Delahunt, and Julianne Smith, *Extraordinary Rendition in U.S. Counterterrorism Policy: The Impact on Transatlantic Relations* (U.S. House of Representatives, 2007), https://fas.org/irp/congress/2007_hr/rendition.pdf.

71. Stephen Grey, "Five Facts and Five Fictions About CIA Rendition," *PBS Frontline*, November 4, 2007, http://www.pbs.org/frontlineworld/stories/rendition701/updates /updates.html.

72. Rice, *No Higher Honor*, 104.

73. Gellman, *Angler*, 129–132.

74. Alexander Hamilton, "The Federalist No. 70: The Executive Department Further Considered," March 15, 1788, http://www.constitution.org/fed/federa70.htm.

75. Ibid.

76. Ibid.

77. Dick Cheney, "Congressional Overreaching in Foreign Policy" (Foreign Policy and the Constitution, American Enterprise Institute, 1989), 4, http://s3.documentcloud.org/documents /339579/congressional-overreaching-cheney.pdf.

78. Gellman, *Angler*, 82.

79. Ibid.

80. Ibid., 190.

81. Ibid.

82. Tenet, *At the Center of the Storm*, 174.

83. Ibid., 170–171.

84. Gellman, *Angler*, 177.

85. Rumsfeld, *Known and Unknown*, 557.

86. Ibid.

87. Goldsmith describes Addington and Cheney: "They had no sense of trading constraint for power. It seemed never to occur to them that it might be possible to increase the President's strength and effectiveness by accepting small limits on his prerogatives in order to secure more significant support from Congress, the courts, or allies. They believed cooperation and compromise signaled weakness and emboldened the enemies of America and the executive branch. When it came to terrorism, they viewed every encounter outside the innermost core of most trusted advisors as a zero-sum game that if they didn't win they would necessarily lose." Goldsmith, *The Terror Presidency*, 126.

88. Alberto R. Gonzales, "Decision Re Application of the Geneva Convention on Prisoners of War to the Conflict with al-Qaeda and the Taliban," in *The Torture Papers: The Road to Abu Ghraib*, ed. Karen J. Greenberg and Joshua L. Dratel (New York: Cambridge University Press, 2005).

6. POW TREATMENT AND INTERROGATORS

1. Donald Rumsfeld, "Pentagon Press Briefing," *CNN*, May 4, 2004, http://www.cnn.com/TRANSCRIPTS/0405/04/se.02.html.

2. Joseph Russomanno, *Tortured Logic: A Verbatim Critique of the George W. Bush Presidency* (Dulles, Va.: Potomac Books, 2011), 269.

3. "Transcript: Bush's Remarks on Iraq at the Army War College," *Washington Post*, May 24, 2004, http://www.washingtonpost.com/wp-dyn/articles/A52723-2004May24_4.html.

4. U.S. Congress Senate Committee on Armed Services, "Inquiry Into the Treatment of Detainees in U.S. Custody," November 20, 2008, xii, http://www.armed-services.senate.gov/imo/media/doc/Detainee-Report-Final_April-22-2009.pdf.

5. Jamie Wilson, "Eight Years for U.S. Soldier Who Abused Prisoners," *The Guardian*, October 22, 2004, http://www.theguardian.com/world/2004/oct/22/usa.iraq.

6. Ben Nuckols, "Military Prosecution in Abu Ghraib Scandal Ends," *Boston Globe*, January 11, 2008, http://www.boston.com/news/nation/articles/2008/01/11/military_prosecution_in_abu_ghraib_scandal_ends/.

7. United Nations, "Convention Against Torture and Other Cruel, Inhuman or Degrading Treatment or Punishment: Addendum—United States of America," June 29, 2005, 65–66, http://www.state.gov/documents/organization/62175.pdf.

8. Tim Golden, "Years After 2 Afghans Died, Abuse Case Falters," *New York Times*, February 13, 2006, http://www.nytimes.com/2006/02/13/national/13bagram.html.

9. Central Intelligence Agency, "CIA Comments on the Senate Select Committee on Intelligence Report on the Rendition, Detention, and Interrogation Program," 44–45, https://www.cia.gov/library/reports/CIAs_June2013_Response_to_the_SSCI_Study_on_the_Former_Detention_and_Interrogation_Program.pdf.

10. James R. Schlesinger, "Final Report of the Independent Panel to Review DoD Detention Operations" (Arlington, Va.: Government Printing Office, August 2004), 28, http://www.npr.org/documents/2004/abuse/schlesinger_report.pdf.

11. Central Intelligence Agency, "CIA Comments on the Senate Select Committee on Intelligence Report on the Rendition, Detention, and Interrogation Program."

12. The SSCI Report highlights several of these instances of congressional testimony on methods and practices. It lists, among others, the CIA testimony to the SSCI on April 24, 2002, regarding Abu Zubaydah's initial interrogation; CIA testimony to the SSCI on September 5, 2002, regarding covert detention facilities and Abu Zubaydah's interrogation; CIA testimony to the SSCI on March 5, 2003, regarding the capture and interrogation of Khalid Sheikh Mohammed; CIA testimony to the SSCI on September 13, 2004, regarding the CIA and abuses at Abu Ghraib prison; and CIA Director Porter Goss's testimony to the SSCI on March 15, 2006, regarding the status of the CIA's detention and interrogation program.

13. In a memo from one of the CIA's overseas black sites discussing the interrogation of Abu Zubaydah, CIA officials wrote: "Our goal was to reach the stage where we have broken any will or ability of subject to resist or deny providing us information (intelligence) to

which he had access. We additionally sought to bring subject to the point that we confidently assess that he does not possess undisclosed threat information, or intelligence that could prevent a terrorist event.'"The Senate Intelligence Committee's Report on the CIA's Detention and Interrogation Program," *Washington Post*, December 9, 2014, 75, http://www.washingtonpost.com/wp-srv/special/national/cia-interrogation-report/document/.

14. Joshua E. S. Phillips recounts the story of U.S. Army prison guards and interrogators in the GWOT. One of them, Jonathan Millantz, is quoted as stating: "'We weren't in the CIA—we were soldiers,' said Millantz. He added that it was reckless 'to give that much power and responsibility to a bunch of guys who were full of hate and resentment—getting shot at and watching their friends get killed . . . seeing people decapitated [in videos]—and then putting those guys in direct control of the people who did these things. [That] was very ironic to me. And I think any human being in that situation would have done similar things.'"Joshua E. S. Phillips, *None of Us Were Like This Before: American Soldiers and Torture* (New York: Verso, 2012), 84.

15. Philippe Sands, *Torture Team: Rumsfeld's Memo and the Betrayal of American Values* (New York: St. Martin's Press, 2008), 124.

16. Carl Levin, "Opening Statement of Senator Carl Levin, Chairman," Treatment of Detainees in U.S. Custody: Hearings Before the Committee on Armed Services, U.S. Senate, Washington, D.C., September 25, 2008, http://www.gpo.gov/fdsys/pkg/CHRG-110shrg47298/html/CHRG-110shrg47298.htm.

17. "The Senate Intelligence Committee's Report on the CIA's Detention and Interrogation Program," 50.

18. "CIA Paid Torture Teachers More Than $80 Million," *NBC News*, December 9, 2014, http://www.nbcnews.com/storyline/cia-torture-report/cia-paid-torture-teachers-more-80-million-n264756.

19. Committee on Armed Services, "Inquiry Into the Treatment of Detainees in U.S. Custody," 23.

20. Scott Shane, "2 U.S. Architects of Harsh Tactics in 9/11's Wake," *New York Times*, August 11, 2009, http://www.nytimes.com/2009/08/12/us/12psychs.html.

21. Ibid.; John Rizzo, *Company Man: Thirty Years of Controversy and Crisis in the CIA*, repr. ed. (New York: Scribner, 2014), 182–183.

22. "The Senate Intelligence Committee's Report on the CIA's Detention and Interrogation Program," n138.

23. "The Senate Intelligence Committee's Report on the CIA's Detention and Interrogation Program."

24. Joseph Tanfani and W. J. Hennigan, "Two Psychologists' Role in CIA Torture Program Comes Into Focus," *Los Angeles Times*, December 14, 2014, http://www.latimes.com/world/afghanistan-pakistan/la-fg-torture-psychologists-20141214-story.html.

25. Department of Defense, "Memorandum for Chief, Inspections Division: 4th Infantry Division Detainee Operations Assessment Trip Report (CONUS Team)," April 2014, 37, https://www.thetorturedatabase.org/files/foia_subsite/pdfs/DOD015937.pdf.

26. Philip Gourevitch, "Exposure: The Woman Behind the Camera at Abu Ghraib," *The New Yorker*, March 24, 2008, http://www.newyorker.com/magazine/2008/03/24/exposure-5.

27. Intelligence Science Board, "Educing Information: Interrogation: Science and Art— Foundations for the Future, Intelligence Science Board (Phase 1 Report)" (Washington, D.C.: National Defense Intelligence College, December 2006), 95, http://www.seas.harvard.edu /courses/ge157/educing.pdf.

28. "The Senate Intelligence Committee's Report on the CIA's Detention and Interrogation Program," 22.

29. R. Jeffrey Smith, "Abu Ghraib Officer Gets Reprimand," *Washington Post*, May 12, 2005, http://www.washingtonpost.com/wp-dyn/content/article/2005/05/11/AR2005051101818 .html.

30. Wilson, "Eight Years for U.S. Soldier Who Abused Prisoners."

31. Antonio M. Taguba, "Taguba Report: AR 15-6 Investigation of the 800th Military Police Brigade," Oversight Report, Investigative File (AR 15-6), May 27, 2004, https://www .thetorturedatabase.org/document/ar-15-6-investigation-800th-military-police -investigating-officer-mg-antonio-taguba-taguba-.

32. Samira Simone, "Abu Ghraib Head Finds Vindication in Newly Released Memos," April 22, 2009, http://www.cnn.com/2009/US/04/22/us.torture.karpinski/.

33. George R. Fay and Anthony R. Jones, "Investigation of the Abu Ghraib Detention Facility and 205th Military Intelligence Brigade" (Baghdad: Department of Defense, 2004).

34. Albert T. Church, "Review of Department of Defense Detention Operations and Detainee Interrogation Techniques" (Washington, D.C.: Office of the Secretary of Defense, March 7, 2005), 6, https://www.aclu.org/sites/default/files/images/torture/asset_upload_file625 _26068.pdf. This review has become known as the Church Report.

35. Ibid., 9.

36. Schlesinger, "Schlesinger Report, 2004," 14.

37. "The Senate Intelligence Committee's Report on the CIA's Detention and Interrogation Program," 57.

38. Rizzo, *Company Man*, 186.

39. Ibid., 182–183.

40. Ibid., 178–179.

41. Sands, *Torture Team*, 61.

42. Church, "Review of Department of Defense Detention Operations," 10.

43. Ibid., 3.

44. Schlesinger, "Schlesinger Report, 2004," 14.

45. Charles H. Jacoby, "Combined Forces Command—Afghanistan Area Operations Report of Inspection," Department of Defense, June 26, 2004, 1, http://www1.umn.edu/humanrts /OathBetrayed/Jacoby%20Report.pdf.

46. Ibid., 5.

47. "The Senate Intelligence Committee's Report on the CIA's Detention and Interrogation Program."

48. Rizzo, *Company Man*, 187.

49. Tom Lasseter, "Day 2: U.S. Abuse of Detainees Was Routine at Afghanistan Bases," *Mc-Clatchy Newspapers*, June 16, 2008, http://www.mcclatchydc.com/news/special-reports/article24484924.html.

50. Phillips, *None of Us Were Like This Before*, 102.

51. Central Intelligence Agency, "KUBARK Counterintelligence Interrogation," July 1963, http://nsarchive.gwu.edu/NSAEBB/NSAEBB122/CIA%20Kubark%201-60.pdf.

52. Ibid.

53. Ibid., 86–87.

54. Central Intelligence Agency, "Memorandum for Executive Secretary, CIA Management Committee: 'Family Jewels,'" May 16, 1973, 5, 23–24, http://nsarchive.gwu.edu/NSAEBB/NSAEBB222/family_jewels_full_ocr.pdf.

55. Rebecca Gordon, *Mainstreaming Torture: Ethical Approaches in the Post-9/11 United States* (New York: Oxford University Press, 2014), 3.

56. Central Intelligence Agency, "Human Resource Exploitation Training," 1983, 46, http://nsarchive.gwu.edu/NSAEBB/NSAEBB122/CIA%20Human%20Res%20Exploit%20H0-L17.pdf.

57. Jennifer K. Harbury, *Truth, Torture, and the American Way: The History and Consequences of U.S. Involvement in Torture* (Boston: Beacon, 2005), 50–52.

58. Ibid., 31.

59. Ibid., 101.

60. Central Intelligence Agency, "The Interrogation of Suspects Under Arrest," July 2, 1996, https://www.cia.gov/library/center-for-the-study-of-intelligence/kent-csi/vol2no3/html/v02i3a08p_0001.htm.

61. "The Senate Intelligence Committee's Report on the CIA's Detention and Interrogation Program," 46–47.

62. James F. Gebhardt, "The Road to Abu Ghraib: U.S. Army Detainee Doctrine and Experience," *Military Review* 85, no. 1 (January 1, 2005), https://www.questia.com/library/journal/1G1-129813229/the-road-to-abu-ghraib-u-s-army-detainee-doctrine.

63. Departments of the Army, the Navy, the Air Force, and the Marine Corps, "Enemy Prisoners of War, Retained Personnel, Civilian Internees and Other Detainees," October 1, 1997, 2, http://www.apd.army.mil/pdffiles/r190_8.pdf.

64. Paul J. Springer, *America's Captives: Treatment of POWs from the Revolutionary War to the War on Terror* (Lawrence: University Press of Kansas, 2010), 154.

65. William T. Bowers, William M. Hammond, and George L. MacGarrigle, *Black Soldier, White Army: The 24th Infantry Regiment in Korea* (Honolulu: University Press of the Pacific, 2005), 206.

66. Eric Weiner, "Waterboarding: A Tortured History," *NPR*, November 3, 2007, http://www.npr.org/2007/11/03/15886834/waterboarding-a-tortured-history.

67. Schlesinger, "Schlesinger Report, 2004," 80.

68. Charles J. Dunlap Jr., "International Law and Terrorism: Some 'Qs & As' for Operators," *The Army Lawyer*, November 2002, http://people.duke.edu/~pfeaver/dunlapterrorism.pdf.

69. Sands, *Torture Team*, 60.

70. Ibid., 125.

71. This view builds on the work by Matthew Evangelista in *Unarmed Forces: The Transnational Movement to End the Cold War* (Ithaca, N.Y.: Cornell University Press, 1999).

72. John Mearsheimer and Stephen M. Walt, "The Israel Lobby," *London Review of Books* 28, no. 6 (March 2006), http://www.lrb.co.uk/v28/n06/john-mearsheimer/the-israel-lobby.

73. Eising Rainer, "Interest Groups in EU Policy-Making," *Living Reviews in European Governance* 3, no. 4 (2008): 15, http://europeangovernance.livingreviews.org/Articles/lreg-2008-4/download/lreg-2008-4BW.pdf.

74. It is important to note, however, that despite Hayden's review and reform of the EIT program, torture still continued under his watch. Hayden's changes may have been motivated by moral concerns as well as concerns about the program's impact on the CIA, but he ultimately decided to keep the majority of it in place. Rizzo, *Company Man*, 246–248.

75. "President Bush's Speech on Terrorism," *New York Times*, September 6, 2006, http://www.nytimes.com/2006/09/06/washington/06bush_transcript.html.

76. Tanfani and Hennigan, "Two Psychologists' Role in CIA Torture Program."

77. Barack Obama, "Executive Order 13491: Ensuring Lawful Interrogations," White House, January 22, 2009, https://www.whitehouse.gov/the_press_office/EnsuringLawfulInterrogations.

78. Eric Schmitt and Thom Shanker, "U.S., Citing Abuse in Iraqi Prisons, Holds Detainees," *New York Times*, December 25, 2005, http://www.nytimes.com/2005/12/25/world/middleeast/us-citing-abuse-in-iraqi-prisons-holds-detainees.html.

79. Cheryl Benard et al., *The Battle Behind the Wire: U.S. Prisoner and Detainee Operations from World War II to Iraq* (Santa Monica, Calif.: RAND Corporation, 2011), 60.

80. Ibid., 58.

81. U.S. Department of Justice, Office of the Inspector General, "A Review of the FBI's Involvement in and Observations of Detainee Interrogations in Guantánamo Bay, Afghanistan, and Iraq," May 2008, ix, https://oig.justice.gov/special/s0805/final.pdf.

82. "Detainee Treatment Act of 2005 (H.R. 2863, Title X)," December 30, 2005, http://www.cfr.org/terrorism-and-the-law/detainee-treatment-act-2005-hr-2863-title-x/p9865.

83. Benard et al., *The Battle Behind the Wire*, 66.

84. "Detainees Chief Sees Koran as Key Ally," *Financial Times*, July 16, 2007, http://www.ft.com/cms/s/0/24c2e12e-3334-11dc-a9e8-0000779fd2ac.html.

85. Samantha L. Quigley, "Lessons Learned at Abu Ghraib Drive Current Detainee Policies," *DoD News*, U.S. Department of Defense, http://archive.defense.gov/news/newsarticle.aspx?id=50081.

86. "Bloggers' Roundtable with Gen. Douglas M. Stone," *Washington Post*, September 18, 2007, http://www.washingtonpost.com/wp-dyn/content/article/2007/09/18/AR2007091801969.html.

87. Benard et al., *The Battle Behind the Wire*, 74.

88. Alissa J. Rubin, "U.S. Readies New Facility for Afghan Detainees," *New York Times*, November 15, 2009, http://www.nytimes.com/2009/11/16/world/asia/16bagram.html.

89. Stanley McChrystal, "United States Force-Afghanistan (USFOR-A), Initial Assessment of the Commander of the NATO International Security Assistance Forces-Afghanistan (COMISAF)" (Kabul: International Security Assistance Forces-Afghanistan, 2009).

90. Jon Boone, "U.S. to Tackle Breeding Ground for Insurgents in Afghan Jails," *The Guardian*, October 14, 2009, http://www.theguardian.com/world/2009/oct/14/afghanistan-prisoners -radicalise-insurgents.

91. Sands, *Torture Team*, 199.

7. IMPLICATIONS AND RECOMMENDATIONS

1. John Yoo, "From Guantanamo to Abbottabad," *Wall Street Journal*, May 4, 2011, http://www .wsj.com/articles/SB10001424052748703834804576301032595527372; "Dick Cheney Calls for the Return of Enhanced Interrogation," *Telegraph*, May 9, 2011, http://www.telegraph .co.uk/news/worldnews/al-qaeda/8503232/Dick-Cheney-calls-for-the-return-of -enhanced-interrogation.html.

2. The SSCI Report examines the claim that the EIT program led to the capture of Osama bin Laden on pages 378 to 400 and finds unequivocally that it is false.

3. Carl von Clausewitz, *On War*, ed. Michael Howard and Peter Paret (Princeton, N.J.: Princeton University Press, 1976), 75.

4. "The Referee as Hypocrite [reproduced on the *New York Times*]," *Boston Globe*, March 14, 2006, http://www.nytimes.com/2006/03/14/opinion/14iht-edchina.html.

5. Mark Weisbrot, "Who Is America to Judge?" *The Guardian*, March 11, 2009, http://www .theguardian.com/commentisfree/cifamerica/2009/mar/11/state-department-human -rights; John Shattuck, "Restoring U.S. Credibility on Human Rights," *American Bar Association Human Rights Magazine* 35, no. 4 (Fall 2008), http://www.americanbar.org /publications/human_rights_magazine_home/human_rights_vol35_2008/human_rights _fall2008/hr_fall08_shattuck.html. The SSCI Report notes in its "Findings and Conclusions" that "the program caused immeasurable damage to the United States' public standing, as well as to the United States' longstanding global leadership on human rights in general and the prevention of torture in particular." From "The Senate Intelligence Committee's Report on the CIA's Detention and Interrogation Program," *Washington Post*, December 9, 2014, 23, http://www.washingtonpost.com/wp-srv/special/national /cia-interrogation-report/document/.

6. "The Referee as Hypocrite."

7. The results of this effort are enshrined in documents such as the U.S. Constitution, with its ban on "cruel and unusual punishment," and the Declaration of the Rights of Man and of the Citizen, with its ban on post-hoc laws, presumed guilt, and unnecessary punishments.

8. Scholars from across the political and ideological spectrum have argued that after World War II, the United States embarked on a mission to transform global affairs by using U.S. power to establish a rules-based international system. For more on this argument, see Robert Kagan, *The World America Made* (New York: Vintage, 2013); G. John Ikenberry, *After Victory: Institutions, Strategic Restraint, and the Rebuilding of Order After Major Wars* (Princeton, N.J.: Princeton University Press, 2000); Henry Kissinger, *World Order* (New York: Penguin, 2014).

9. "Prosecute Torturers and Their Bosses," editorial, *New York Times*, December 21, 2014, http://www.nytimes.com/2014/12/22/opinion/prosecute-torturers-and-their-bosses.html; Erwin Chemerinsky, "Prosecute the Torturers: It's the Law," *Los Angeles Times*, December 9, 2014, http://www.latimes.com/opinion/op-ed/la-oe-torture-report-20141209-story.html; Peggy Noonan, "A Flawed Report's Important Lesson," *Wall Street Journal*, December 12, 2014, http://www.wsj.com/articles/a-flawed-reports-important-lesson-1418345866; George Tenet et al., "Ex-CIA Directors: Interrogations Saved Lives," *Wall Street Journal*, December 10, 2014, http://www.wsj.com/articles/cia-interrogations-saved-lives-1418142644; Steven Mufson, "Six Years Later, Political Debate Over CIA Interrogations Hasn't Gone Away," *Washington Post*, December 9, 2014, http://www.washingtonpost.com/business /economy/six-years-later-political-debate-over-cia-interrogations-hasnt-gone -away/2014/12/09/6e1be114-7fd4-11e4-81fd-8c4814dfa9d7_story.html.

10. "ACLU, Amnesty International, Human Rights Watch Urge DOJ to Appoint Special Prosecutor for CIA Torture," *American Civil Liberties Union*, June 23, 2015, https://www .aclu.org/news/aclu-amnesty-international-human-rights-watch-urge-doj-appoint-special -prosecutor-cia-torture.

11. Jack L. Goldsmith, *Power and Constraint: The Accountable Presidency After 9/11* (New York: Norton), 237.

12. Barack Obama, "Statement of President Barack Obama on Release of OLC Memos," April 16, 2009, https://www.whitehouse.gov/the-press-office/statement-president-barack -obama-release-olc-memos; Dan Balz, "Confronting the Bush Legacy, Reluctantly," April 22, 2009, http://voices.washingtonpost.com/44/2009/04/22/confronting_the_bush _legacy_re.html; "Statement of Attorney General Eric Holder on Closure of Investigation Into the Interrogation of Certain Detainees," Department of Justice, August 30, 2012, http:// www.justice.gov/opa/pr/statement-attorney-general-eric-holder-closure-investigation -interrogation-certain-detainees.

13. Andrew Rawnsley, "The Greatest Moral Failure of Tony Blair's Premiership," *The Guardian*, February 7, 2009, http://www.theguardian.com/commentisfree/2009/feb/08/tony-blair -human-rights-torture.

14. Iain Hollingshead, "Whatever Happened to . . . Impeaching Blair?" *The Guardian*, January 20, 2006, http://www.theguardian.com/politics/2006/jan/21/iraq.iraq.

15. Jack L. Goldsmith, *The Terror Presidency: Law and Judgment Inside the Bush Administration* (New York: Norton, 2007), 116–117.

16. Barton Gellman, *Angler: The Cheney Vice Presidency*, repr. ed. (New York: Penguin, 2009), 346–347.

17. Ibid.

18. For the full story of Zelikow's proposal and its rejection, see ibid., 346–349.

19. For example, Bush signed Executive Order (EO) 13440 on July 20, 2007 in which he used his authority as president to interpret the requirements of Common Article 3 for CIA detention policy. This was necessary because in 2006 the Supreme Court had found in *Hamdan v. Rumsfeld* that Common Article 3 applied to the conflict with al-Qaeda and its associated forces. Against the backdrop of this legal requirement, Bush moved to limit its

impact on the CIA's interrogation program. As such, EO 13440 essentially posited that all CIA interrogation and detention programs that complied with the administration's rulings on the definition of torture and cruel and inhumane treatment—such as the OLC opinions issued throughout Bush's presidency—would satisfy U.S. obligations under Common Article 3. Likewise, Bush vetoed the 2008 Intelligence Authorization Act specifically because it would have ended the CIA program. George W. Bush, "Executive Order 13440: Interpretation of the Geneva Conventions Common Article 3 as Applied to a Program of Detention and Interrogation Operated by the Central Intelligence Agency," White House, July 20, 2007, http://fas.org/irp/offdocs/eo/eo-13440.htm; George W. Bush, "The President's Radio Address," March 8, 2008, http://www.gpo.gov/fdsys/pkg/PPP-2008-book1 /pdf/PPP-2008-book1-doc-pg336.pdf.

20. "Obama 2008 Debate Promise: I'll Restore America's Standing in the World," 2008, https://www.youtube.com/watch?v=GdE9ZiooUrw.

21. David H. Petraeus, "Commanding General David H. Petraeus' Letter About Values," Multi-National Force—Iraq, May 10, 2007, http://www.washingtonpost.com/wp-srv /nation/documents/petraeus_values_051007.pdf.

22. "Biden Says Prison at Guantanamo Bay Should Be Closed," *Washington Post*, June 6, 2005, http://www.washingtonpost.com/wp-dyn/content/article/2005/06/05/AR2005060501043.html.

23. "*Meet the Press* Transcript for February 21, 2010," *MSNBC*, February 21, 2010, http://www .nbcnews.com/id/35493976/ns/meet_the_press/t/meet-press-transcript-february/.

24. "Osama Bin Laden Tape Transcript," *MSNBC*, May 23, 2006, http://www.nbcnews.com /id/12939961/ns/us_news-security/t/osama-bin-laden-tape-transcript/.

25. See #28 in Anwar Al Awlaki, *44 Ways to Support Jihad* (Victorious Media), http://ebooks .worldofislam.info/ebooks/Jihad/Anwar_Al_Awlaki_-_44_Ways_To_Support_Jihad.pdf.

26. "They Plot and Allah Plots: Foreword," *Dabiq*, no. 9 (June 2015): 4, http://media.clarion project.org/files/islamic-state/isis-isil-islamic-state-magazine-issue%2B9-they-plot-and -allah-plots-sex-slavery.pdf. Emphasis added.

27. Michael D. Shear, Walter Pincus, and R. Jeffrey Smith, "In Obama's Inner Circle, Debate Over Memos' Release Was Intense," *Washington Post*, April 24, 2009, http://www.washington post.com/wp-dyn/content/article/2009/04/23/AR2009042304718.html?hpid=topnews&si d=ST2009042304720.

28. David S. Kris, "Law Enforcement as a Counterterrorism Tool," *Journal of National Security and Law Policy* 5, no. 1 (June 15, 2011), http://jnslp.com/wp-content/uploads/2011/06/01 _David-Kris.pdf.

29. Robin Wright and Bradley Graham, "U.S. Works to Sustain Iraq Coalition: 4 Nations Have Left, 4 More Are Getting Ready to Leave International Force," *Washington Post*, July 15, 2004.

30. "Hungary Announces Iraq Pull-Out," *BBC*, November 3, 2004, http://news.bbc.co.uk/2 /hi/europe/3979349.stm.

31. Goldsmith, *The Terror Presidency*, afterword.

32. Alberto Mora, "Complete Text: Alberto Mora Discussing Torture and Cruel and Inhuman Treatment of Detainees in Georgetown's William V. O'Brien Lecture in International Law

and Morality," *Anthony Clark Arend*, May 3, 2013, http://anthonyclarkarend.com/human rights/complete-text-alberto-mora-discussing-torture-and-cruel-and-inhuman-treatment -of-detainees-in-georgetowns-william-v-obrien-lecture-in-international-law-and-morality/.

33. Edward Cody, "Friendly Persuasion-Stick, Then Carrot; Torrent of Leaflets Promise Embattled Iraqis 'Arab Hospitality' If They Surrender," *Washington Post*, February 9, 1991; Tom Clancy and Chuck Horner, *Every Man a Tiger* (New York: G. P. Putnam's Sons, 1999), 477; Rick Atkinson, *Crusade: The Untold Story of the Persian Gulf War* (Boston: Houghton Mifflin, 1993), 377; M. S. White, ed., *Gulf Logistics: Blackadder's War* (London: Brassey's, 1995), 217, 234.

34. Paul J. Springer, *America's Captives: Treatment of POWs from the Revolutionary War to the War on Terror* (Lawrence: University Press of Kansas, 2010), 193.

35. "Hearing on Guantanamo Detention Facility Outlook," *C-SPAN*, February 5, 2015, http://www.c-span.org/video/?324186-1/hearing-guantanamo-detention-facility-outlook.

36. Committee on Armed Services, U.S. Senate, "Inquiry Into the Treatment of Detainees in U.S. Custody," November 20, 2008, xii, http://www.armed-services.senate.gov/imo/media /doc/Detainee-Report-Final_April-22-2009.pdf.

37. John McCain, "Floor Statement by Senator John McCain on Senate Intelligence Committee Report on CIA Interrogation Methods," December 9, 2014, http://www.mccain.senate .gov/public/index.cfm/2014/12/floor-statement-by-sen-mccain-on-senate-intelligence -committee-report-on-cia-interrogation-methods.

38. "Department of the Army Field Manual (FM 34-52): Intelligence Interrogation" (United States Government Printing Office, September 28, 1992), sec. 1–8, https://fas.org/irp /doddir/army/fm34-52.pdf.

39. Philippe Sands, *Torture Team: Rumsfeld's Memo and the Betrayal of American Values* (New York: St. Martin's Press, 2008), 15.

40. Colin S. Gray, "Irregular Warfare: One Nature, Many Characters," *Strategic Studies Quarterly* 1, no. 2 (Winter 2007): 43.

41. Andrew Mack, "Why Big Nations Lose Small Wars: The Politics of Asymmetric Conflict," *World Politics* 27, no. 2 (January 1975): 175–200.

42. From pages 172 to 430, the SSCI Report examines the CIA's claims that the program produced useful intelligence. The *New York Times* provides a brief snapshot of some of the claims the SSCI Report rebukes: Haeyoun Park, Larry Buchanan, and Matt Apuzzo, "Does Torture Work? The C.I.A.'s Claims and What the Committee Found," *New York Times*, December 9, 2014, http://www.nytimes.com/interactive/2014/12/08/world/does -torture-work-the-cias-claims-and-what-the-committee-found.html. The CIA strongly disagreed with the committee's assessment of the intelligence and put its disagreements, including supporting evidence, in writing. The response can be found here: "C.I.A.'s Response to the Senate Torture Report," *New York Times*, December 9, 2014, http://www .nytimes.com/interactive/2014/12/09/world/document-cias-response-to-the-senate -torture-report.html. Others have examined the claim that the coercive techniques produced invaluable information and have challenged the conclusions of the SSCI Report: David Cole, "Did the Torture Report Give the CIA a Bum Rap," *New York Times*, February 20, 15, http://www.nytimes.com/2015/02/22/opinion/sunday/did-the-torture-report-give

-the-cia-a-bum-rap.html?_r=0; Benjamin Wittes, "Thoughts on the SSCI Report, Part III: The Program's Effectiveness," *Lawfare*, December 28, 2014, https://www.lawfareblog .com/thoughts-ssci-report-part-iii-programs-effectiveness; and Robert Jervis, "The Torture Blame Game," *Foreign Affairs*, May/June 2015, https://www.foreignaffairs.com/reviews /2015-04-20/torture-blame-game.

43. Wayne Sandholtz, *Prohibiting Plunder: How Norms Change* (Oxford: Oxford University Press, 2007), 264.

44. Bruce Drake, "Americans' Views on Use of Torture in Fighting Terrorism Have Been Mixed," *Pew Research Center*, December 9, 2014, http://www.pewresearch.org/fact-tank/2014/12/09 /americans-views-on-use-of-torture-in-fighting-terrorism-have-been-mixed/.

45. "United in Remembrance, Divided Over Policies: Ten Years After 9/11," *Pew Research Center*, September 1, 2011, 11, http://www.people-press.org/2011/09/01/united-in-remembrance -divided-over-policies/.

46. "Majority Says CIA Harsh Interrogations Justified," *Washington Post*, January 4, 2015, http://www.washingtonpost.com/politics/polling/majority-says-cia-harsh-interrogations -justified/2015/01/04/b6f9d79e-8518-11e4-abcf-5a3d7b3b20b8_page.html.

47. John Rizzo, *Company Man: Thirty Years of Controversy and Crisis in the CIA*, repr. ed. (New York: Scribner, 2014), 246–248.

48. Barack Obama, "Executive Order 13491: Ensuring Lawful Interrogations," White House, January 22, 2009, https://www.whitehouse.gov/the_press_office/EnsuringLawfulInterrogations.

49. Jane Mayer outlines the history of how Alberto Mora, then–general counsel of the Navy, pushed back against the Haynes memo and the administration's detainee policy. Jane Mayer, "The Memo," *The New Yorker*, February 27, 2007, http://www.newyorker.com/magazine /2006/02/27/the-memo.

50. "Working Group Report on Detainee Interrogations in the Global War on Terrorism: Assessment of Legal, Historical, Policy, and Operational Considerations" (Department of Defense, April 4, 2003).

51. Donald Rumsfeld, "Memorandum for the Commander, U.S. Southern Command: Counter-Resistance Techniques in the War on Terrorism" (Department of Defense, April 16, 2003).

52. Rizzo, *Company Man*, 216.

53. Ibid., 214–215, 243.

54. David Cole, "'New Torture Files': Declassified Memos Detail Roles of Bush White House and DOJ Officials Who Conspired to Approve Torture," *Just Security*, March 2, 2015, https://www.justsecurity.org/20553/new-torture-files-declassified-memos-detail-roles -bush-wh-doj-officials-conspired-approve-torture/.

55. Rizzo, *Company Man*, 246–48.

56. Obama, "Executive Order 13491."

57. Goldsmith, *Power and Constraint*, 189–190.

58. Ibid., 176–177.

59. Ibid., 177.

60. Bush, "Executive Order 13440."

61. Goldsmith, *Power and Constraint*, 167–168.

62. Goldsmith, *The Terror Presidency*, 140.

63. Richard A. Posner, *Not a Suicide Pact: The Constitution in a Time of National Emergency* (New York: Oxford University Press, 2006), 43.

64. The ACLU and Center for Constitutional Rights are two examples of organizations that largely adhere to this philosophy.

65. Posner, *Not a Suicide Pact*, 47.

66. Laura W. Murphy, Michael W. Macleod-Ball, and Michael German, "Written Statement of the American Civil Liberties Union Before the Subcommittee on Terrorism, Nonproliferation and Trade: 'Strategy for Countering Jihadist Websites'" (House Committee on Foreign Affairs, September 29, 2010), https://www.aclu.org/files/assets/Statement_House _Financial_Services_Countering_Jihadist_Websites_Sept_2010.pdf.

67. Peter Singer, "How Many Lives Is This War Worth?" *Los Angeles Times*, March 27, 2003, http://articles.latimes.com/2003/mar/27/news/war-oesinger27.

68. W. Arkin, "Iraq Rules Need More Airing," *Washington Post*, February 4, 2008.

69. Donald Rumsfeld and Richard Myers, "Defense Department Briefing, February 19, 2003," *IIP Digital*, February 19, 2003, http://iipdigital.usembassy.gov/st/english/texttrans/2003 /02/20030219191407ross@pd.state.govo.704632.html#axzz300QFdi5U.

70. Stephen M. Walt, "A Christmas Pardon," *Foreign Policy*, December 22, 2014, https:// foreignpolicy.com/2014/12/22/a-christmas-pardon-torture-report-obama-bush-cheney/; Anthony D. Romero, "Pardon Bush and Those Who Tortured," *New York Times*, December 8, 2014, http://www.nytimes.com/2014/12/09/opinion/pardon-bush-and-those-who-tortured .html; Barack Obama, "Statement by the President Report of the Senate Select Committee on Intelligence," White House, December 9, 2014, https://www.whitehouse.gov /the-press-office/2014/12/09/statement-president-report-senate-select-committee -intelligence; Harry Stout, "Obama History Project," *NYMag.com*, January 11, 2015, http:// nymag.com/news/politics/obama-history-project/harry-stout; Jay Parini, "How America Hurt Itself Over Torture" *CNN*, December 10, 2014, http://www.cnn.com/2014/12/09 /opinion/parini-torture-report/index.html; Jonathan Bernstein, "Pardon the People Who Allowed Torture," *BloombergView*, December 9, 2014, http://www.bloombergview.com /articles/2014-12-09/pardon-the-people-who-allowed-torture.

71. William Roberts, "Calls for Prosecution After 'Torture Report,'" *Al Jazeera*, December 10, 2014, http://www.aljazeera.com/indepth/features/2014/12/calls-prosecution-after-torture-report-2014121052353558637.html; Ben Emmerson, "Feinstein Report: UN Expert Calls for Prosecution of CIA Officers and Other US Government Officials," United Nations Office of the High Commissioner for Human Rights, December 9, 2014, http://www.ohchr.org /EN/NewsEvents/Pages/DisplayNews.aspx?NewsID=15397&LangID=E#sthash.E4r VzPRZ.dpuf; Rick Gladstone and Robert Mackey, "Overseas, Torture Report Prompts Calls for Prosecution," *New York Times*, December 9, 2014, http://www.nytimes.com /2014/12/10/world/europe/overseas-torture-report-prompts-calls-for-prosecution.html; Jordan Paust, "The Senate Torture Report and Prior Admissions," *Jurist* (University of Pittsburgh), December 9, 2014, http://jurist.org/forum/2014/12/jordan-paust-senate-torture.php.

72. Springer, *America's Captives*.

BIBLIOGRAPHY

9/11 Commission. "Final Report of the National Commission on Terrorist Attacks Upon the United States (The 9/11 Commission Report)." July 22, 2004. http://www.9-11commission .gov/report/911Report.pdf.

Adler, Emmanuel. "Constructivism and International Relations." In *Handbook of International Relations*, ed. Walter Carlsnaes, Thomas Risse, and Beth A. Simmons. London: Sage, 2002.

Allen, Michael J. *Until the Last Man Comes Home: POWs, MIAs, and the Unending Vietnam War.* Chapel Hill: University of North Carolina Press, 2012.

American Civil Liberties Union, "ACLU, Amnesty International, Human Rights Watch Urge DOJ to Appoint Special Prosecutor for CIA Torture." June 23, 2015. https://www.aclu .org/news/aclu-amnesty-international-human-rights-watch-urge-doj-appoint-special -prosecutor-cia-torture.

Army Concept Team in Vietnam. "Accountability, Classification, and Record/Reporting System for Captured Enemy Personnel." Suitland, Md.: U.S. National Archives, 1970.

Atkinson, Rick. *Crusade: The Untold Story of the Persian Gulf War.* Boston: Houghton Mifflin, 1993.

Awlaki, Anwar al-. *Forty-Four Ways to Support Jihad.* Victorious Media. http://ebooks.worldofislam .info/ebooks/Jihad/Anwar_Al_Awlaki_-_44_Ways_To_Support_Jihad.pdf.

Bacque, James. "The Last Dirty Secret of World War Two." *Saturday Night* (September 1989): 31–39.

Ballenger, Lee. *The Outpost War: The U.S. Marine Corps in Korea*, vol. 1: *1952.* Dulles, Va.: Potomac Books, 2005.

Barrett, Nicole. "Holding Individual Leaders Responsible for Violations of Customary International Law: The U.S. Bombardment of Cambodia and Laos." *Columbia Human Rights Law Review* 32 (2001): 429–476.

Beaver, Diane E. "Memorandum for Commander, Joint Task Force 170." U.S. Department of Defense, October 11, 2002.

Benard, Cheryl, et al. *The Battle Behind the Wire: U.S. Prisoner and Detainee Operations from World War II to Iraq.* Santa Monica, Calif.: RAND Corporation, 2011.

Best, Geoffrey. *Humanity in Warfare: The Modern History of the International Law of Armed Conflicts.* London: Methuen, 1983.

Betts, Richard K. "Compromised Command." *Foreign Affairs,* July/August 2001. https://www.foreignaffairs.com/reviews/review-essay/2001-07-01/compromised-command.

——. *The Enemies of Intelligence.* New York: Columbia University Press, 2007.

Bialke, Joseph P. "United Nations Peace Operations: Applicable Norms and the Application of the Law of Armed Conflict." *Air Force Law Review* 50 (2001).

Bin-Ladin, Shaykh Usamah Bin-Mohammed, et al. "Jihad Against Jews and Crusaders: World Islamic Front Statement." February 23, 1998. http://fas.org/irp/world/para/docs/980223-fatwa.htm.

Black, Joseph Cofer. "Statement of Cofer Black: Joint Investigation Into September 11." U.S. Congress, September 26, 2012. http://fas.org/irp/congress/2002_hr/092602black.html.

Borch, Frederic L. *Judge Advocates in Combat: Army Lawyers in Military Operations from Vietnam to Haiti.* Washington, D.C.: Government Printing Office, 2001.

——. *Judge Advocates in Vietnam: Army Lawyers in Southeast Asia, 1959–1975.* Fort Leavenworth, Kan.: U.S. Army Command and General Staff College, 2003. http://www.loc.gov/rr/frd/Military_Law/pdf/JAs_Vietnam.pdf.

Bowers, William T., William M. Hammond, and George L. MacGarrigle. *Black Soldier, White Army: The Twenty-Fourth Infantry Regiment in Korea.* Honolulu: University Press of the Pacific, 2005.

Bowman, Marion (Spike). "Witness to Guantanamo." March 2015. http://witnesstoguantanamo.com/interviews/marionspikebowman/.

Brennan, John, Donald Rumsfeld, Michael Bloomberg, and Rudy Giuliani. *Face the Nation* transcript: September 11, 2011. Interview by Bob Schieffer. http://www.cbsnews.com/news/face-the-nation-transcript-september-11-2011/3/.

Brinkerhoff, John R. *United States Army Reserve in Operation Desert Storm. Enemy Prisoner of War Operations: The 800th Military Police Brigade.* Arlington, Va.: ANDRULIS Research Corporation, 1992.

Burgers, J. Hermann. *The United Nations Convention Against Torture: A Handbook on the Convention Against Torture and Other Cruel, Inhuman, or Degrading Treatment or Punishment.* Dordrecht: Martinus Nijhoff, 1988.

Bush, George H. W. "Remarks at the Annual Convention of the National Religious Broadcasters." January 28, 1991. http://www.presidency.ucsb.edu/ws/?pid=19250.

——. "Remarks to the National League of Families of American Prisoners and Missing in Southeast Asia in Arlington, Virginia." Arlington, Va., July 24, 1992. http://www.presidency.ucsb.edu/ws/?pid=21263.

Bush, George W. "Executive Order 13440: Interpretation of the Geneva Conventions Common Article 3 as Applied to a Program of Detention and Interrogation Operated by the Central Intelligence Agency." The White House, July 20, 2007. http://fas.org/irp/offdocs/eo/eo-13440.htm.

——. "Guard and Reserves 'Define Spirit of America': Remarks by the President to Employees at the Pentagon." September 17, 2001. http://georgewbush-whitehouse.archives.gov/news/releases/2001/09/20010917-3.html.

——. "Military Order of November 13, 2001: 'Detention, Treatment and Trial of Certain Non-Citizens in the War Against Terrorism.'" National Archives and Records Administration, November 16, 2001. Federal Register. http://www2.gwu.edu/~nsarchiv/torturingdemocracy/documents/20011113.pdf.

——. "The President's Radio Address." Government Publishing Office, March 8, 2008. http://www.gpo.gov/fdsys/pkg/PPP-2008-book1/pdf/PPP-2008-book1-doc-pg336.pdf.

Bybee, Jay. "Memorandum for John Rizzo, Acting General Counsel of the Central Intelligence Agency: Interrogation of Al Qaeda Operative." Department of Justice, August 1, 2002. http://www.washingtonpost.com/wp-srv/nation/pdf/OfficeofLegalCounsel_Aug2Memo_041609.pdf.

——. "Standards of Conduct for Interrogation under 18 U.S.C. §§ 2340–2340a." In *The Torture Papers: The Road to Abu Ghraib*, ed. Karen J. Greenberg and Joshua L. Dratel. New York: Cambridge University Press, 2002.

Carnahan, Burrus M. "Lincoln, Lieber, and the Laws of War: The Origins and Limits of the Principle of Military Necessity." *American Journal of International Law* 92, no. 2 (April 1, 1998): 213–231.

Carr, E. H. *The Twenty Years' Crisis, 1919–1939: An Introduction to the Study of International Relations.* New York: Harper Perennial, 1964.

Carter, Jimmy. "Inaugural Address." January 20, 1977. http://www.presidency.ucsb.edu/ws/?pid=6575.

——. "State of the Union Address." January 23, 1980. http://www.jimmycarterlibrary.gov/documents/speeches/su80jec.phtml.

——. "University of Notre Dame—Address at Commencement Exercises at the University." May 22, 1977. http://www.presidency.ucsb.edu/ws/?pid=7552.

Carvin, Stephanie. *Prisoners of America's Wars: From the Early Republic to Guantanamo.* New York: Columbia University Press, 2010.

Central Intelligence Agency. "Central Intelligence Agency, Office of Inspector General Special Review: Counterterrorism Detention and Interrogation Activities," May 7, 2004. http://www2.gwu.edu/~nsarchiv/torture_archive/20040507.pdf.

——. "CIA Comments on the Senate Select Committee on Intelligence Report on the Rendition, Detention, and Interrogation Program." https://www.cia.gov/library/reports/CIAs_June2013_Response_to_the_SSCI_Study_on_the_Former_Detention_and_Interrogation_Program.pdf.

——. "Human Resource Exploitation Training." 1983. http://nsarchive.gwu.edu/NSAEBB/NSAEBB122/CIA%20Human%20Res%20Exploit%20H0-L17.pdf.

——. "The Interrogation of Suspects Under Arrest." July 2, 1996. https://www.cia.gov/library/center-for-the-study-of-intelligence/kent-csi/vol2no3/html/v02i3a08p_0001.htm.

——. "KUBARK Counterintelligence Interrogation." July 1963. http://nsarchive.gwu.edu/NSAEBB/NSAEBB122/CIA%20Kubark%201-60.pdf.

——. "Memorandum for Executive Secretary, CIA Management Committee: 'Family Jewels.'" May 16, 1973. http://nsarchive.gwu.edu/NSAEBB/NSAEBB222/family_jewels_full_ocr.pdf.

Chang, Iris. *The Rape of Nanking: The Forgotten Holocaust of World War II*. New York: Basic Books, 1997.

Checkel, Jeffrey T. "Why Comply? Social Learning and European Identity Change." *International Organization* 55, no. 3 (June 2001): 553–588.

Cheney, Dick. "Cheney in His Own Words." *PBS Frontline*, June 20, 2006. http://www.pbs.org /wgbh/pages/frontline/darkside/themes/ownwords.html#1.

——. "Congressional Overreaching in Foreign Policy." American Enterprise Institute, 1989. http://s3.documentcloud.org/documents/339579/congressional-overreaching-cheney.pdf.

——. *In My Time: A Personal and Political Memoir*. Repr. ed. New York: Threshold Editions, 2012.

——. "Remarks at the 56th Annual Alfred E. Smith Memorial Foundation Dinner." Waldorf-Astoria Hotel, New York, October 18, 2001. http://georgewbush-whitehouse.archives.gov /vicepresident/news-speeches/speeches/vp20011018.html.

Cherneva, Iveta. "The Drafting History of Article 2 of the Convention Against Torture." *Essex Human Rights Review* 9, no. 1 (June 2012). http://projects.essex.ac.uk/ehrr/V9N1 /CHERNEVA.pdf.

Church, Albert T. "Review of Department of Defense Detention Operations and Detainee Interrogation Techniques." Washington, D.C.: Office of the Secretary of Defense, March 7, 2005. https://www.aclu.org/sites/default/files/images/torture/asset_upload_file625_26068.pdf.

Clancy, Tom, and Chuck Horner. *Every Man a Tiger*. New York: G. P. Putnam's Sons, 1999.

Clapper, James R., et al. *Current and Projected National Security Threats to the United States*. United States Senate, 2013. http://fas.org/irp/congress/2013_hr/threat.pdf.

Clark, Kathleen. "Ethical Issues Raised by the OLC Torture Memorandum." *Journal of National Security Law and Policy* 1, no. 455 (2005).

Clarke, Jeffrey J. *Advice and Support: The Final Years, 1965–1973*. Washington, D.C.: Government Printing Office, 1988.

Clinton, William J. "Remarks at the Legislative Convention of the American Federation of State, County, and Municipal Employees." March 23, 1999. http://www.presidency.ucsb.edu /ws/?pid=57294.

——. "Remarks at the University of Connecticut in Storrs." October 15, 1995. http://www.presidency .ucsb.edu/ws/?pid=50655.

——. "Statement on Kosovo." March 24, 1999. http://millercenter.org/president/speeches /speech-3932.

Clodfelter, Mark. *The Limits of Air Power: The American Bombing of North Vietnam*. Lincoln: Bison Books, 2006.

Cole, David. "Enemy Aliens." *Georgetown Law Faculty Publications and Other Works*, January 1, 2002. http://scholarship.law.georgetown.edu/facpub/956.

——. "'New Torture Files': Declassified Memos Detail Roles of Bush White House and DOJ Officials Who Conspired to Approve Torture." *Just Security*, March 2, 2015. https://www.justsecurity .org/20553/new-torture-files-declassified-memos-detail-roles-bush-wh-doj-officials-conspired -approve-torture/.

——. "Taking Responsibility for Torture." *The New Yorker*, December 9, 2014. http://www.newyorker .com/news/news-desk/taking-responsibility-torture.

——., ed. *Torture Memos: Rationalizing the Unthinkable*. New York: The New Press, 2009.

"Convention Between the United States of America and Other Powers, Relating to Prisoners of War." The Avalon Project, Yale University, July 27, 1929. http://avalon.law.yale.edu/20th_century /geneva02.asp.

"Convention for the Amelioration of the Condition of the Wounded and Sick in Armies in the Field (The Convention of 1906)," July 6, 1906. https://www.icrc.org/ihl/INTRO /180?OpenDocument.

"Convention Relative to the Treatment of Prisoners of War," July 27, 1929. https://www.icrc.org /applic/ihl/ihl.nsf/INTRO/305?OpenDocument.

"Convention Relative to the Treatment of Prisoners of War (III)," August 12, 1949. https://www .icrc.org/ihl/INTRO/375?OpenDocument.

Cooke, John S. "Introduction: Fiftieth Anniversary of the Uniform Code of Military Justice Symposium." *Military Law Review* 165 (September 2000). http://www.loc.gov/rr/frd/Military _Law/Military_Law_Review/pdf-files/276085~1.pdf.

Cortell, Andrew P., and James W. Davis Jr. "How Do International Institutions Matter? The Domestic Impact of International Rules and Norms." *International Studies Quarterly* 40, no. 4 (December 1996): 451–478.

Daugirdas, Kristina, and Julian Mortenson. "Contemporary Practice of the United States Relating to International Law." *American Society of International Law* 60, no. 1 (1966). http://repository .law.umich.edu/articles/948.

Davis, Vernon E. *The Long Road Home: U.S. Prisoner of War Policy and Planning in Southeast Asia*. Washington, D.C.: Office of the Secretary of Defense, 2000.

"Detainee Treatment Act of 2005 (H.R. 2863, Title X)." Government Printing Office, December 30, 2005. http://www.cfr.org/terrorism-and-the-law/detainee-treatment-act-2005-hr-2863 -title-x/p9865.

Dickinson, Laura A. "Using Legal Process to Fight Terrorism: Detentions, Military Commissions, International Tribunals, and the Rule of Law," *Southern California Law Review* 75, no. 1 (2001–2002).

Dower, John W. *War Without Mercy: Race and Power in the Pacific War*. New York: Pantheon, 1987.

Doyle, Robert. *The Enemy in Our Hands: America's Treatment of Prisoners of War from the Revolution to the War on Terror*. Repr. ed. Lexington: University Press of Kentucky, 2011.

Drake, Bruce. "Americans' Views on Use of Torture in Fighting Terrorism Have Been Mixed." *Pew Research Center*, December 9, 2014. http://www.pewresearch.org/fact-tank/2014/12/09 /americans-views-on-use-of-torture-in-fighting-terrorism-have-been-mixed/.

Draper, Gerald I. A. D. *The Red Cross Conventions*. London: Stevens & Sons, 1958.

Dunlap, Jr., Charles J. "International Law and Terrorism: Some 'Qs & As' for Operators." *The Army Lawyer* (November 2002). http://people.duke.edu/~pfeaver/dunlapterrorism.pdf.

——. "Law and Military Interventions: Preserving Humanitarian Values in 21st-Century Conflicts." Washington, D.C.: Carr Center for Human Rights Policy, Kennedy School of Government, Harvard University, 2001. http://people.duke.edu/~pfeaver/dunlap.pdf.

Emmerson, Ben. "Feinstein Report: UN Expert Calls for Prosecution of CIA Officers and Other US Government Officials." United Nations Office of the High Commissioner for Human

Rights, December 9, 2014. http://www.ohchr.org/EN/NewsEvents/Pages/DisplayNews.aspx ?NewsID=15397&LangID=E#sthash.E4rVzPRZ.dpuf.

Erwin, Marshall C., and Amy Belasco. "Intelligence Spending and Appropriations: Issues for Congress." Congressional Research Service, September 18, 2013. http://fas.org/sgp/crs/intel /R42061.pdf.

Evangelista, Matthew. *Unarmed Forces: The Transnational Movement to End the Cold War*. Ithaca, N.Y.: Cornell University Press, 1999.

Fay, George R., and Anthony R. Jones. "Investigation of the Abu Ghraib Detention Facility and 205th Military Intelligence Brigade." Baghdad: Department of Defense, 2004.

Finnemore, Martha. *National Interests in International Society*. Ithaca, N.Y.: Cornell University Press, 1996.

Finnemore, Martha, and Kathryn Sikkink. "International Norm Dynamics and Political Change." *International Organization* 52, no. 4 (October 1998): 887–917.

Fisher, Louis. *The Politics of Shared Power*. College Station: Texas A&M University Press, 1998.

Fisher, Tracy. "At Risk in No-Man's Land: United States Peacekeepers, Prisoners of War, and the Convention on the Safety of United Nations and Associated Personnel." *Minnesota Law Review* 85 (2000/2001): 663.

Flores, Richard R. "Memory-Place, Meaning, and the Alamo." *American Literary History* 10, no. 3 (Autumn 1998): 428–445.

Ford, Gerald R. "Executive Order 11905: United States Foreign Intelligence Activities." The White House, February 18, 1976. http://fas.org/irp/offdocs/eo11905.htm.

——. "Imperiled Not Imperial." *Time*, November 10, 1980.

Ford, Worthington Chauncey, ed. *Journals of the Continental Congress, 1774–1789*. Washington, D.C.: Government Printing Office, 1906.

Foreign Intelligence Surveillance Act of 1978. 92 Stat. 1783. Vol. 92, 1978. http://www.gpo.gov/fdsys /pkg/STATUTE-92/pdf/STATUTE-92-Pg1783.pdf.

Friedel, Frank. *Francis Lieber: Nineteenth-Century Liberal*. Baton Rouge: Louisiana State University Press, 1947.

Garner, James Wilford. *International Law and the World War*. Vol. 1. London: Longman, Green & Co., 1920.

Gebhardt, James F. "The Road to Abu Ghraib: U.S. Army Detainee Doctrine and Experience." *Military Review* 85, no. 1 (January 1, 2005). https://www.questia.com/library /journal/1G1-129813229/the-road-to-abu-ghraib-u-s-army-detainee-doctrine.

Gellman, Barton. *Angler: The Cheney Vice Presidency*. Repr. ed. New York: Penguin, 2009.

"The Geneva Convention and the Treatment of Prisoners of War in Vietnam." *Harvard Law Review* 80, no. 4 (February 1, 1967): 851–868.

George, Alexander L., and Andrew Bennett. *Case Studies and Theory Development in the Social Science*. Cambridge, Mass.: MIT Press, 2005.

Goldsmith, Jack L. *Power and Constraint: The Accountable Presidency After 9/11*. New York: Norton, 2012.

——. *The Terror Presidency: Law and Judgment Inside the Bush Administration*. New York: Norton, 2007.

Goldsmith, Jack L., and Robert Chesney. "Terrorism and the Convergence of Criminal and Military Detention Models." *Stanford Law Review* 60, no. 4 (February 1, 2008): 1079.

Goldsmith, Jack L., and Eric A. Posner. *The Limits of International Law.* Oxford: Oxford University Press, 2006.

Goldstein, Judith, and Robert Keohane, eds. *Ideas and Foreign Policy: Beliefs, Institutions, and Political Change.* Ithaca, N.Y.: Cornell University Press, 1993.

Gonzales, Alberto R. "Decision Re Application of the Geneva Convention on Prisoners of War to the Conflict with Al Qaeda and the Taliban." In *The Torture Papers: The Road to Abu Ghraib,* ed. Karen J. Greenberg and Joshua L. Dratel, 1st ed., 118–121. New York: Cambridge University Press, 2005.

Gordon, Rebecca. *Mainstreaming Torture: Ethical Approaches in the Post-9/11 United States.* New York: Oxford University Press, 2014.

Gourevitch, Philip. "Exposure: The Woman Behind the Camera at Abu Ghraib." *The New Yorker,* March 24, 2008. http://www.newyorker.com/magazine/2008/03/24/exposure-5.

Govern, Kevin H. "Sorting the Wolves From the Sheep (Military Police PB 19-04-2)." U.S. Army, October 2004. http://www.wood.army.mil/ENGRMAG/pdfs/Oct%2004%20pdfs/Govern.pdf.

Gray, Colin S. "Irregular Warfare: One Nature, Many Characters." *Strategic Studies Quarterly* 1, no. 2 (Winter 2007).

Greenberg, Karen J., and Joshua L. Dratel, eds. *The Torture Papers: The Road to Abu Ghraib.* New York: Cambridge University Press, 2005.

Grey, Stephen. "Five Facts and Five Fictions About CIA Rendition." *PBS Frontline,* November 4, 2007. http://www.pbs.org/frontlineworld/stories/rendition701/updates/updates.html.

"Hague Convention Respecting the Laws and Customs of War on Land and Its Annex: Regulations Concerning the Laws and Customs of War on Land (Hague IV)." October 18, 1907. https://www.icrc.org/applic/ihl/ihl.nsf/INTRO/195.

Hamilton, Alexander. "The Federalist No. 8: The Consequences of Hostilities Between the States." November 20, 1787. http://www.constitution.org/fed/federa08.htm.

——. "The Federalist No. 70: The Executive Department Further Considered." March 15, 1788. http://www.constitution.org/fed/federa70.htm.

Harbury, Jennifer K. *Truth, Torture, and the American Way: The History and Consequences of U.S. Involvement in Torture.* Boston: Beacon, 2005.

Hartigan, Richard Shelly. *Lieber's Code and the Law of War.* Chicago: Precedent, 1983.

Hattem, Julian. "Senate Votes to Ban Use of Torture." *The Hill,* June 16, 2015. http://thehill.com/policy/national-security/245117-senate-votes-to-permanently-ban-use-of-torture.

Henkin, Louis. *Foreign Affairs and the United States Constitution.* 2nd ed. Oxford: Clarendon, 1997.

Hickey, Donald R. *The War of 1812: A Short History.* Champaign: University of Illinois Press, 1995.

Hogue, L. Lynn. "Lieber's Military Code and Its Legacy." In *Francis Lieber and the Culture of the Mind,* ed. Charles R. Mack and Henry H. Lesesne. Columbia: University of South Carolina Press, 2005.

Howell, William G., and Jon C. Pevehouse. *While Dangers Gather: Congressional Checks on Presidential War Powers.* Princeton, N.J.: Princeton University Press, 2007.

Hull, Roger H., and John C. Novogrod. *Law and Vietnam: Roger H. Hull and John C. Novogrod.* New York: Oceana, 1968.

ICRC. "Annex to Report on Visit to Phu Quoc Pw Camp." Suitland, Md.: U.S. National Archives, 1968.

———. "Report on Visit Made to Phu Quoc Pw Camp." Suitland, Md.: U.S. National Archives, 1968.

Ikenberry, G. John. *After Victory: Institutions, Strategic Restraint, and the Rebuilding of Order After Major Wars.* Princeton, N.J.: Princeton University Press, 2000.

Inouye, Daniel K., and Lee H. Hamilton. "Report of the Congressional Committees Investigating the Iran-Contra Affair with Supplemental, Minority, and Additional Views." Washington, D.C.: U.S. Government Printing Office, November 17, 1987. https://archive.org/stream /reportofcongress87unit#page/n7/mode/2up.

Intelligence Science Board. "Educing Information: Interrogation: Science and Art—Foundations for the Future, Intelligence Science Board (Phase 1 Report)." Washington, D.C.: National Defense Intelligence College, December 2006. http://www.seas.harvard.edu/courses/ge157 /educing.pdf.

International Committee of the Red Cross. "International Review of the Red Cross," 1965. http://www.loc.gov/rr/frd/Military_Law/pdf/RC_Nov-1965.pdf.

———. "South Sudan: World's Newest Country Signs up to the Geneva Conventions." News release, July 19, 2012. https://www.icrc.org/eng/resources/documents/news-release/2012 /south-sudan-news-2012-07-09.htm.

International Court of Justice. *Military and Paramilitary Activities in and Against Nicaragua: Nicaragua v. United States of America.* The Hague, 1986.

Jacoby, Charles H. "Combined Forces Command-Afghanistan Area Operations Report of Inspection." Department of Defense, June 26, 2004. http://www1.umn.edu/humanrts /OathBetrayed/Jacoby%20Report.pdf.

Jervis, Robert. "The Torture Blame Game." *Foreign Affairs*, May/June 2015. https://www .foreignaffairs.com/reviews/2015-04-20/torture-blame-game.

Johnson, Lock K. *A Season of Inquiry: The Senate Intelligence Investigation.* Lexington: University Press of Kentucky, 1985.

———. *The Threat on the Horizon: An Inside Account of America's Search for Security After the Cold War.* New York: Oxford University Press, 2011.

"Joint Resolution Concerning the War Powers of Congress and the President." The Avalon Project, Yale University, now 1973. http://avalon.law.yale.edu/20th_century/warpower.asp.

Judge Advocate General's Corps. "The Corps at the End of the 20th Century." *The Judge Advocate General's Corps Regimental History.* https://www.jagcnet.army.mil/8525736A005BE1BE/0/05 FE336414E1920D8525735C00642BC0?opendocument&noly=1.

Kagan, Robert. *The World America Made.* New York: Vintage, 2013.

Keeva, Steven. "Lawyers in the War Room." *American Bar Association Journal* 77, no. 12 (December 1, 1991): 52–59.

Kissinger, Henry. *World Order.* New York: Penguin, 2014.

Koch, J. A. *The Chieu Hoi Program in South Vietnam, 1963–1971.* Washington, D.C.: RAND Corporation, 1973.

Koh, Harold Hongju. *Libya and War Powers.* Washington, D.C.: U.S. Department of State, 2011. http://www.state.gov/s/l/releases/remarks/167250.htm.

———. *The National Security Constitution: Sharing Power After the Iran-Contra Affair.* New Haven, Conn.: Yale University Press, 1990.

———. "Statement of Harold Hongju Koh Before the Senate Judiciary Committee, Subcommittee on The Constitution on Restoring the Rule of Law." U.S. Senate, September 16, 2008. http://fas.org/irp/congress/2008_hr/091608koh.pdf.

———. "War and Responsibility in the Dole-Gingrich Congress," *University of Miami Law Review* 50, no. 1 (January 1996).

———. "Why Do Nations Obey International Law?" *Yale Law Journal,* Faculty Scholarship Series, 106 (1997): 2,599–2,659.

Kris, David S. "Law Enforcement as a Counterterrorism Tool." *Journal of National Security and Law Policy* 5, no. 1 (June 15, 2011). http://jnslp.com/wp-content/uploads/2011/06/01_David-Kris.pdf.

Lambert, Andrew. "A British Perspective on the War of 1812." *PBS.* http://www.pbs.org/wned /war-of-1812/essays/british-perspective/.

"Laws and Customs of War on Land (Hague II); July 29, 1899." http://avalon.law.yale.edu/19th _century/hague02.asp.

Legro, Jeffrey. *Rethinking the World: Great Power Strategies and International Order.* Ithaca, N.Y.: Cornell University Press, 2005.

Levie, Howard S. *Documents on Prisoners of War.* Newport, R.I.: Naval War College, 1979. http:// archive.org/details/documentsonpriso60levi.

———. "Maltreatment of Prisoners of War in Vietnam." In *The Vietnam War and International Law,* vol. 2, ed. Richard A. Falk. Princeton, N.J.: Princeton University Press, 1969.

Levin, Carl. "Opening Statement of Senator Carl Levin, Chairman." Presented at the Treatment of Detainees in U.S. Custody: Hearings Before the Committee on Armed Services, U.S. Senate, Washington, D.C., September 25, 2008. http://www.gpo.gov/fdsys/pkg/CHRG -110shrg47298/html/CHRG-110shrg47298.htm.

Levitt, Matthew. "The Origins of Hezbollah." *The Atlantic,* October 23, 2013. http://www .theatlantic.com/international/archive/2013/10/the-origins-of-hezbollah/280809/.

Lewis, George G., and John Mewha. *History of Prisoner of War Utilization by the United States Army, 1776–1945.* Washington, D.C.: Department of the Army, 1955.

Lewy, Guenter. *America in Vietnam.* New York: Oxford University Press, 1980.

Lieber, Francis. "General Orders No. 100 : The Lieber Code—Instructions for the Government of Armies of the United States in the Field." April 24, 1863. The Avalon Project, Yale University. http://avalon.law.yale.edu/19th_century/lieber.asp.

Lippman, Matthew. "The Development and Drafting of the United Nations Convention Against Torture and Other Cruel Inhuman or Degrading Treatment or Punishment." *Boston College International and Comparative Law Review* 17, no. 2 (August 1, 1994): 275.

Mack, Andrew. "Why Big Nations Lose Small Wars: The Politics of Asymmetric Conflict." *World Politics* 27, no. 2 (January 1975): 175–200.

MacKenzie, S. P. "The Treatment of Prisoners of War in World War II." *Journal of Modern History* 66, no. 3 (September 1, 1994): 487–520.

Madison, James. "James Madison to Thomas Jefferson," April 2, 1798. http://press-pubs.uchicago .edu/founders/documents/a1_8_11s8.html.

Markels, Alex. "Will Terrorism Rewrite the Laws of War?" *NPR*, December 6, 2005. http://www .npr.org/2005/12/06/5011464/will-terrorism-rewrite-the-laws-of-war.

Mayda, Jaro. "The Korean Repatriation Problem and International Law." *American Journal of International Law* 47, no. 3 (July 1, 1953): 414–438.

Mayer, Jane. *The Dark Side: The Inside Story of How the War on Terror Turned Into a War on American Ideals*. Repr. ed. New York: Anchor, 2009.

——. "The Memo." *The New Yorker*, February 27, 2007. http://www.newyorker.com/magazine /2006/02/27/the-memo.

McCain, John. "Floor Statement by Senator John McCain on Senate Intelligence Committee Report on CIA Interrogation Methods." December 9, 2014. http://www.mccain.senate.gov /public/index.cfm/2014/12/floor-statement-by-sen-mccain-on-senate-intelligence-committee -report-on-cia-interrogation-methods.

McChrystal, Stanley. "United States Force-Afghanistan (USFOR-A), Initial Assessment of the Commander of the NATO International Security Assistance Forces-Afghanistan (COMISAF)." Kabul: International Security Assistance Forces-Afghanistan, 2009.

Mearsheimer, John, and Stephen M. Walt. "The Israel Lobby." *London Review of Books* 28, no. 6 (March 2006). http://www.lrb.co.uk/v28/n06/john-mearsheimer/the-israel-lobby.

Melman, Seymour. "Prisoners of War and the Wounded in the Field." In *In the Name of America*, 66. Annandale, Md.: Turnpike, 1968.

Meron, Theodor. "The Time Has Come for the United States to Ratify Geneva Protocol I." *American Journal of International Law* 88, no. 4 (October 1994): 678–686.

——. *War Crimes Law Comes of Age: Essays*. New York: Oxford University Press, 1999.

Miles, Donna. "Operation Homecoming for Vietnam POWs Marks 40 Years." *American Forces Press Service*. February 12, 2013. http://www.defense.gov/news/newsarticle.aspx?id=119272.

"Military Order of November 13, 2001: 'Detention, Treatment and Trial of Certain Non-Citizens in the War Against Terrorism.'" National Archives and Records Administration, November 16, 2001. Federal Register. http://www2.gwu.edu/~nsarchiv/torturingdemocracy /documents/20011113.pdf.

Miller, John C. *Triumph of Freedom, 1775–1783*. Boston: Little, Brown, 1948.

Moorehead, Caroline. *Dunant's Dream: War, Switzerland, and the History of the Red Cross*. New York: Carroll & Graf, 1999.

Mora, Alberto. "Complete Text: Alberto Mora Discussing Torture and Cruel and Inhuman Treatment of Detainees in Georgetown's William V. O'Brien Lecture in International Law and Morality." *Anthony Clark Arend*, May 3, 2013. http://anthonyclarkarend.com /humanrights/complete-text-alberto-mora-discussing-torture-and-cruel-and-inhuman -treatment-of-detainees-in-georgetowns-william-v-obrien-lecture-in-international-law -and-morality/.

Morgan, Edmund M. "The Background of the Uniform Code of Military Justice." *Military Law Review* 28 (April 1965). http://www.loc.gov/rr/frd/Military_Law/Military_Law_Review /pdf-files/277077~1.pdf.

Murphy, Laura W., Michael W. Macleod-Ball, and Michael German. "Written Statement of the American Civil Liberties Union Before the Subcommittee on Terrorism, Nonproliferation and Trade: 'Strategy for Countering Jihadist Websites.'" House Committee on Foreign Affairs, September 29, 2010. https://www.aclu.org/files/assets/Statement_House_Financial _Services_Countering_Jihadist_Websites_Sept_2010.pdf.

Murphy, Sean D. *United States Practice in International Law*: Vol. 1, *1999–2001*. Cambridge: Cambridge University Press, 2003.

Nixon, Richard. "Address to the Nation Announcing Conclusion of an Agreement on Ending the War and Restoring Peace in Vietnam." January 23, 1973. http://www.presidency.ucsb.edu /ws/?pid=3808.

Nowak, Manfred, and Elizabeth McArthur. *The United Nations Convention Against Torture: A Commentary*. New York: Oxford Commentaries on International Law, 2008.

Nowlan, Robert A. "George Washington, Charge to the Northern Expeditionary Force, September 14, 1775." In *The American Presidents, Washington to Tyler: What They Did, What They Said*. Jefferson, N.C.: McFarland, 2012.

Obama, Barack. "Executive Order 13491: Ensuring Lawful Interrogations." White House, January 22, 2009. https://www.whitehouse.gov/the_press_office/EnsuringLawfulInterrogations.

——. "Statement by the President Report of the Senate Select Committee on Intelligence." White House, December 9, 2014. https://www.whitehouse.gov/the-press-office/2014/12/09 /statement-president-report-senate-select-committee-intelligence.

——. "Statement of President Barack Obama on Release of OLC Memos." White House, April 16, 2009. https://www.whitehouse.gov/the-press-office/statement-president-barack-obama -release-olc-memos.

Office of the District Marshal for Massachusetts. "Document Regarding the Parole of Captain Henry Nelles, Prisoner of War, August 10, 1814." August 10, 1814. Archives of Ontario. http:// www.archives.gov.on.ca/en/explore/online/1812/big/big_073_parole_terms.aspx.

Office of the Historian. "Carter and Human Rights, 1977–1981." U.S. Department of State, October 31, 2013. https://history.state.gov/milestones/1977-1980/human-rights.

"Osama Bin Laden Tape Transcript." *MSNBC*, May 23, 2006. http://www.nbcnews.com /id/12939961/ns/us_news-security/t/osama-bin-laden-tape-transcript/.

Osiel, Mark J. "Obeying Orders: Atrocity, Military Discipline, and the Law of War." *California Law Review* 86, no. 5 (October 1998): 943–1,129.

Paust, Jordan. "The Senate Torture Report and Prior Admissions." *Jurist* (University of Pittsburgh), December 9, 2014. http://jurist.org/forum/2014/12/jordan-paust-senate-torture.php.

Petraeus, David H. "Commanding General David H. Petraeus' Letter about Values." Multi-National Force—Iraq, May 10, 2007. http://www.washingtonpost.com/wp-srv/nation/documents /petraeus_values_051007.pdf.

Pew Research Center. "United in Remembrance, Divided Over Policies: Ten Years After 9/11." September 1, 2011. http://www.people-press.org/2011/09/01/united-in-remembrance-divided -over-policies/.

Phillips, Joshua E. S. *None of Us Were Like This Before: American Soldiers and Torture*. New York: Verso, 2012.

Pictet, Jean. *Humanitarian Law and the Protection of War Victims.* Geneva: Henry Dunant Institute, 1975.

Posner, Richard A. *Not a Suicide Pact: The Constitution in a Time of National Emergency.* New York: Oxford University Press, 2006.

Prendergast, Catherine. "Extract from an Original Letter from Catherine Prendergast (Mayville) to William Merritt (Greenbush)." September 7, 1814. Archives of Ontario. http://www.archives.gov.on.ca/en/explore/online/1812/prisoners.aspx#merritt.

Prugh, George S. "The Code of Conduct for the Armed Forces." *Columbia Law Review* 56, no. 5 (May 1, 1956): 678–707.

———. *Law at War: Vietnam, 1964–1973.* Washington, D.C.: Department of the Army, 1975.

"Punishment for War Crimes: Duty: Or Discretion?" *Michigan Law Review* 69, no. 7 (June 1, 1971): 1,312–1,346.

Quigley, Samantha L. "Lessons Learned at Abu Ghraib Drive Current Detainee Policies." *DoD News, U.S. Department of Defense.* http://archive.defense.gov/news/newsarticle.aspx?id=50081.

Rainer, Eising. "Interest Groups in EU Policy-Making." *Living Reviews in European Governance* 3, no. 4 (2008). http://europeangovernance.livingreviews.org/Articles/lreg-2008-4/download/lreg-2008-4BW.pdf.

Raines, Jr., Edgar F. *The Rucksack War: U.S. Army Operational Logistics in Grenada, 1983.* Washington, D.C.: Center of Military History, 2010.

Raymond, Gregory A. "Lieber and the International Laws of War." In *Francis Lieber and the Culture of the Mind,* ed. Charles R. Mack and Henry H. Lesesne. Columbia: University of South Carolina Press, 2005.

Reagan, Ronald. "Address to the Nation on Events in Lebanon and Grenada." October 27, 1983. http://www.reagan.utexas.edu/archives/speeches/1983/102783b.htm.

Rice, Condoleezza. *No Higher Honor: A Memoir of My Years in Washington.* New York: Broadway Paperbacks, 2012.

Rivkin, David B., Jr., and Lee A. Casey. "The Rocky Shoals of International Law." *The National Interest* (Winter 2000–2001). http://nationalinterest.org/article/the-rocky-shoals-of-international-law-523.

Rizzo, John. *Company Man: Thirty Years of Controversy and Crisis in the CIA.* Repr. ed. New York: Scribner, 2014.

Robinson, Ralph. "Retaliation for the Treatment of Prisoners in the War of 1812." *American Historical Review* 49, no. 1 (October 1, 1943): 65–70.

Rove, Karl. *Hardball with Chris Matthews*: Karl Rove Q&A—In-Depth Discussion on Bolton, Iraq, and Downing St. Memo. Interview by Chris Matthews. June 22, 2005. http://www.nbcnews.com/id/8306049/ns/msnbc-hardball_with_chris_matthews/t/karl-rove-q/.

"Rules of Land Warfare." Government Printing Office, 1914. http://www.loc.gov/rr/frd/Military_Law/pdf/rules_warfare-1914.pdf.

Rumsfeld, Donald. *Known and Unknown: A Memoir.* Repr. ed. New York: Sentinel, 2012.

———. "Memorandum for the Commander, US Southern Command: Counter-Resistance Techniques in the War on Terrorism." U.S. Department of Defense, April 16, 2003.

——. "Pentagon Press Briefing." *CNN*, May 4, 2004. http://www.cnn.com/TRANSCRIPTS/0405/04 /se.02.html.

Rumsfeld, Donald, and Richard Myers. "Defense Department Briefing, February 19, 2003." *IIP Digital*, February 19, 2003. http://iipdigital.usembassy.gov/st/english/texttrans/2003/02/2003 0219191407ross@pd.state.gov0.704632.html#axzz300QFdi5U.

Rumsfeld v. Padilla: Brief of Louis Henkin, Harold Hongju Koh, and Michael H. Posner as Amici Curiae in Support of Respondents (U.S. Supreme Court 2004).

Russomanno, Joseph. *Tortured Logic: A Verbatim Critique of the George W. Bush Presidency*. Dulles, Va.: Potomac Books, 2011.

Sandholtz, Wayne. *Prohibiting Plunder: How Norms Change*. Oxford: Oxford University Press, 2007.

Sands, Philippe. *Torture Team: Rumsfeld's Memo and the Betrayal of American Values*. New York: St. Martin's Press, 2008.

Sartre, Jean-Paul. Preface to *The Question*, by Henri Alleg, trans. John Calder. New York: Bison, 2006.

Scheuer, Michael F., Bill Delahunt, and Julianne Smith. *Extraordinary Rendition in U.S. Counterterrorism Policy: The Impact on Transatlantic Relations*. U.S. House of Representatives, 2007. https://fas.org/irp/congress/2007_hr/rendition.pdf.

Schimmelfennig, Frank. "Strategic Calculation and International Socialization: Membership Incentives, Party Constellations, and Sustained Compliance in Central and Eastern Europe." *International Organization* 59, no. 4 (2005).

Schlesinger, James R. "Final Report of the Independent Panel to Review DoD Detention Operations." Arlington, VA: Government Printing Office, August 2004. http://www.npr.org /documents/2004/abuse/schlesinger_report.pdf.

Schlesinger, Jr., Arthur M. *The Imperial Presidency*. Repr. ed. Boston: Mariner, 2004.

——. *War and the American Presidency*. New York: Norton, 2005.

Schneider, Mark L. "Human Rights Policy Under the Carter Administration." *Law and Contemporary Problems* 43 (Spring 1979): 261–267.

Shannon, Vaughn P. "Norms Are What States Make of Them: The Political Psychology of Norm Violation." *International Studies Quarterly* 44, no. 2 (June 1, 2000): 293–316.

Shattuck, John. "Restoring U.S. Credibility on Human Rights." *American Bar Association Human Rights Magazine* 35, no. 4 (Fall 2008). http://www.americanbar.org/publications/human _rights_magazine_home/human_rights_vol35_2008/human_rights_fall2008/hr_fall08 _shattuck.html.

Smist Jr., Frank J. *Congress Oversees the United States Intelligence Community, 1947–1994*. 2nd ed. Knoxville: University of Tennessee Press, 1994.

Spiro, Peter J. "The New Sovereigntists: American Exceptionalism and Its False Prophets." *Foreign Affairs*, December 2000. https://www.foreignaffairs.com/articles/united-states/2000-11-01 /new-sovereigntists-american-exceptionalism-and-its-false-prophets.

Springer, Paul J. *America's Captives: Treatment of POWs from the Revolutionary War to the War on Terror*. Lawrence: University Press of Kansas, 2010.

Starkey, Armstrong. "Paoli to Stony Point: Military Ethics and Weaponry During the American Revolution." *Journal of Military History* 58, no. 1 (1994).

Stout, Harry. "Obama History Project." *NYMag.com*, January 11, 2015. http://nymag.com/news/politics/obama-history-project/harry-stout.

Strauss, Ulrich. *The Anguish of Surrender: Japanese POWs of World War II*. Seattle: University of Washington Press, 2003.

Taguba, Antonio M. "Taguba Report: AR 15-6 Investigation of the 800th Military Police Brigade." Oversight Report, Investigative File (AR 15-6), May 27, 2004. https://www.thetorturedatabase.org/document/ar-15-6-investigation-800th-military-police-investigating-officer-mg-antonio-taguba-taguba-.

Tenet, George. *At the Center of the Storm: The CIA During America's Time of Crisis*. Repr. ed. New York: Harper Perennial, 2008.

——. "We're At War." Central Intelligence Agency, September 16, 2001. http://nsarchive.gwu.edu/news/20051209/at_war.pdf.

——. "Written Statement for the Record of the Director of Central Intelligence Before the National Commission on Terrorist Attacks Upon the United States." Central Intelligence Agency, March 24, 2004. https://www.cia.gov/news-information/speeches-testimony/2004/tenet_testimony_03242004.html#Role.

Thompson, Waddy. *Recollections of Mexico*. New York: Wiley and Putnam, 1846.

Tocqueville, Alexis de. *Democracy in America*. Ed. Isaac Kramnick. Trans. Gerald Bevan. London: Penguin, 2003.

Toosi, Nahal. "Koh in the Cross Hairs," *POLITICO*, April 19, 2015, http://social.politico.com/story/2015/04/harold-koh-in-the-crosshairs-117110.html.

"Treaty of Amity and Commerce Between His Majesty the King of Prussia, and the United States of America." September 10, 1785. The Avalon Project, Yale University. http://avalon.law.yale.edu/18th_century/prus1785.asp.

"Treaty of Peace and Amity Between His Britannic Majesty and the United States of America (Treaty of Ghent)." 1814. The Avalon Project, Yale University. http://avalon.law.yale.edu/19th_century/ghent.asp.

"Treaty with Morocco." July 28, 1786. The Avalon Project, Yale University. http://avalon.law.yale.edu/18th_century/bar1786t.asp.

Trooboff, Peter D., ed. Introduction to *Law and Responsibility in Warfare: The Vietnam Experience*. Chapel Hill: University of North Carolina Press, 1975.

"Understanding the Iran-Contra Affair: The Minority Report." Brown University, 2010. http://www.brown.edu/Research/Understanding_the_Iran_Contra_Affair/h-thereport.php.

United Nations. "Convention Against Torture and Other Cruel, Inhuman, or Degrading Treatment or Punishment." December 10, 1984. http://www.un.org/en/ga/search/view_doc.asp?symbol=A/RES/39/46.

——. "Convention Against Torture and Other Cruel, Inhuman or Degrading Treatment or Punishment: Addendum—United States of America." June 29, 2005. http://www.state.gov/documents/organization/62175.pdf.

——. "Resolutions Adopted on the Reports of the First Committee, United Nations General Assembly, 399th Plenary Meeting, 7th Session." United Nations, December 3, 1952. http://www.worldlii.org/int/other/UNGARsn/1952/101.pdf.

——. "UN Document E/CN.4/L.1470: Cruel, Inhuman or Degrading Treatment or Punishment." March 11, 1979.

United Nations International Criminal Tribunal for the Former Yugoslavia. "Final Report to the Prosecutor by the Committee Established to Review the NATO Bombing Campaign Against the Federal Republic of Yugoslavia." June 13, 2000. http://www.icty.org/sid/10052.

U.S. Army Chief of Staff. "U.S. Actions to Prevent War Crimes by U.S. and Republic of Vietnam Armed Forces." Suitland, Md.: U.S. National Archives, 1970.

U.S. Catholic Bishops. "The Challenge of Peace: God's Promise and Our Response," May 3, 1983. http://www.osjspm.org/the_challenge_of_peace_1.aspx.

U.S. Congress Senate Committee on Armed Services. *General Ridgway: Hearings Before the United States Senate Committee on Armed Services, Eighty-Second Congress, Second Session, on May 21, 1952.* U.S. Government Printing Office, 1952.

——. "Inquiry Into the Treatment of Detainees in U.S. Custody." November 20, 2008. http://www.armed-services.senate.gov/imo/media/doc/Detainee-Report-Final_April-22-2009.pdf.

U.S. Department of Defense. "Department of Defense Directive: DoD Law of War Program." February 22, 2011. http://www.dtic.mil/whs/directives/corres/pdf/231101e.pdf.

——. "Final Report to Congress: Conduct of the Persian Gulf War." April 1992. http://www.globalsecurity.org/military/library/report/1992/cpgw.pdf.

——. "Memoranda: Counter-Resistance Techniques." 2002. http://nsarchive.gwu.edu/NSAEBB/NSAEBB127/02.12.02.pdf.

——. "Memorandum for Chief, Inspections Division: 4th Infantry Division Detainee Operations Assessment Trip Report (CONUS Team)." April 2014. https://www.thetorturedatabase.org/files/foia_subsite/pdfs/DOD015937.pdf.

——. "Working Group Report on Detainee Interrogations in the Global War on Terrorism: Assessment of Legal, Historical, Policy, and Operational Considerations." April 4, 2003.

U.S. Department of Justice. "Office of Professional Responsibility's Report of Investigation: The Office of Legal Counsel's Memoranda on Issues Relating to the Central Intelligence Agency's Use of 'Enhanced Interrogation Techniques' on Suspected Terrorists." July 29, 2009. http://fas.org:8080/irp/agency/doj/opr-2nddraft.pdf.

——. "Statement of Attorney General Eric Holder on Closure of Investigation into the Interrogation of Certain Detainees." August 30, 2012. http://www.justice.gov/opa/pr/statement-attorney-general-eric-holder-closure-investigation-interrogation-certain-detainees.

U.S. Department of Justice, Office of the Inspector General. "A Review of the FBI's Involvement in and Observations of Detainee Interrogations in Guantánamo Bay, Afghanistan, and Iraq." May 2008. https://oig.justice.gov/special/s0805/final.pdf.

U.S. Department of State. "Foreign Relations of the United States, 1952–1954. Korea: Volume XV, Part 1. Document 30." United States Department of State, February 8, 1952. http://history.state.gov/historicaldocuments/frus1952-54v15p1/d30.

——. "Foreign Relations of the United States, 1952–1954. Korea: Volume XV, Part 1. Document 197," June 30, 1952. http://history.state.gov/historicaldocuments/frus1952-54v15p1/d197.

——. "Foreign Relations of the United States, 1952–1954. Korea: Volume XV, Part 1. Document 286," October 8, 1952. http://history.state.gov/historicaldocuments/frus1952-54v15p1/d286.

——. "Foreign Relations of the United States, 1952–1954. Korea: Volume XV, Part 1. Document 554." United States Department of State, May 26, 1953. http://history.state.gov/historical documents/frus1952-54v15p1/d554.

——. "Foreign Relations of the United States, 1964–1968, Volume III, Vietnam." United States Department of State, 1968. https://www.state.gov/www/about_state/history/vol_iii/109 .html.

——. "Foreign Relations of the United States, 1964–1968 Volume III, Vietnam, June–December 1965, Document 117." United States Department of State, August 10, 1965. https://history .state.gov/historicaldocuments/frus1964-68v03/d117.

——. "Foreign Relations of the United States, 1964–1968 Volume III, Vietnam, June–December 1965, Document 167." United States Department of State, October 13, 1965. https://history .state.gov/historicaldocuments/frus1964-68v03/d167.

——. "Foreign Relations of the United States, 1964–1968 Volume III, Vietnam, June–December 1965, Document 172." United States Department of State, October 20, 1965. https://history .state.gov/historicaldocuments/frus1964-68v03/d172.

——. "Foreign Relations of the United States, 1964–1968 Volume III, Vietnam, June–December 1965, Document 182." United States Department of State, October 25, 1965. https://history .state.gov/historicaldocuments/frus1964-68v03/d182.

——. "Foreign Relations of the United States, 1964–1968, Volume V, Vietnam, 1967." United States Department of State, 1967. https://history.state.gov/historicaldocuments/frus1964 -68v05.

——. "Foreign Relations of the United States Diplomatic Papers, 1941. General, The Soviet Union." United States Department of State, 1941. http://digicoll.library.wisc.edu/cgi-bin /FRUS/FRUS-idx?type=header&id=FRUS.FRUS1941v01.

——. "Papers Relating to the Foreign Relations of the United States, 1918. Supplement 2, The World War." 1918. http://digicoll.library.wisc.edu/cgi-bin/FRUS/FRUS-idx?type=article&did=FRUS .FRUS1918Supp02.i0007&id=FRUS.FRUS1918Supp02&isize=M.

——. "Papers Relating to the Foreign Relations of the United States, 1918. Supplement 2, The World War: Prisoners of War." 1918. http://digicoll.library.wisc.edu/cgi-bin/FRUS/FRUS -idx?type=div&did=FRUS.FRUS1918Supp02.i0007&isize=text.

——. "Remarks with UK Foreign Secretary David Miliband and Google Senior Vice President David Drummond." May 22, 2008. http://2001-2009.state.gov/secretary/rm/2008/05/105182 .htm.

U.S. Department of the Army. "Army Regulation (AR 350-216): Training in the Provisions of the Geneva Conventions for the Protection of War Victims of 1949." U.S. Government Printing Office, April 24, 1967. http://usahec.contentdm.oclc.org/cdm/ref/collection/p16635coll11/id/2587.

——. "Army Training Circular: Prisoners of War (TC 27-10-2)." Department of the Army, September 17, 1991. http://www.loc.gov/rr/frd/Military_Law/pdf/prisoners-of-war-1991.pdf.

——. "Department of the Army Field Manual (FM 19-40): Enemy Prisoners of War and Civilian Interests." United States Government Printing Office, August 1964. http://www.survivalebooks .com/free%20manuals/1964%20US%20Army%20Vietnam%20War%20Enemy%20Prison-ers%20of%20War%20&%20Civilian%20Internees%2056p.pdf.

——. "Department of the Army Field Manual (FM 34-52): Intelligence Interrogation." United States Government Printing Office, September 28, 1992. https://fas.org/irp/doddir/army /fm34-52.pdf.

——. "Report of the Department of the Army Review of the Preliminary Investigations into the My Lai Incident (Volume III: Exhibits, Book I—Directives)." Department of the Army, March 14, 1970. http://www.loc.gov/rr/frd/Military_Law/pdf/RDAR-Vol-IIIBook1.pdf.

U.S. Departments of the Army, the Navy, the Air Force, and the Marine Corps. "Enemy Prisoners of War, Retained Personnel, Civilian Internees and Other Detainees." October 1, 1997. http://www.apd.army.mil/pdffiles/r190_8.pdf.

U.S. Senate. "Foreign and Military Intelligence: Final Report of the Select Committee to Study Governmental Operations with Respect to Intelligence Activities." Washington, D.C. April 26, 1976. http://www.intelligence.senate.gov/sites/default/files/94755_I.pdf.

Von Clausewitz, Carl. *On War.* Ed. Michael Howard and Peter Paret. Princeton, N.J.: Princeton University Press, 1976.

Waldron, Jeremy. *Torture, Terror, and Trade-Offs: Philosophy for the White House.* Oxford: Oxford University Press, 2012.

Walt, Stephen M. "A Christmas Pardon." *Foreign Policy,* December 22, 2014. https://foreign policy.com/2014/12/22/a-christmas-pardon-torture-report-obama-bush-cheney/.

"War Department Basic Field Manual (FM 19-5): Military Police." U.S. Government Printing Office, June 14, 1944. http://www.ibiblio.org/hyperwar/USA/ref/FM/PDFs/FM19-5.PDF.

"War Department Field Manual (FM 27-10): Rules of Land Warfare." U.S. Government Printing Office, October 1, 1940. http://armypubs.army.mil/doctrine/DR_pubs/dr_a/pdf/fm27_10 .pdf.

Warner, Denis, and Peggy Warner. *The Sacred Warriors: Japan's Suicide Legions.* New York: Avon, 1984.

Wedgwood, Ruth. "Al Qaeda, Terrorism, and Military Commissions." *American Journal of International Law* 96, no. 2 (April 2002).

White, Joseph Robert. "Humanity in a 'War Without Mercy.'" *H-War,* H-Review, January 2007. http://www.h-net.org/reviews/showrev.php?id=12797.

——. "Review of Straus, Ulrich, *The Anguish of Surrender: Japanese POWs of World War II." H-War,* H-Review, January 2007. http://www.h-net.org/reviews/showrev.php?id=12797.

White, M. S., ed. *Gulf Logistics: Blackadder's War.* London: Brassey's, 1995.

White, William Lindsay. *The Captives of Korea: An Unofficial White Paper on the Treatment of War Prisoners.* New York: Scribner, 1957.

White House. "President's Statement on Signing of H.R. 2863, the 'Department of Defense, Emergency Supplemental Appropriations to Address Hurricanes in the Gulf of Mexico, and Pandemic Influenza Act, 2006.'" December 30, 2005. http://georgewbush-whitehouse .archives.gov/news/releases/2005/12/20051230-8.html.

Whitman, Bryan, W. Hays Parks, and Pierre-Richard Prosper. "Department of Defense Briefing on Humane Treatment of Iraqi and U.S. Prisoners of War Under Geneva Convention." International Information Programs, 2003. http://www.defense.gov/Transcripts/Transcript .aspx?TranscriptID=2281.

Wippman, David. "Kosovo and the Limits of International Law." *Fordham International Law Journal* 25, no. 1 (2001): 129–150.

Wittes, Benjamin. *Law and the Long War: The Future of Justice in the Age of Terror.* New York: Penguin, 2009.

——. "Thoughts on the SSCI Report, Part III: The Program's Effectiveness." *Lawfare*, December 28, 2014. https://www.lawfareblog.com/thoughts-ssci-report-part-iii-programs-effectiveness.

Yingling, Raymond T., and Robert W. Ginnane. "The Geneva Conventions of 1949." *American Journal of International Law* 46, no. 3 (July 1, 1952): 393–427.

Yoo, John C. "Application of Treaties and Laws to Al Qaeda and Taliban Detainees." In *The Torture Papers: The Road to Abu Ghraib*, ed. Karen J. Greenberg and Joshua L. Dratel, 38–79. New York: Cambridge University Press, 2005.

——. "Memorandum Opinion for the Deputy Counsel to the President." In *The Torture Papers: The Road to Abu Ghraib*, ed. Karen J. Greenberg and Joshua L. Dratel, 3–24. New York: Cambridge University Press, 2005.

——. *The Powers of War and Peace: The Constitution and Foreign Affairs After 9/11*. Chicago: University of Chicago Press, 2005.

——. *War by Other Means: An Insider's Account of the War on Terror.* New York: Atlantic Monthly Press, 2006.

Yoo, John C., and Robert J. Delahunty. "Authority for Use of Military Force to Combat Terrorist Activities Within the United States." U.S. Department of Justice, October 23, 2001. http://nsarchive.gwu.edu/torturingdemocracy/documents/20011023.pdf.

Young, Oran R. "Regime Dynamics: The Rise and Fall of International Regimes." In *International Cooperation: Building Regimes for Natural Resources and the Environment*. Ithaca, N.Y.: Cornell University Press, 1989.

Zinni, Anthony. "The SJA in Future Operations." *Marine Corps Gazette* 80, no. 2 (February 1996). https://www.mca-marines.org/gazette/1996/02/sja-future-operations.

INDEX

Eager, Charles ("Chuck"), 46
education, 65–66
800th Military Police Brigade, 77, 148
EITs. *See* enhanced interrogation techniques
Enemies of Intelligence, The (Betts), 219n93
"Enemy in Your Hands, The," 65
England, Lynndie, 142, 194
enhanced interrogation techniques (EITs),
    4–5, 86, 134, 179; DoD stopping, 183–84;
    Rizzo and, 219n74; torture and, 230n74;
    veto of, 152
EO. *See* Executive Order
executive authority, 85–86, 92, 107–10; of G. W.
    Bush, 186; cooperation and compromise
    in, 225n87; foreign affairs and, 102–3; in
    foreign relations, 108–10; Goldsmith and,
    186; international law and, 115–16; lawyer's
    role and, 95–96; push to expand, 138–39;
    unitary, 110–13. *See also* authority
executive branch: authority of, 136–39; OLC
    and, 103–4; oversight of, 87–89, 96
Executive Order (EO), 185; 11905, 121, 195;
    13440, 196, 232n19; 13491, 160, 183, 185, 196
Ex parte Quirin, 48
Ex Parte Vallandigham, 41

Fay-Jones report, 148
FBI. *See* Federal Bureau of Investigation
Federal Antitorture Statute, U.S., 10, 17, 18,
    72, 195
Federal Bureau of Investigation (FBI), 178
Federalist No. 70, 136
Federal War Crimes Act, 10, 72, 195
Feinstein, Dianne, 151–52
Feith, Doug, 133
Field Manual, DoD (FM), 39; "2-22.3," 160,
    196; "19-5," 63; "19-40," 27, 63, 156; "27-10,"
    63, 76; "30-15," 63–64, 78
Field Manual on Military Intelligence
    (FM 34–52), 95, 156, 158, 160–61, 177–78,
    184, 195–96; Gulf War lessons in, 78–79;
    interrogation techniques in, 149

Finnemore, Martha, 22–23
FISA. *See* Foreign Intelligence Surveillance
    Act
FM. *See* Field Manual
Foley, James, 24, 177
food rations, 51
Ford, Gerald, 89, 121–22
foreign affairs, 102–3, 108–10
Foreign Affairs and the U.S. Constitution
    (Henkin), 89–90
Foreign Intelligence Surveillance Act (FISA),
    88
foreign policy, 85–86; British model of, 87–88;
    embedded norms and, 199n5; human rights
    in, 123; torture decision influencing, 171–73
foreign relations, 108–9
"44 Ways to Support Jihad," 175
Fourth Geneva Convention, 26–27, 49–51, 69,
    161, 187–88
Franks, Tommy, 188
Frederick, Ivan L., 142, 148, 194
Fredman, Jonathan, 202n40
Free World Military Assistance Force
    (FWMAF), 60–61, 67

Gardner, John, 161, 194
Gates, Robert, 162
Gelles, Mike, 144, 158, 194
Gellman, Barton, 105, 108, 111, 136, 138, 172
General Orders No. 100, 39
Geneva Conventions, 4, 9, 32–33, 49–52,
    195–96; Additional Protocol I to, 11–12,
    172; Article 24 of, 42–43, 206n58; Article
    38 of, 54; commitment to uphold, 81;
    Common Article 3 of, 10–11, 49–51, 64,
    133, 172–73, 186, 232n19; expansive view
    of, 26, 58; human rights laws and, 182–83;
    Japan not ratifying, 45–46; in Korean
    War, 52–55; mandated repatriations in, 55;
    1929 Geneva Convention Relative to the
    Treatment of Prisoners of War, 45–46;
    norms and protections of, 11–13; prisoners